For years, I've combed through piles of information on the serious use of firearms in self-defense searching for useful nuggets of wisdom. When I read *Handgun Combatives, 2nd Edition* I realized I had struck a major vein! Spaulding is extremely knowledgeable and highly accomplished but he doesn't shoot over the heads of his readers. His understandable, modest and effective teaching style makes this newest release required reading for anyone studying and using arms.

JIM HIGGINBOTHAM
Military Contract Weaponcraft
Coordinator/Marksmanship Specialist
Deputy Sheriff / Officer Survival Instructor

Packed with simple, sensible and street-proven concepts, skills, and cutting-edge techniques *Handgun Combatives, 2nd Edition* is a ***tactical goldmine*** for real-world operators, law enforcement, and citizens alike. If you're dead serious about prevailing under the gravest of circumstances, this book is an indispensable training resource.

SGT. CHARLES E. HUMES, JR.
Director of the A.P.P.L.E. P.I.T.T. LLC
Police Institute of Tactical Training
Columnist for LawOfficer.Com

I keep copies of different books in my classroom that I believe have important information on specific subjects, but when it comes to the best all-around personal information book out there, *Handgun Combatives, 2nd Edition* is it!

JOHN BENNER
Tactical Defense Institute

Dave has the rare ability to look at movement, technique and results and discard anything that doesn't contribute to greater effectiveness or improve a shooter's personal safety "in the moment."

You'll enjoy reading the second edition of *Handgun Combatives* even if you've read the first edition. You'll be glad you spent your hard-earned money on it if you're reading it for the first time; it's destined to be a timeless classic in the genre.

KELLY MCCANN, USMC (Ret)
– Founder of Crucible
– Author of *Combatives for Street Survival:*
Hard-Core Countermeasures for High-Risk Situations

HANDGUN COMBATIVES

2nd Edition

Dave Spaulding

43-08 162nd Street
Flushing, NY 11358
www.LooseleafLaw.com
800-647-5547

1st Printing – January 2011   5th Printing — September 2014
2nd Printing – July 2011   6th Printing — January 2016
3rd Printing — August 2012   7th Printing — January 2017
4th Printing — July 2013   8th Printing — December 2018

Library of Congress Cataloging-in-Publication Data

Spaulding, Dave, 1955-
  Handgun combatives / by Dave Spaulding. -- 2nd ed.
      p. cm.
  Includes index.
  ISBN 978-1-60885-024-2
  1. Firearms--Law and legislation. 2. Combatants and noncombatants
(International law) I. Title.
  K3661.S68 2010
  363.33--dc22

                                                  2010030855

Cover design by: Armen Edgarian
                    armenjohn@mac.com &
                    Sans Serif, Saline, Michigan

Dedication

To Diane......First, last and forever; the best is yet to come.

To Amber, Misty and Thomas, the best children that God could bless parents with.

To the new "sons" in the family, Steve and Daryn, as well as the latest "additions," Isabel and Joey.

To Mom and Dad; for everything else.

Another great book by *Dave Spaulding*, co-authored with *Ed Lovette*

Defensive Living, *2ⁿᵈ Edition*
Preserving Your Personal Safety Through Awareness, Attitude and Armed Action

Foreword by *Bruce Siddle*

"Ed Lovette and Dave Spaulding have distilled over 50 years of hard-earned experience into 100 pages of street-proven wisdom. There's everything you need to know and not one word more."

Marcus Wynne
Trips Magazine

Table of Contents

Acknowledgments

While I hope that what is contained in this book is a new package, the individual tactics and techniques are really nothing new. Without the information provided by the following people, this book would never have been possible:

Bert DuVerney and the staff of the Smith & Wesson Academy.

John Meyer, Gene Zink and Mark Kunnath of the original Heckler & Koch International Training Division.

John Shaw and the staff of the Mid-South Institute of Self-Defense Shooting (MISS).

Bank Miller, George Harris and John Peterson of the original Sig-Arms Academy.

Dennis Martin of CQB Services Limited of Liverpool, England.

Ed Lovette, former CIA operations officer.

Clint and Heidi Smith and the staff of Thunder Ranch.

Colonel Jeff Cooper, Greg Morrison, Dave Harris, Giles and Ed Stock, Ed Head and the staff of the Gunsite Academy.

John Benner, Chris Wallace, John Motil and the staff of the Tactical Defense Institute.

John and Vicki Farnum of Defense Training International

Dennis Anderson and Chuck Remsberg of the "old" Calibre Press.

Bill Groce (RIP), Sam Faulkner and Larry Scott (RIP) of the Ohio Peace Officer Training Academy

Kelly McCann, Phil Motzer, John Garman and the staff of Crucible.

Tom Ahonen, Brad Ross and Jeff Brown of Law Enforcement Targets

Paul Schohlem of Porta-Target

Kyle Burdette of Action Target

Mike Janich of Martial Blade Concepts

Ken Hackathorn, Evan Marshall, Ed Nowicki, Greg Foster, Dennis Tueller, Chuck Humes, Mike Boyle, Tom Marx, Ken Jorgenson, Alan "Opie" Howard, Massad Ayoob, Laura Burgess, Joyce Laituri, JoAnne Powers, Jimmi Nasser, Scott Ralston, Ralph Mroz, Ernest Langdon, Rich Grassi, Lou Chiodo, Marcus Wynne, Vince O'Neill, John Rau, Aaron Davis, Bob Bossey, David Morrell, Mike Sisino, T.C. Fuller, Dick Reinheimer and the rest of "Team Woodchuck."

Arthur Viani of Ghost, Inc.

To a group of gunsmiths who I think are the best in the world:
Karl Sokol of Chestnut Mountain Sports; Tony Jamakis of TJ's
Custom Gun Works, David Bowie of Bowie Tactical Concepts and
Robbie Barrkman of the Robar Companies.

To the finest holster makers in the world:
Lou Alessi (R.I.P.) of Alessi Holsters; Chuck Buis of Blackhawk; Dan
Donohue of Strong Holsters; Jim Murnack of Fist Holsters; Kim
Fideler of G.G & G Holsters; Tim Wegner of Blade-Tech, Brian
Hoffner of Hoffner's Holsters, Gregg Garrett of Comp-Tac, Jason
Shafer of JS Holsters, Mike Barnham of Galco and Tony Kanaly of
Milt Sparks Holsters.

To the men and women of the Montgomery County (Ohio) Sheriff's
Office: Retired Sheriff Tom Wilson, Sheriff Gary Haines (R.I.P.),
Major Sam Mains (Ret.), Major Roland Cox (Ret.), Lt. Dan Pierron
(Ret.), Sgt. Jack Yahle (Ret.), Sgt. Pete Snyder (Ret.), Sgt. Dave
Parin and Deputy Bob Freeze (Ret.). It was a great time, but I'm glad
it's over… but I do miss free ammo!

To the men and women of the former Combined Agencies for
Narcotics Enforcement (CANE) Task Force:
1st Asst. Prosecutor Deb Armanini, Sgt. "Wild" Bill Dillon, Det. Mike
Franklin, Det. Diane Taylor, Det. Don Williams, Det. Jess Wimberly,
Agt. Dean Derenberger, Det. Mike Gabrielson, Det. Dennis Castle,
Det. "Ash" Hutsonpillar, Det. Randy Miller, Det. Greg "Goofy"
Andrews, Det. Doug Yarnall, Sgt. Dave Hale, Sgt. Daryl Wilson, Sgt.
Larry Schroeder and Dep. Troy Bodine and K-9 "Jake." I would go
through "The Door" with you guys anytime!

To the fine editors (and gentlemen) who have supported my "writing
career" over the last two decades:
Harry Kane of Harris Publications; Denny Hansen of SWAT
Magazine; Dan Burger and David Griffiths of Police Magazine; Dave
Arnold (RIP), Scott Rupp and Jerry Lee of Intermedia Publications;
Dale Stockton, Crawford Coates and Nicole Reino of LAW OFFICER
magazine, Roy Huntington of FMG Publications , Michael & Mary
Loughrey and Hilary McKeon of Looseleaf Law Publications.

To my typist Liz Miller

And finally, to all of the readers who have found "something" in my
articles and books, it is most appreciated.

About The Author

DAVE SPAULDING is a retired lieutenant and 28-year veteran of the Montgomery County Sheriff's Office in Dayton, Ohio. He has worked in all facets of law enforcement including communications, jail operations, court security, patrol, evidence collection and investigations. As an investigator he investigated homicides and worked undercover targeting career criminals. He was a member of the SWAT team for 12 years, 8 of which were spent as a training officer. He supervised his department's training operation and worked full time as a use of force instructor. He was the commander of the CANE Drug Task Force, a federally funded multi-jurisdictional operation that targets upper, mid and street level dealers. Between his time in SWAT and narcotics assignments, he has been a participant in several hundred forced entries/search warrants and vehicle take-downs. He currently works in the private security sector.

He is a graduate of most of the better-known shooting schools and is the author of over 1,000 articles that have appeared in such publications as COMBAT HANDGUNS, GUNS AND WEAPONS FOR LAW ENFORCEMENT, SWAT, GUNS AND AMMO, HANDGUNS, AMERICAN HANDGUNNER, AMERICAN COP, POLICE, LAW AND ORDER and LAW OFFICER. He is the coauthor of the best selling book DEFENSIVE LIVING. He has taught nationally and has been a staff instructor at such prestigious events as the international training conferences of ASLET, IALEFI and ILEETA.

Dave has taught his Handgun Combatives course all over North America, as well as having been an adjunct instructor for the Tactical Defense Institute and the Heckler & Koch International Training Division. He has been a member of the American Society of Law Enforcement Training (ASLET), the International Association of Law Enforcement Firearms Instructors (IALEFI), The International Association of Counter Terrorist and Security Professionals, The International Law Enforcement Educators & Trainers Association (ILEETA) and is a past president and board member of the Ohio Tactical Officer's Association.

ILEETA (the world's largest police training organization) and *Law Officer* magazine named Dave the 2010 Law Enforcement Trainer of the Year.

A Note from the Author

I have been studying armed conflict all of my adult life. HANDGUN COMBATIVES is the result of this study. My one regret from the first edition was that I did not make it clear that what was contained in its pages was the *simplest* way to accomplish the needed task(s)! Not the slickest, coolest looking or latest trend, but the most simple/easy methodology I have found. This latest edition offers the same message.

I can remember attending the basic police academy and questioning a number of the things that I was taught, especially in the firearms lesson plan. It was the mid-1970s and the Practical Pistol Course was the popular course of fire. The PPC had stages of fire that started at 60 yards and moved forward to 7, but none closer. No instruction was given for what I now call "bad breath" distances. The saving grace of the time was that we were actually trained in real hand to hand combat techniques consisting of punches, kicks, head butts and finger gouges (warm and fuzzy, don't hurt the suspect, minimum force "subject control" techniques did not become vogue until the 90's) which are the correct solution to such close quarter combat situations, but the area between three feet and 21 feet was largely unaddressed. As we now know, this area is where the action is, regardless of whether it is a law enforcement officer or legally armed citizen.

Due to this experience, I felt that I needed to know *exactly* what happens in a gunfight so that I could better prepare myself when and if it happened to me. I started to talk with every person that I could find who had been in a gunfight. I started with people from the "Greatest Generation"...those WWII veterans who were still plentiful at the time. While these men did not talk easily about their experiences, they were all willing to help the young cop make sense of what many of them called "a crazy business." All spoke matter of factly and none tried to embellish their tale(s), as many who "research" armed conflict from laboratories, Airsoft or Simunitions scenarios would have you believe. Regardless of what these "research gurus" tell you, "war stories" are worth hearing. As time went by, Korean and Vietnam war veterans were added to the mix. I sought out every cop that I could who had "seen the elephant" as well as armed citizens who bravely defended their homes and families against human predators. I did not forget those who prey upon us. While working in the county jail, I spoke with many felons who would tell me amazing stories (not about themselves mind you, but "others" they had "heard" about) and I learned much. Seeing it through their eyes was priceless for me. Now, it's returning soldiers, sailors and Marines from the War on Terror where fighting insurgents in the urban environment is revealing much about close quarter combat. It was never intended to be a published research project for public consumption, just A WAY to answer the questions in MY own mind. But as HANDGUNS Editor Dave Arnold told me before he died way too young, "You care too much about good guys and gals not to share this" and he was right.

What follows in this book is my "take" on how the semi-automatic pistol should be used in personal defense. As many of my interviews revealed to me, one must begin with making themselves *combative* or all else is a waste of time and effort. The first edition was criticized for the title because I did not include revolvers as they are handguns. This is true, but the large majority of people who select a handgun for personal protection select the pistol (9 out of 10 I am told) thus, I have concentrated my effort here. The title "Pistol Combatives" was considered, but it was decided that it just did not sound as good. In addition, my partner from my first book, *Defensive Living,* Ed Lovette, has written the consummate revolver book *"The Snubby Revolver."* While directed at snubbies, it is full of wisdom for any revolver shooter.

As the motto for the now defunct Heckler & Koch International Training Division used to say, this book "is A way, not THE way." Again, it is my take on the subject matter, there are alternate methodologies that are quite good... learn from all of them...but LEARN! The threat of attack is too great to ever stop learning. Be careful and look out for the garbage techniques that are out there, but learn. When and if the time comes, you will be glad you did.

Dave Spaulding
July 2010

Foreword

You know why Dave Spaulding is thin? Why he's fit? Because he swims upstream that's why – he swims against the current. Among the many reasons I've grown to like Dave so much and respect him as an authority on combat handgunning is that he isn't swept along with any latest craze or gee-whiz trend in handgun shooting. No, Dave's as honest a "student" and as earnest a practitioner of the use of handguns as I have ever known.

He's analytical. His opinions are valuable because he has a vast amount of personal and professional experience in which to consider the validity of any tactic, technique or procedure. He isn't just another gun rag author. He's forgotten more about the use of handguns than most people have the time, interest or opportunity to amass. I've found him self-effacing, self-deprecating and just a damn panic to be around. His wry wit will catch you off-guard, so pay attention.

He's attended most of the more well-known shooting schools and always presents himself as a student, not as a seasoned and accomplished shooter (which he is). His shooting skills are immediately apparent, yet he insists on not speeding through any instruction and painstakingly listens to each teaching point, then puts it to use rather than defaulting to his own "style." He sincerely wants to experience what the particular curriculum has to offer in order to objectively evaluate it.

An excellent instructor himself, Dave doesn't brook foolishness and demands critical self-appraisal from his students. I think over the years he's arrived at the correct conclusion that to develop personal skill further, a shooter has to open himself/herself up (becoming vulnerable in the process) and explore objectively what their true personal level of skill is. After all, that's what he does so he's not asking anyone to do anything he personally doesn't do each time he attends training or practices.

Dave has the rare ability to look at movement, technique and results and discard anything that doesn't contribute to greater effectiveness or improve a shooter's personal safety "in the moment."

You'll enjoy reading the second edition of *Handgun Combatives* even if you've read the first edition. You'll be glad you spent your hard-earned money on it if you're reading it for the first time; it's destined to be a timeless classic in the genre.

I'm glad to know Dave Spaulding and call him a friend. He's game, will jump on the mat willingly and takes his pucks without complaint then deals them right back. He'll stand on the firing line and shoot with the best, or a struggling novice, and be the same Dave Spaulding to either.

Dave's an unapologetic "what you see is what you get" kind of guy who loves to crack a few cold beers after some hard training and will make you laugh 'til your sides hurt. He's the consummate professional whose depth of knowledge is considerable. In this book you'll learn the last few things about Dave worth knowing: that he'll take a stand and state his opinion based on well-reasoned logic and personal experience and that he's not a "my way or the highway" kind of guy. And that speaks well of him.

Kelly McCann, USMC (Ret)
  – Founder of Crucible
  – Author of *Combatives for Street Survival:*
     Hard-Core Countermeasures for High-Risk Situations

Chapter One

DEVELOPING THE COMBATIVE MIND

"The final weapon is the brain, all else is supplemental."
John Steinbeck

For as long as I have been studying combative skills, it has always been understood that the mind is the ultimate weapon. Mr. Steinbeck understood this a century ago and it is still valid today. Through the years, this concept has been called several things, primarily the "survival mindset" or the "winning mind." As I have studied this topic over the last three decades, I have come to the realization that the whole idea of using the mind as a weapon is far more than just survival or even winning. The words survival and win, at least to my way of thinking, mean that you are already involved in some sort of confrontation that you are trying to bring to a conclusion in your favor. However, more often than not, what you do prior to a contest is going to determine the outcome. Whether it be in the starting blocks when the gun goes off; when the whistle is blown for a jump ball; or a life or death confrontation; the person who is caught unprepared to respond is likely to lose... lag time can, and will, kill! Thus, our mindset must deal with more than just the confrontation itself. It must deal with what happens prior to the confrontation. As a matter of fact, how the mind functions is a lifestyle commitment, not something that occurs just during conflict. This said, I have shrugged off titles such as "Survival Mind" or the "Winning Mind" and have adopted an attitude that I call the **Combative Mind**. Yes, it is an attitude. It is a life style commitment. It is something that you must live, something that must be part of your being...your soul!

The mind "sees" things in pictures. This being the case, I prefer to be visually/verbally descriptive...i.e., saying things in such a way that you would hopefully get a visual representation in the brain of what is being said. For example, I will use the term "press," which is short for "depress" meaning "a constant pressure to a breaking point," when working the trigger as I think that it is the best visual/verbal representation of what one does with an individual finger versus "squeeze" which, in my mind, is done with the entire hand like squeezing a rubber ball. For this same reason, I will dispense with the word "survival" as survival means "to remain in existence", which is not the vision I want to implant in your mind. Survival is what you do when you are cast adrift in a lifeboat — a situation over which you have no control. Hopefully you have control over your own safety! What I want you to focus on is **TO PREVAIL** which means "to be victorious"...something that conjures a picture to me beyond just winning. Superman actor Christopher Reeve "survived" the accident with his horse, though few will say that he prevailed (though he did prevail in many fine causes after his accident) after his fall from his horse. This is the perfect "picture" that I want you to see when you think of the difference between survive and prevail. Surviving a confrontation to live on a ventilator or in a wheel chair is just not good enough! I want you to walk away from any confrontation thrust at you VICTORIOUS...and to feel *good about doing so!* When was the last time that any athlete felt bad about prevailing over his opponents? Not the same thing as a life or death confrontation, you say? Well, to my way of thinking, the fight to the death may be the ultimate competition and if you can't feel good about that, what can you feel good about?

While the Boy Scouts of America may not appreciate their motto being used in a combative forum, it is true you must "be prepared" at all times to deal with whatever life brings your way, including a life threatening, do or die confrontation. You must prepare ahead of time. Trying to play catch up, once a confrontation arises, is quite likely to result in a no-win situation FOR YOU! You must see any potential threat coming long before any attack occurs. Then respond appropriately with just a moment's notice, with a fury that is both final and decisive, for you to prevail! Remember, the person(s) who are attacking you have already made the decision to act. You must now **AVOID**, **EVADE** or **COUNTER** (what I call the "Hierarchy of Confrontation Management") the attack and, if you must counter it, counter it with a level of force that is far greater than what they are attacking you with. It is furious, it is final and there is no going back. Be enthusiastic in your own rescue!

Thus, I have adopted a life style that I call the Combative Mind. The reason for this, is because it takes place prior, during and after any type of confrontation. It is more than just learning a martial art or a firearm skill and hoping that it is enough when the situation occurs. It is a train of thought. A life style commitment to WHEN it happens, not IF it happens. While survival is certainly instinctive, the ability to PREVAIL is not.... it is learned. It is a skill that must be practiced over and over again or the razor's edge will dull.

Personal combative skills, whether they are hand-to-hand, edged weapon, impact weapon, or firearms are perishable. In order for them to stay at their best they must be practiced. This is well understood by scholastic, collegiate and professional athletes. These people practice five days a week, several hours a day. Professional competitive shooters, even on their days off, will go out and shoot fifty rounds, just to keep the trigger finger sharp. Sports physiologists have known for many years that you can spend weeks building a skill to its sharpest edge and on Friday be able to do the skill to an exceptional level that can be accomplished without thought. Take a weekend off and get up Monday morning and as much as 20% of that skill can be lost, yet law enforcement officers and legally armed citizens practice infrequently with their handguns. If you think you are potentially in danger, the thought must have at least crossed your mind or you would not be reading this book, you realize that you need to develop life saving skills, and once these skills are learned they must be practiced. Being aware that this practice is necessary is part of developing the Combative Mind.

Like any other life style commitment, you must realize that your personal defenses are important, learn the skills, then practice them. Think about an NFL quarterback with all of the natural ability that he possesses. How often do you think he would be able to connect with a receiver if he only threw the ball two or three times a year? Not very likely, is it? Yet, we go to the range, practice two or three times a year and think we're going to be good enough to save our own lives. You wouldn't bet five bucks on the unpracticed quarterback, but many people bet their lives on being an unpracticed shooter every day!

Reading this, or any other book is only the beginning. It is only the first of many steps in helping you develop a new lifestyle in which you have decided it is necessary for your own well being to be constantly vigilant. From here, seek out quality hands on training. Continue to read books and magazines, watch videos, and try to absorb all the information that you can. Be forewarned, much of the information available out there is for profit only and does not really enhance your skills. Let me let you in on a little secret, an evaluation that I do in order to determine whether a piece of information, tactic or technique is worth your time and effort to learn. I call this evaluation process the "Three S Test." The first S is, does the tactic, technique or piece of information makes SENSE to you? You are a person with a long life experience. You have seen and done many things in your life, whether or not you're a soldier, police officer or intelligence official doesn't really matter. Most of us have faced tragedy, trauma and stress in our lives and we have developed experience from this. Look at this new piece of information or technique and decide; does it make sense to you? If it doesn't, seek out the instructor or author and ask them to clarify it. See if they can make sense of it for you. If in the end it doesn't make good common sense (I know... common sense isn't!), then a red flag should go up.

The second S is; is the technique SIMPLE to perform? If it seems complex in the controlled environment of the gym or on the range, then think about how difficult the technique is going to be to perform in a stress filled, life saving environment. As we will discuss later, your skills are going to deteriorate, if it isn't simple to perform under controlled conditions then it certainly will not be simple to perform during a life-threatening event. PLEASE do not succumb to the phenomenon I call "shooting cool" in which how you look is more important than how you shoot. This is a phenomenon that I have noted since the first edition of this book and it seems to be spreading across the shooting community like a prairie fire. People are showing up for training dressed like commandos, wearing the latest in military or SWAT "fashion", adopting stances and weapon positions that have little to do with true skill, but really look "great" to those around them. In one basic police academy program I instructed, a cadet showed up wearing 5.11 clothing, wrap around Oakley sunglasses, Adidas GSG-9 boots and a thigh rig. He stepped up to the line and when I told the shooters to assume a ready shooting position, this student squatted like he was preparing for a bowel movement in the woods, pulled his gun to his chest and pointed it at his groin. At this point I took him off the line and asked him what he thought he was doing. He told me, "this is the latest in tactical clothing which will give me an edge in armed conflict. The stance I have assumed is called "Sul"...*it is what all of the high speed tactical operators are using!*" This is a direct quote! This young man had no prior firearms experience, but he knew what was current and cool. Its hard to keep things simple when you are concerned about looking cool. Lord, help me, it now appears that we can look good, feel good or shoot good, but not all three.

While it's important to practice your life saving skills, I realize that you are husbands, wives, parents, soccer coaches, volunteers, employees and many other things in your life, so you are only going to be able to commit so much time to keeping your combative skills sharp. It makes sense that the simpler the technique is to perform, the easier it will be to keep skills sharp with a minimal amount of practice time. Simple is easy and easy is, well... easier to maintain!

Finally, is the technique STREET proven? Check with the instructor and find out if what he or she is teaching has ever been used in a real world high threat situation. If it has not, do you really want to be the guinea pig for this instructor's technique...especially if they have their name on it? For the vast majority of us, the answer would be no. Does it make **Sense**? Is it **Simple**? Is it **Street proven**? Three questions that we all want to know as we develop our skill set. It's not really too much to ask in exchange for our training dollars and limited time.

Developing the Combative Mind is just like fighting alcoholism or drug addiction – you have to want to do it. If not, it's not going to happen on its own. The desire must be there ahead of time. My primary reason for writing this book is to ensure that the readers prevail in every confrontation they face. A lofty goal, most certainly, but one that I think can be achieved. After thirty-plus years in law enforcement and security, I can assure you there are a lot of vermin out there ready to prey upon you. The police cannot be everywhere. As a matter of fact, the U.S. Supreme Court has ruled that the police do not have the responsibility to protect individual citizens, they are empowered to protect society as a whole. It is the responsibility of each of us to protect ourselves against attack. It will not be pretty. It will not be Hollywood antiseptic. It will be down, dirty, ugly and bloody. Decide now that you are willing to do whatever it takes to prevail. If you have made this decision, then read on and I will tell you what you need to know to develop the Combative Mind. Understand that the Combative Mind is something that is with you always. You must access it in milliseconds, you can't keep it locked away in a box and when it's needed, run, get the key, unlock the box, open it and hope that it will be there. It is something that must be kept spring-loaded, instantly accessible for when the time comes.

Let's look at the word "combat." According to Webster's Dictionary it means "to counter or actively oppose; to fight back." Taking it further, being combative means "ready and willing to fight." Mindset is defined as "a course of action based on a previous decision. A set path based on reason and intellect." Putting it all together – combative mindset – means "to counter or actively oppose, to fight back. Ready and willing to fight based on a previous decision, a set path based on reason and intellect." This reason and intellect are going to be a compilation of your life experience as well as any training and formal education you may possess. What this book is about is personal security. The path to combative proficiency is going to be an ongoing journey in which you will probably never reach the end. If you visualize the path of such proficiency, it should look like a pyramid, with a base foundation and building blocks continually building to a summit. The first building block in this pyramid must be creating the right mindset, for without it all of the skills that will follow will amount to nothing. Let's talk about what I call the "Concept of the Harsh Reality." The truth is, fighting is not fun (at least for most of us). Faced with a hostile threat there are four things that the human organism has been proven to do: fight, flee, posture, or submit. Without a doubt, fighting is the best option. Yet, sometimes it is not always the most advantageous. Thus, fleeing a situation in which there is no chance of winning would certainly be a good option. If the term fleeing disturbs you, then call it "tactical withdraw," however you can place it in your mind to make the situation more palatable is certainly okay with me. Posturing and submitting are unacceptable. Submission means that you are "folding your cards" and accepting whatever your attacker decides to do to you. Let me give you a little bit of the harsh reality – it is not going to be pleasant, it is not going to be fun and it will not be what you have envisioned. They have attacked you for a reason and they are going to carry it out and it will either hurt or kill you. The only thing that will deter them from doing so is to fight back or flee the situation. Remember, avoidance and evasion are THE BEST way to deal with any confrontation! No matter how well trained or prepared you are, you always run the risk of losing, so avoid/evade, if possible. Nature has shown that a predator will more viciously attack the bird that is helpless with a broken wing than the bird that is totally healthy and may put up a fight.

Posturing is also unacceptable. I must admit that as an instructor for almost 30 years, I have spoken with many a student who has come to me and said, "Oh, I will never shoot anyone. I'm just going to use the gun to scare them away." Well, let me tell you something, this seldom works! If you can scare them away, that's great. However, over the last three decades of law enforcement I have learned that criminals, AKA human predators, can tell when someone has the resolve to fight versus someone who is just trying to fake their way through. I spent seven years of my career working in the County Jail dealing with criminals on a daily basis. When my shift was slow and book-ins were few, I would take the opportunity and get some of these predators out of their cells and sit them down in the officer's dining room and talk to them about criminal behavior. It was amazing, for a few moments of freedom, a bologna sandwich and a can of soda the information these predators would reveal. I never ceased to be amazed by the amount of "street intellect" they possessed. Their ability to size people up is uncanny. Without a doubt, criminals, human predators and even those people who live and breathe the street can tell when someone is willing to fight and someone is only posturing. I would caution anyone who buys a firearm with this intention to rethink his or her solution. They have a 75% to 80% chance of failure in the event they brandish a firearm with no will to use it.

The person that submits or postures is nothing more than a victim. Webster's Dictionary defines victim as "a sufferer from a force or action; a dupe." A dupe is someone who is "cheated, someone who is less than sharp." Someone who is less than sharp is someone who is less than intelligent. Think about the victim mindset. I don't think it is unfair to say that someone who allows him or her self to be a victim is less than sharp, less than intelligent. Anyone who believes that the police will protect them as individuals is naive at best. It is up to each and every one of us to protect ourselves against any hostile threat. In direct contradiction to victim, predator is defined as "one who selfishly exploits others, a roving killer or attacker. One who preys upon others." The predator is one who selfishly exploits others while the victim is someone who is less than sharp. The fact of the matter is if you look like prey, you will be preyed upon. Thunder Ranch founder Clint Smith says, "if you look like food, you will be eaten." Without a doubt the biggest part of developing the combative mind is preparing oneself psychologically to enter a fight. Not just physiologically to develop the skills to fight, we must mentally prepare ourselves to engage in combat—to fight back!

Chic Gaylord was never a soldier, was never a police officer, he made holsters. But he was very wise to the ways of the world. Back in 1960 Mr. Gaylord understood this concept when he made the statement, "the peace officer who is psychologically unprepared for a gunfight is fighting two men when he goes into combat. He must conquer both himself and his adversary." In other words, if you must take the time to develop the will to fight, the fight will be over before you can even become an active participant. Col. Jeff Cooper probably said it best in his well-known book *The Principles of Personal*

Defense, in which he advises that personal defense requires the following:

1. Alertness ("a commander may be forgiven for being defeated, but never for being surprised.")

2. Decisiveness ("when it becomes evident that you are faced with a violent physical assault, your life depends on you selecting a correct course of action and carrying it through without hesitation or deviation.")

3. Aggressiveness ("the best personal defense is an explosive counterattack.")

4. Speed ("on the very instant that we know our assailant intends us serious harm, we must work just as fast as we can.")

5. Coolness ("you must keep your head. If you lose your cool under attack, you will probably not survive to make excuses"...)

6. Precision ("if you are fortunate enough to have access to any sort of firearm when under attack remember that it is only as good as your ability to keep cool and shoot carefully.")

7. Ruthlessness ("if you find yourself under attack, don't be kind. Be harsh, be tough, be ruthless.")

8. Surprise ("by doing what our assailant least expects us to do, we may throw him completely off.")

A very important aspect of the Combative Mind is to be aware of what's going on around us. Awareness is something that is not so easy to do as we go about our daily lives. With so many responsibilities facing us, it is easy to be distracted from what is going on around us. For example, several years ago I was at a local mall eating a chocolate chip ice cream cone. I was so deeply involved in the wonderful taste of the ice cream that one of my former students was able to come up behind me, tap me on the back and say "Hey,

Dave, how you doing?" I was so startled by this that I dropped the ice cream cone on the ground. The end result was not only that I was caught flatfooted and unaware, but also I lost the object of my attention and enjoyment. The moral of this story is that if we want to enjoy those things that life has to offer, it is a good idea to be aware of what is going on around us. Such enjoyment can easily come to an end. In this case it was only an ice cream cone, in a worse case scenario it could have been my life.

As a vehicle to remind ourselves that we must stay aware at all times, Colonel Cooper introduced what is now known as the Color Codes of Awareness. Each color has a corresponding mental picture of a state of awareness that an individual should be in whenever in that condition. Cooper noted that the intensity of the colors elevates with the level of awareness. White is a soothing color, known to be used in hospitals and other medical institutions because of its soothing qualities.

Condition White is no perception of danger, period! There is no reason whenever you are outside your home that you should be in Condition White. Yes, we must all go to Condition White sometime in a 24-hour period, i.e., sleep, but we should only do so when we are secure in a location in which we have total control. For example, locked in your own home, lying on the couch, watching your favorite television show. I think we could all agree that if we are attacked in this state, it is unlikely we could catch up in a fight. However, because we are locked in our home, surrounded by security devices we control, we are much more likely to be warned of an attack than if we were outside.

Condition Yellow, which is still a soothing color, but certainly more intense than white, is a relaxed state of awareness. This is a state anyone should be in anytime they are out and about. Whether it is going to school, a place of business or to a social event, this is a state in which we are aware of our 30/360 environment. This translates to knowing what's going on around us in a 30' area in a 360° circle, including up and down if you are in a location that allows people to be either above or below you. It is even more important whenever we are armed we are in Condition Yellow, because any location that we travel to is a potential armed confrontation due to our firearm being present. Being aware of people near the firearm is just as important as people who may need the attention of your gun in the event that they try and attack.

Color Codes of Awareness	
White	No perception of danger
Yellow	Relaxed awareness
Orange	Alerted: unknown danger. (High-level of sensory awareness)
Red	Armed Confrontation (You or another are in danger of serious bodily harm)
Black**	Mental Shutdown (You have "folded your cards" and placed your fate in the hands of another)

Not all instructors include the level black in their coding system.

The next level on the color code is **Condition Orange**, certainly a more intense color than yellow. This is being alerted to unknown danger, a high level of sensory awareness. Those of us who have been in the military or in law enforcement have been in situations where "the hair on the back of our neck stood up," or we "felt a churning in our stomach" because something just didn't seem to be correct. This feeling is a direct result of our training as well as our life experience. Most of us live and work in environments in which we have a good understanding of what is normal and what is not. If something is out of the norm, most of us will know something is not right and it should get out attention. If nothing else, we are alerted to what is going on in our immediate vicinity. DO NOT IGNORE THESE FEELINGS! The vast majority of us, whether we have advanced college degrees or not, are intelligent people. We have a certain amount of street sense that tells us something that is not correct and is not harmonious with our environment. We should pay attention to these "feelings."

Not too long ago a young lady, who was almost a rape victim, told me an interesting story. It is a perfect example of listening to this intuition.... or not listening! She said that she was working late in an office building and was alone on her floor waiting for the elevator. When it opened, there was an individual on the elevator that she described as looking like a "biker." He had long hair, beard, greasy looking with dirty blue jeans and a leather jacket. She told me that "everything in her being" told her not to get on the elevator, but she did anyway. You know why? Because she DIDN'T WANT TO OFFEND him! Who cares if we offend this person? We don't know him, we don't care what his opinion is. But very often people want to be perceived as being kind, nice, and not offensive, so she goes ahead and gets on the elevator with this guy. Poor reason and bad move! Unfortunately, she realized this too late, because once the doors closed she was sexually attacked. This biker looking person went so far as to get underneath her clothing and was removing her undergarments when she was saved by nothing more than a complete stroke of luck. The elevator stopped and the doors opened on another floor because another late worker had pushed the elevator button. Fortunately for this young woman the attacker fled with nothing more than a little groping. It could have been a lot worse. It is certainly a prime example of not listening to your intuition, which is important. I have never ridiculed people who have made decisions based on intuition, as I think there is more to it than many realize. Intuition starts with recognition. Many incidents are avoided by recognizing an atypical situation as it is developing. If the situation is typical, it is very likely that intuition will never be engaged as we will go through the normal decision making process. However, when a situation is atypical, it is not unusual for an almost "animal sense" to develop. Intuition is about perception. You can perceive it as not being the norm or incorrect, then you should act on that perception/intuition.

The final level on the awareness chart is **Condition Red**. I am talking about blood red, one of the most intense colors in the color spectrum. Condition Red is associated with armed confrontation. You or another are in danger of serious bodily harm or death. If you do not fight or flee, you are going to end up injured or dead. It's as simple as that! There is no way around it. It is at this moment, with no hesitation whatsoever, that the Combative Mindset must kick in and you must engage in combat. There are no ifs, ands, or buts, you must fight and it is fight right now!

There is one other color that is often discussed, but it is not really a code of awareness. It is the color code of shutdown. Colonel Cooper never included this in his color code system, but I like it. It is called **Condition Black**. Notice it is not called a color code of awareness but it is called "a condition known as black." This is mental shutdown. You have folded your cards and placed your fate in the hands of another. You are prey, you are food, and you have decided to posture or submit. You are the deer in the headlights of the semi-truck of life. Condition Black, regardless at how you look at it, is unacceptable.

Over the years many people have said that the Color Codes of Awareness are a good way of understanding awareness, however, many people would like to know how to stay at a high level of awareness for a period of time. This is most certainly an area of concern. Anyone who has ever been in the police or military service or has ever worked as an executive protection specialist/bodyguard, understands that staying at a high level of awareness for a long period of time is most difficult. One of the best reminders of how to do this is known as the OODA Loop. OODA standing for Observation, Orientation, Decision and Action. The OODA Loop was the creation of Colonel John Boyd of the United States Air Force, who died of cancer at the age of 70. However, Boyd will not be forgotten due to his contributions to the world of individual combat. The concept of the OODA Loop was forged in war. Colonel Boyd flew about 20 combat missions in an F-86 during the Korean War. He noticed that American fighter pilots had achieved roughly a ten to one kill ratio over their North Korean enemies and Chinese adversaries, even though the Mig 15 could out-maneuver the F-86. Credit for the U.S. fighter's performances was given to better training. Colonel Boyd agreed, stating that people are far more important than hardware in war. Machines don't fight wars, people do and they use their minds. Certainly Colonel Boyd understood the concept of the Combative Mind. Colonel Boyd was a ferocious reader and researcher, reading all of the great military theorists. He analyzed campaigns and great battles. Colonel Boyd never attempted to publish his research but did assemble it into a 13-hour briefing called "The Discourse on Winning and Losing." He gave briefings to enlisted men and Generals alike, also congressman, newspaper reporters, scientists, futurists, academics, and most anyone interested in military science and personal security who would listen. Boyd felt that conflict could be viewed as a duel where in the adversary observes his opponents action, orients himself to the unfolding situation, decides on the appropriate course or counter move and then acts on his adversary. The individual who moves through the OODA Loop cycle the fastest, gains an incredible advantage over his enemy by being able to disrupt his enemy's response. Essentially both adversaries are going through the OODA cycle. The person who can go through the cycle the fastest or interrupt their opponent's cycle will be the victor.

What many people do not realize regarding Boyd's loop is that his version is much more complex than what is normally depicted in current training doctrine (Figure 1). His loop is actually much more complex with a great deal of the loop cycle being spent in the orientation phase (Figure 2). In reality, the combatant that spends a lot of time trying to figure out what is going on will loose the fight, something that Boyd makes clear in his writings. The person who can *move from observation to action with little, if any, delay will be the one who will prevail.* Boyd insisted that the *observant and prepared individual will spend less time orienting and deciding...* something that is critical when the victor of a life and death event will be decided in a few seconds. The truth is, if you must orient yourself to what is happening, it might be too late. As you can see from Boyd's loop, many factors are involved in the orientation phase— factors that can slow a decision. Boyd realized via "implicit guidance and control" a person can go from observation to action. An argument can be made that "implicit guidance and control" is the same as mindset, training and preparation. No one understood this concept better than WWII German Ace Erich Hartman. Hartman flew 1,000 combat missions with 352 confirmed dogfight kills. This level of life and death success is not achieved without a high level of preparation and awareness. Hartman created a four step "system to victory" which he taught to other Nazi pilots. The steps were SEE-DECIDE-ATTACK-REVERSE...a process quite similar to Boyd's action/response loop. Hartman told other pilots, "The pilot that sees the other first already has half the victory" and "most of the pilots I killed on a given day did not know I was in the same sky with them."

An excellent example of interrupting the OODA cycle would be the use of a distraction device or flash bang which is very common in military special ops and police SWAT teams. During a hostage situation, the suspect has observed, oriented and decided on a course of action and has expressed this course of action to the authorities. It is at this moment that the tactical team enters. They force the door and throw in the flash bang, which interrupts the suspect between his decision and action phase, allowing the tactical team to enter his OODA Loop and complete their cycle faster. Either going faster or interrupting your opponent's cycle is certainly a means to victory. Numerous military special operations units, particularly during the

Gulf War, to ensure victory over their opponents have used the OODA Loop.

The OODA Loop works hand in hand with Cooper's Color Codes of Awareness. When in Condition White, the loop will be large and moving slowly. The ability to observe, orient, decide and act will also

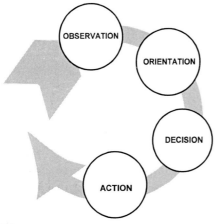

be slow. As you go up in the color code to yellow, it will cycle faster. Visualize each stage of the OODA cycle moving faster as you move up in the intensity of the colors. You will observe faster, you will orient faster and you will decide and act faster. At Condition Orange the cycle will be moving at almost "warp speed." The observation to action time frame will be based on your experience and in-depth training. The more life experience, the more training you

Figure 2

have the better you will respond. When Condition Red is reached and combat is obvious, there will be no cycle. One will merely be responding to the threat from a gut level, from a preprogramed state

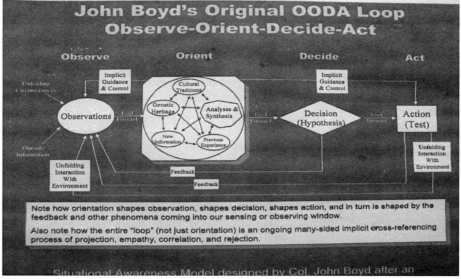

Figure 3

that will totally take any thought process out of the equation. It will be see—act. Understanding the Color Codes of Awareness, the OODA Loop and how the two work hand-in-hand will help any real world operator understand how to maintain high levels of awareness.

How important is awareness to any combat situation? By knowing what is happening we are much less likely to be a victim of what is known as Startle Reflex. Startle Reflex simply means you have been caught unaware. When startled we crouch, we throw our hands up around our heads, we vibrate with surprise, we are completely unprepared to fight. This startle response creates what is known as Lag Time. Lag Time is the amount of time it takes you to see, identify, and react to danger. Since most attacks, both unarmed and armed, are over in a matter of seconds, lag time can mean the difference between life and death. Former U.S. Navy SEAL Richard Machowicz in his book *UNLEASHING THE WARRIOR WITHIN* (Hyperion Publishing, New York) revealed seven keys to minimizing lag time, some of which we will deal with in other sections of the book. Mr. Machowicz's book is certainly recommended reading.

Let's highlight them now so that you can familiarize yourself with them. The comments after each point are mine and should not be considered the thoughts of Mr. Machowicz.

1. **Limit your responses.** Later in the book we will refer to Hick's Law. It basically states that when going from one trained response to two, lag time will increase by 58%.

2. **Simple techniques are faster techniques.** I am a firm believer in what I call the SIG principle (this doesn't refer to the excellent line of SIG-Sauer handguns). It means that Simple Is Good. A high intensity situation is not the time to experiment with techniques. Remember the three "S" test? This is certainly addressed here.

3. **Practice your techniques.** While perfect practice does make for perfect, any practice of any technique is better than none. Any type of preparation is better than no preparation at all.

4. **Make your actions natural, smooth and efficient.** Later on when we deal with handgun techniques we will talk about the continuous motion principle and how the

natural and smooth actions make you faster and more efficient.

5. **You can react later with a fast, simple technique, than earlier with a slow, complicated technique.**

6. **Anticipate correctly and gain a little, anticipate incorrectly and lose a lot.** Know thy enemy and know thyself. Good information is always critical.

7. **All reaction time is shortened with advanced information.** As we have already stated, awareness is so important.

At the moment you observe danger, if you can overcome the startle reflex, you will also experience a chemical dump known as Body Alarm Reaction. This is adrenaline and other chemicals dumping into your system all at once preparing (hopefully) for flight or fight. This chemical dump will result in physical and psychological manifestations such as general muscle tightening, loss of digital dexterity, tunnel vision, auditory exclusion and unreliable mental track. Critical decision-making ability will be impaired as well as time/space distortions. In a nutshell, you will not have the physical and mental abilities in an actual armed confrontation that you have in the gym or on the range. Because your ability to respond will be impaired, your motor skill performance will also be impaired. Fine motor skills, things that are performed by small muscle groups such as the hands or fingers, will suffer. Your body will revert to what is known as gross motor skills, things which involve the action of large muscle groups. Bulk strength like a punch or a kick will take precedence over fine dexterity moves such as a pressure point. Dexterity and complex coordination will be reduced under high stress due to the fight or flight response. This occurs due to reduced blood flow to the small muscle groups in order to feed the large muscle groups as they allow you to fight or flee. You are going to punch, kick and run, activities that require very little coordination. This being reality, it is essential that your hand-to-hand or your combative firearm skills need to involve simple activities.

Unfortunately for many of us, at the same time these chemicals are entering your body, many people will enter a state of denial, "This can't be happening to me" thoughts. Remember, part of developing the Combative Mind is understanding it's not IF something will happen to you, but knowing WHEN something happens. You must preprogram this *when/then thinking* into your database, i.e., your brain. At the moment of engagement, will you have a lack of commitment or willingness? Or will you do whatever it takes, no matter how distasteful, to fight back and prevail? All that should concern you at this point is to prevail! It is up to you, the fact is that most people don't plan to fail, they just fail to plan and pre-planning is essential to any combative activity. Developing a state of awareness is absolutely critical to developing the combative mind. Again, it is not just about winning or survival; it is about fighting.

I like to equate awareness to the common light switch. You are either switched on or you are switched off. When you are switched on the light is bright, you can see easily and respond to many situations with a much better command of your skill and abilities. When you are switched off, it is dark, it is hard to see, it is difficult to make decisions, it is difficult to know where your adversary is at; it is hard to respond. Without a doubt, the best state of mind to be in is to be switched on. Switch off only when you have the advantage of a safe location.

Situational awareness is heightened by the use of all of our senses, but the primary sense used is vision (though sound is also quite important!). Observation and scanning techniques are critical, and you should begin to develop them as soon as possible. The biggest mistake many people make is that they are observing their environment they look at things far away before they look at things that are close. Let me relate a test that was performed on me during a training course. Get two objects, they could be quarters, poker chips, anything small that can be held in your hand. Have an individual cover their eyes and ears and tell them to turn away. Take the two objects, placing one right at their feet and the other approximately 20 feet away. Tell the person to turn around and look for the objects. Without fail, the object they will see first is the one that is twenty feet away. The one at their feet may be one of the last things they see in the room. Since we are going to be engaged by a hostile threat, which is more dangerous to us? The one close to our personal proximity or the one 20 feet away? Certainly the type of weapon they hold in their hand is a factor, but it is a general rule that the closest threat is the greatest threat. When we begin observation and scanning to heighten our awareness, it is absolutely essential that we first look near and then far. Make this part of your lifestyle, scan from near to far and from right to left. This is why the 30'/360° rule is so important. Know those things that are inside that

30' area first and then move out. Think of potential targets as primary and secondary targets. Primary targets are those things closest to you as a general rule. Yes, it is possible that someone fifty yards away with a rifle can present the same threat as someone two feet away with a knife. However, I think we all agree there is little we can do about a person fifty yards away with a rifle, but the person two feet away can hurt us immediately. Maybe the response to this situation is to use the primary target as cover from the secondary target! Deserves thought, don't you think? Observe and scan the area, deal with primary and secondary targets, be aware of what is going on around you and it will be less likely that startle reflex and lag time will affect your response.

What must now be developed for the Combative Mind is desire! Instructors can tell you what to do, can give you the tools to do it, what they can't make you is willing to do it. You must have the will to fight back, the will to do whatever it takes to come out on top. I have long felt that will beats skill. Create willingness by writing down all the things you will lose if you do not survive an armed confrontation, things that you will give up: loved ones, cherished possessions, and the feelings of those loved ones when you are no longer around. As Sean Connery said to Kevin Costner in the Academy Award winning movie *The Untouchables*; "the first rule of law enforcement is to make sure that when your shift is over, you go home alive." It doesn't matter if you are a law enforcement officer, a soldier, or a legally armed citizen. What is important is that every day you go home to your family alive and unharmed, the same way both physically and mentally as when you left. There have been any number of military and police training films that have tried to deal with the concept of willingness. The one film clip that I have found to be the best came from the 1976 movie, *The Shootist*, with John Wayne and Ron Howard. This was John Wayne's last movie and as most fans of the "Duke" know, he was fighting a life-losing battle with cancer. It was kind of apropos that in this movie he was playing an aging gun fighter battling cancer. In the movie, he befriends a boy played by Howard and takes him for a shooting lesson. They fire the Duke's revolver at a tree and it is clear that the young stable boy is just as good a shot as the aging gunman. Perplexed by this turn of events, the Howard character turns and looks at Wayne and says "wait a minute, you've killed upwards of 30 men and you always come out on top. I nearly tied you shooting!" Wayne's response to this statement could not be any more profound. He says, "Friend, there is nobody out there shooting back at you. It isn't always being fast or even accurate that counts, it's being willing. I found out early that most men, regardless of cause or need, are not willing. They blink an eye or draw a breath before they pull the trigger and I won't." The history of gun fighting has shown that the man who has no reservation about killing has a *huge* advantage.

This state of willingness has been known but not quite understood throughout history. In the book *Triggernometry* by Eugene Cunningham, a study of the old west gun fighters was undertaken. During the research for this book, the author tried to determine exactly what separated these men from the average man of the old west. On page 418 the author wrote "yesterday I asked an old buscadero who does sheer twinkling magic with his six-guns, what he perceived to be the difference between target shooting and the ancient business of gun play. He hesitated not one split second in answering, 'state of mind.' Even if your target shot could make Clay Allison or Harvey Logan or John Wesley Hardin or Billy the Kid look like a bunch of amateurs, not that I believe he could, aerie one of them could walk off the range where they'd be beat and kill the target expert before he could say Jack Robinson or a heap shorter name than that. Chances are he couldn't give St. Peter the beginning of an idea about what happened or why, much less how. The average shooting gallery shot is used to doing this or doing that. Not used to having the split part of a second make the difference between his living and his dying. The gunfighter was schooled to kill." Whether you call it willingness or state of mind, it is something that these Old West gunmen preprogramed into their psyche. There is no hesitation when the time comes. They will do what they do best and that is to act against the threat.

In the interest of simplifying how to develop the Combative Mind, I have developed what I call a "mind-equation," which I call the NESS Brothers. Essentially it puts awareNESS and willingNESS into a common addition problem.

It looks like this:

$$\begin{array}{c} \text{AwareNESS} \\ + \\ \underline{\text{WillingNESS}} \\ \text{PREVAIL!} \end{array}$$

The NESS brothers are a visual model for the installation of a see—act response for personal combat. The NESS brothers is a lifestyle commitment. Awareness means many things. It means, certainly, knowing what's going on around you. It means being aware of your environment and always being vigilant, using the corresponding color codes and an action/response when necessary. It is also being aware of new tactics and techniques that may become available through advanced training, reading and viewing videos. It means being aware of anything that is new and notable that may assist you in your quest for proficiency. It also means willingness. Being willing to do whatever it takes, no matter how distasteful to come out on top of your armed confrontation. It means being willing to train, yes, spending your own time and money to develop proper, needed skills. Many people are not willing to do this. It makes one wonder if people are not willing to invest their own money and time in their ability to prevail, how are they possibly willing to do whatever it takes to prevail in a confrontation?! Part of being willing means controlling fear. It doesn't mean overcoming fear, because I truly believe that fear is your friend, but you need to know how to channel it to willingness. Fear should make you mad, it shouldn't overpower you. How do you control fear? Here is a list, compiled by former Portland, Oregon Police Psychologist Dr. Alexis Artwohl, of just a few things you can do to diminish and control fear. The added comments are mine:

1.   Stay up to date on tactics in all areas of your life. Train regularly with them. Don't just pick one skill, such as firearms. Develop a whole range of needed skills.

2.   Develop confidence backed by real skill. Know that your techniques will work when you need them. The more competent you believe you are, the more you train, and the less likely you are to feel overwhelmed by fear.

3.   Practice mental imagery (aka visualization) of high-risk situations at least once a week. We will deal with how to do this in chapter two.

4.   Learn what the physiological responses are to the flight or fight and understand that it will happen to you no matter

how brave you are. These flight or fight responses have been reviewed earlier in this chapter.

5. Understand and totally accept the possibility that you may one day have to use deadly force. As distasteful as it is, not if, but when you engage you may have to take a life. Yes, it's dirty, it's ugly, it's distasteful, and it's not warm and fuzzy. But it is real.

6. Review past high-risk situations that have come to your attention and determine what was done well and what needed to be improved. Constantly try to improve your observation and assessment skills. The threat that you see coming can be avoided or evaded, making engagement less likely.

7. Trust your instincts. Remember the young lady we talked about earlier in the elevator? Don't worry about social pressures. Do what you think is right. You are the number one important person in your life.

8. Develop a powerful will to prevail, no matter what the situation. Do whatever it takes, no matter how distasteful. Do be willing!

9. Maintain a high level of physical fitness, which we will deal with in another chapter.

10. Be knowledgeable of crime trends and criminals in your area. Certainly a good idea to know your neighborhood and to know your neighbors.

11. Don't let life beat you down. I realize that this is hard at times. In chapter two we will talk about ways to stay mentally positive.

12. Make sure you and your family get any psychological briefing available after any traumatic events. I'm not a warm and fuzzy guy. I'm not a firm believer in all this post-traumatic stress disorder, however, I realize that some people may suffer an aftermath. My feeling is to deal with

these professionally. But also realizing that it can and will happen to you and that you will have to deal with it accordingly. I feel that posttraumatic stress will be reduced, if you accept this beforehand.

To bring this chapter to a close I would like to offer a quote from Clint Smith of Thunder Ranch, which I think sums this up very well. "Get the best training you can afford. But train with the understanding that firearms practice is about 75% physical and 25% mental. However, a gun fight is about 25% physical and 75% mental." Don't ever, ever give up. Stay in the fight as long as you can. They may have pre-planned their attack, but they were not planning on you fighting back. So they, too, are going to be in a state of denial and startle. You never know, if you can just fight on for another second or another minute, it may be just enough for your opponent to give up. Don't be the one that quits as quitters NEVER WIN...they never prevail! They just DIE...

As I was preparing to send this second edition to press, I asked my friend and co-worker, Alan "Opie" Howard, to read it one more time just to make sure I had it right. Opie is a former marine, reitred cop and one of the true pioneers in the field of police mountain biking. As he handed the manuscript back to me, he said,

> *"Dave, once someone cares about you or loves you, you give up the right to give up. You owe it to them to do everything you can to come home."*

Well said, Opie... well said.

Chapter Two

NLP SKILL DEVELOPMENT AND THE WAY OF THE JEDI

"The iron ore thinks itself senselessly tortured in the blast furnace: the tempered steel blade looks back and knows better."
Tibetan Proverb

S ince the last edition, I have been told by other trainers that NLP is "Junk Science," but I don't buy it. Too much of what is involved in NLP has proven its worth. In the early 1980s the U.S. Army's Intelligence and Security Command (INSCOM) commissioned a study of alternative human learning technologies (alternative meaning "new age" type systems such as biofeedback, hypnosis, visualization, etc.) and specifically the use of Neuro-Linguistic Programming. The object of this project was to apply the concepts of NLP, the modeling of excellence, to identify individuals who are working at a superior performance level and model their behaviors, so that training processes could be instilled in others going through a specific training course. The primary model utilized for this was pistol shooting. This project became to be known as the Jedi Project after the mythical Jedi warriors of George Lucas' STAR WARS movies. This project was covered in great detail in a now out of print book entitled *The Warrior's Edge*. The statistical results of the Jedi Project were exciting. While the database was too small to provide any absolutes, the results were undeniable. They showed indisputable effectiveness in performance in terms of different, more effective and modern ways of training combative skills around pistol shooting. Since that time, additional research has shown a great congruence between NLP and various combative training systems, especially traditional martial arts systems. However, NLP has continued to be an excellent way to accelerate a student in advanced combative shooting skills.

One of the suppositions of NLP is that you manage your own internal mental state. This is an incredible challenge, along with recognizing mental state in other human beings and communicating more effectively. NLP has turned out to be an extraordinary learning tool. One of the direct applications, something that many instructors have learned to appreciate, is that with repeated practice in a given technique, it is quickly turned into a long term database that is difficult to do improperly once it is imbedded. The techniques of NLP enable us to anchor, that is recreate, a desired mental state technique on demand (as stated over and over again in Chapter One, instantaneous combative mind, on demand, is essential). This adds that emotional content which gives much more focus to the intensity and the effectiveness of a given technique of the battle to be fought! Besides enhancing combative skills, NLP can specifically provide to the student a more effective tool in which to recreate, emotionally anchor and access those powerful emotional states in combat or in any hostile environment scenario. It gives a strategy to access those states rather than as we have always relied on in the past, by sheer blind luck, fall into the right state of mind. It is a short cut to effective, results in terms of the ability to bring about your resources, physical, emotional, spiritual and mental to bear on the resolution of a combative problem. What NLP does is allow you to do more in the training time available, or cut down on the training time taken to achieve the same goal. It's kind of like accelerated learning, it is the study of excellence in any given field.

The term Neuro-Linguistic Programming roughly translates to "the language of the brain." It is a system for a person to use the brain's capability to copy the correct performance of another and incorporate it into your personal performance. Think of it as a Xerox machine for combative applications. NLP enables the user to recreate a desired mental state or skill on demand. NLP can be used in three formats:

Mental Imagery
Modeling
Anchoring

Mental Imagery, or "visualization," uses the pictures in your brain to pre-set a particular situation. As I said in Chapter One, it is a good idea to play out high-risk situations by using mental imagery at least weekly. What is meant here is to put yourself into a situation that you are likely to encounter. Play it out in your brain like you are watching a DVD, not losing but winning the particular confrontation. By pre-planning, using mental imagery, it is possible to reduce your lag time because you have actually "experienced" the event in your head. No, you haven't experienced it in real life, but you have played out a like-type scenario in your brain so an end result is already pre-programmed, as the brain does not differentiate between what it images and what it experiences. This will allow you to respond instantly without having to orient to it. Remember we said that most people don't plan to fail, they just fail to plan.

What mental imagery does is preprogram a plan of action in your brain for situations that you are likely to face. Let me give you an example. In that same class I told you about earlier, where I was talking to women concerned about sexual assault, I had a woman approach me at a break and told me that her number one nightmare scenario was the parking garage where she worked. She said that quite often she had to work late and her car was parked in the garage, which was fine during the day with people coming and going, but at night she would possibly be alone. She said she was concerned about leaving her office and being attacked in the garage. She could picture in her head a suspect coming out of nowhere with a knife and sexually assaulting her. I asked her how this particular scenario played out in her mind and she said it always ended pretty much with her doing what the guy wanted. Using mental imagery, I asked this woman to replay this particular scenario in her head but coming out with a different ending. The first thing I asked her was how she saw herself walking out of the office and she said that she usually wore a skirt and high heels. I asked her if this type of dress was inhibiting to her in a fight and she said, yes, it was. The skirt was tight fitting for the most part and the heels made it difficult to stand upright and stable. I asked her if this mode of dress was work policy and she stated that it wasn't. I asked her if, on the days that she worked late, it would be possible that she could wear slacks and flat shoes or maybe change into sneakers before she left the office. She said this was possible. I then had her begin the scenario in her head again but this time walking into the parking garage wearing a pair of slacks and tennis shoes. When the subject attacked, instead of "folding her cards" and allowing whatever to happen, I asked her, in her mind, to take a combative stance and as the subject approached her, to go below his reach and strike him in the knee. Then visualize this knee strike disabling him and fleeing to her car or an elevator, whichever would be easier and offer the most security. We then replayed this scenario over and over again with several different outcomes, all of which came out to her benefit. You could see, as we went through this, that her confidence level grew as she was playing this out in her head. Not the first strike or blow had ever been landed on a criminal, but in her head she was capable of doing this and we re-programmed an entire new outcome in her head. As we went through the remainder of the class, you could see a greater level of confidence in this young lady as to how a situation would come to her in the event that a crisis would arise. This is also an excellent example as to how you can anchor a particular response to your repertoire of skills.

One of the best examples of using mental imagery in a combative environment is in Mark V. Wiley's book *FILIPINO MARTIAL CULTURE* published by the Charles E. Tuttle Company. On page 83, the author reveals how Grandmaster Floro Villabrille prepared for his matches. "Prior to his last opponent in a challenge in Hawaii, he spent some time in quiet, visualizing himself repeatedly knocking down his opponent. He claimed that his ability to visualize his opponent's defeat before the actual fight gave him strength, courage, and will to fight until his opponent was unconscious. Villbrille won this match but claims that had he not already been victorious in his mind prior to the fight, he would have lost."

We've already discussed how lag time needs to be reduced. By accessing a combating state of mind, we can respond instantly to situations in which we are threatened. By playing likely scenarios over and over in our head and responding to them instantaneously, with whatever skills and weapons we normally have, we can pre-program a state of mind and action. "State access," as it is known, is used to handle the situation with as much force and fury as necessary. This state access will allow us to go from condition yellow to condition red instantaneously, thus getting inside their reaction loop and responding more quickly. Accessing the combat state of mind is essential and the person who can do it first will be the victor. Remember the person attacking has already made the decision on what they are going to do and how they are going to do it. In order for you to catch up and surpass them you need to move instantaneously and with violence of action in a way that they do not anticipate. This is definitely part of the combative mind. By anchoring this state (and the appropriate response) in your head, you can access this state almost instantaneously. However, it does require some work on your part.

Mental imagery is also used to "see" both the color codes and OODA Loop as you go about your daily routine. Be keeping a mental picture of both of these "mind charts," you can keep yourself at the desired state of awareness/preparation without a great deal of conscious thought. If you think about something long enough, it will become part of your lifestyle. As we have said over and over again, this is a life style commitment.

How will NLP help the combat shooter? By using the techniques known as modeling, which is the copying of a given skill. Everyone reading this book has a good idea of what we need to do in order to shoot well. We need a solid body position, good grip, trigger control, and alignment of the weapon on the target. All of these things must be done over and over again. Let's think about this for a minute, why do we need to recreate a technique when we already know there are techniques that work well? For example, let's look at the wheel. The round configuration of the wheel allows it to roll. We may improve on the materials used to make the wheel, but the basic concept of the wheel has been the same for centuries. You just cannot improve on the concept of the wheel. In regard to shooting, what we need to do is to determine what is necessary in order to save ourselves in a gun fight and train toward this. This is the process used in the Jedi Project by the U.S. Army. They took two groups of soldiers; one went through the basic combat pistol qualification course lasting four and one/half days. The second group was the test group and was given the new NLP-based pistol training which lasted one and one/half days. The NLP group watched the performance of a master shooter and copied his techniques as much as their body would allow. At the end of training, each group fired the same pistol qualification course and scores were evaluated. Among the findings were: Group One had 73% pass the test with 10% scoring at an expert ranking. Group Two, the NLP group, had a 100% pass ratio with 25% qualifying as expert. The Jedi Project demonstrated that advanced human technologies had advantages in both reduction of training time and increase proficiency levels. For those of us in firearms training, and for those who are students, this technology is certainly encouraging. The modeling of excellence is the modeling of those who can already do it well...just do what they do within the limits of your individual skill!

In regard to shooting skills, what do we really need to accomplish? We need to base it on correct fundamentals, which is a great deal of what this book is about. We need to have good concentration followed by consistency. If we concentrate on performing the correct fundamentals consistently, accuracy will result. Speed is a result of lack of unnecessary motion, not spastic muscle manipulation. If we were to put this into a "combative pistol" skill building pyramid, it would look like this:

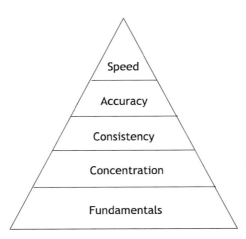

What do we really need to know in an armed confrontation? There are a number of excellent schools and some that are not so excellent, so let's take a look at what we REALLY need to know:

1. How to hit what we are shooting at (which is accuracy) as quickly as possible without complicating the process. I've always liked the SAS motto: "Train hard, fight easy." Don't make this complicated. Remember you're going to deteriorate in skill level. So you want to make your techniques as simple as possible. Remember the seven keys to minimizing reaction time in Chapter One? We need to make this simple so that we can perform at our highest level.

2. How to draw the weapon quickly while keeping a shooting grip. In a situation that is going to be over in milliseconds, we haven't got the time to be fumbling around with our gun to get it in line with our arm. The grip on the gun has to be absolutely correct the minute it clears leather (or in some cases Kydex), in order for us to prevail in a gun fight. Of course, having the gun in your hand is actually the fastest draw and this comes down to your level of awareness, but few of us can walk around with a pistol in our hand.

3. Learning to look for, recognize and make use of available cover, i.e., stopping fire. A bad guy shooting at you is not

a good thing! In addition, your opponent decides what is cover as cover is not the same for a .25 auto and an AK-47!

4. If cover is not available, removing ourselves from incoming fire. Let's be honest, incoming rounds have the right of way. Avoiding this means doing things like shooting and moving, thinking on the run and engaging multiple hostiles while not standing flat-footed. While it is true that armed confrontations are not simple affairs, your skills will deteriorate. Don't make things unnecessarily complicated.

Hopefully, what we will do for the remainder of this book, is deal with these subjects in a simple, straightforward manner so the student can get a good basis of learning before they go forward for additional hands on training. But remember the advantages of using NLP when developing your combative skills. By modeling what you want to do, practicing it as perfectly as possible as often as possible, concentrating hard, visualizing the skills perfectly in your mind and using all of the above to anchor quality performance and response, your road to combative proficiency will be an easier and more enjoyable journey.

To conclude this complex chapter, I would like to introduce the reader to Marcus Wynne. Marcus is a lifetime martial artist in Kali and has an abundance of real world combative experience including time in the U.S. Army playing "hide and seek" with North Korean soldiers in the DMZ, duty as a U.S. Air Marshal flying high risk counter-terrorist missions to the world's hot spots, as a bodyguard/executive protection specialist and finally as a researcher/trainer for his own company, Jedi Ventures. Marcus closed the doors on his company to become a novelist. His trio of action/espionage books were best sellers and gave an excellent look into the world of special operations. In my opinion, Marcus is the master in regard to using NLP as a combative training system.

D: *How did you get started with NLP and combative skills?*

M: I was first exposed to neuro-linguistic programming through a book called *The Warrior's Edge*, by Alexander, Morris, and Groller. That book outlined what was called the Jedi Project, which I think you mention elsewhere in your book. There has been for many years a great deal of official government interest in enhancing human performance, and NLP techniques have been used for everything from interrogation to improving pistol shooting. I took some classes from an influential figure in the NLP field, Paul Scheele, and began to experiment with the techniques to see how I could influence my performance the way the subjects in the Jedi Project did.

I was doing this before I was recruited for the Federal Air Marshal Program. After I had been through training, I was asked to take over tactical training for the Air Marshal Teams, so I had plenty of opportunity to apply NLP and neural-based learning techniques on the students that were going through the Air Marshal Basic Course, which was a fourteen-week course of instruction at the Federal Law Enforcement Training Center at Marana, Arizona, where a lot of the counter-terrorist training for the Feds was going on.

While I was involved in training, I had access to, on a regular basis, the trainers from the FBI HRT, CIA paramilitary, DOD Spec Ops and Special Forces. I asked these guys what they knew about using neural-based learning for combatives and none of them knew anything about it, even though the government had drawn from some of those organizations people who were to be trained in advanced mental concepts. So with the encouragement of these guys, I continued my research during training and continued using my students and me as guinea pigs to see how it all worked out.

After I left the Air Marshal Program and federal service in 1993 (I started doing the research and applications in the late 1980s) I continued to refine the techniques and continue the research. I published two short articles in *Combat Handguns Magazine* about the OODA loop and using NLP for pistol skills in the mid-90s – I've seen those articles in a number of classrooms as training aids, and I've seen myself quoted (though not always attributed) from those same articles in other people's writings and classroom presentations.

The places I focused on in training were using NLP to increase situational awareness through the OODA loop, create an ideal emotional/physical state I called state access, and enhance the manipulation of the weapon while under stress. The laboratory I continued to use were students – I was doing freelance training at the time and taught dignitary protection in a high-threat environment to a wide range of students, from military to private sector. After I had refined the material somewhat, I took it out of the realm of combatives and generalized it as critical skill performance while under high stress. I was hired to consult with NASA's Astronaut Program and the BMW Factory Racing Team, among other organizations.

So that's how I got started.

D: *How did you use NLP to enhance situational awareness?*

M: Elsewhere in your book you talk about Colonel John Boyd and the OODA loop. Boyd was a tactical genius whose work has been applied everywhere from fighter pilot tactics to business strategy. I researched his work after being exposed to it while consulting with NASA, and wrote the first article that applied the OODA loop to pistol combatives in *Combat Handguns* in June of 1996.

The critical thing about the OODA loop is the initial entry point, OBSERVATION. From the NLP perspective, OBSERVATION is more than just the visual skill of looking around, it involves total involvement in the environment you happen to be in. Whether you're conscious of it or not, your body and brain are simultaneously processing millions of bits of information about your environment and the other humans in it each and every second. The thing is we have filters, born of our genetic predisposition, experiences, and training, that filter all that information so that we're not overwhelmed with it. Filters take raw subjective data from your senses and either delete it, generalize from it, or distort it – hence the saying that no two people see the same thing at the same time, especially when under stress.

So what's important in applying NLP in the OODA loop is using all your senses and paying attention to what they're telling you, which sometimes requires a reeducation of our sensory filters.

Your filters start working at an early age, when your parents and other people start literally telling you what to pay attention to. We learn primarily from our genetic predisposition (which leads some people to be more visual, more auditory, or more kinesthetic in their perceptions than others), our life experiences, and lastly from training. The variable that is most flexible is that of training – and you can multiply the effect if you give the student experiences in training. By that I mean using scenario-based training far more than most organizations do, with the scenarios built for giving the student the specific experiences that will benefit them in their job. For instance, teaching observation in the classroom can be a sterile experience – but if you put students into a scenario with skilled role players, with some role players coached on providing the body language cues that indicate that they're armed and may be considering violence (and we have plenty of real videotape from the street to show that sort of thing) and give them immediate feedback and correction on their decisions, then you've really accomplished something in giving them an experience, rather than a lecture about what to look for.

It's important that we maximize our observation, because that's the entry point into the OODA loop. The more you observe and are engaged in your environment the faster your personal OODA loop turns, which means you have that much more time to formulate the appropriate response. Remember, OBSERVATION leads you into ORIENTATION, so half the OODA loop is about perceiving threat, and DECISION and ACTION are based on what you perceive.

NLP-based exercises can develop great observational skills in the student, which enhances their overall state of situational awareness.

D: *You talk a lot about state, and state access...what is that?*

M: A state is a combination of two things: your physiology, or your body chemistry and neurological workings; and your internal representation. That is how and what you're thinking about. Being happy is a specific set of internal chemistry working which is reflected in your posture, your smile, your sense of lightness and all that, combined with your thinking and internal representation in the brain, which is a set of feelings: light, relaxed, all those things that add up to happy.

Everyone has a set of states that they go through in the course of the day: sleepy, happy, alert, worried, bored, fatigued, sleepy, etc. What's important for combative purposes are a state of general alertness, or being in the most observant state so as to maximize your OODA loop; and a trained state, the fighting state.

I talked about the state of general alertness as being one of the most important components of the combative mind, to use your term. It doesn't matter how great a shot you are or what a great fighter you are if you don't see trouble coming soon enough to prepare for it. So alertness, being cued into your environment, that's the important aspect. But just as important, actually the two go hand in hand, is the fighting state, the physiology and internal representations that add up to ferocious resolve.

I use those words specifically, and they're drawn from the work of Richard Bandler, who was one of the co-founders of NLP. A state of general alertness will cue you in to what's happening and give you the time and options to decide whether to fight or not. But if you're going to fight, you need to have all your mental attributes lined up and ready to go, and that is what we call fighting state. I'm presupposing that anybody reading this book has made a conscious decision that if necessary, they will fight with everything they have up to and including deadly force.

How do you create that state? Well, everybody (or at least most normally functioning human beings) has it in them. The brain has four major triggers deep in the reptile brain feed, fu*k, flee, and fight, the four Fs. The thing is that the fight reflex gets socialized at an early age and people learn how to use words and other actions to prevent and avoid actual physical violence. But the brain and the body are hard wired for fighting. The easiest way to get a student in touch with that is to have them get calm, close their eyes, and visualize vividly someone attacking someone they love, like their wife or husband or child. Have them vividly experience the internal representation of what they imagine, because remember that the brain doesn't distinguish between reality and something vividly imagined enough. If they do their work, they'll feel a kinesthetic change in their body, the body will tilt forward, weight will shift to the balls of the feed, their hands may clench, they'll hunch the head...when you see that and some other body cues, then you know that they've found the fighting state.

Then you want to anchor that – have people practice their defensive skills while they're in that fighting state, and they'll have access to both the state and their physical skills, whether it's shooting, hand to hand, blades, whatever.

That's where most traditional firearms and combative training go awry – people learn their defensive skills in the classroom and on the range, but the state that they're in is one of being a student, not of a fighter. Some people pick it up naturally because by genetic predisposition they're combative. But a lot, maybe most, don't. So when they have to use the skills for real, there's significant lag time as they fight first to get into the right state and then manipulate the weapon under stress. You can watch this in police videotape when an officer is taken by surprise and must retreat...watch how the body language changes when they overcome their surprise and present the weapon to defend themselves. You can watch the state access taking place right in front of your eyes. As an instructor, you have to create experiences like that for your students so they don't have to discover it on their own in the street.

D: *You mention manipulating the weapon under stress. How do you use NLP to enhance that performance under stress?*

M: Well, you mention elsewhere in the book using visualization and imagery for training. That's important, but one real foundation stone is having students do intense emotionally vivid visualizations while they're using the weapon. If a student is firing each shot at his target in the same state of excitation as he would be if it was a human being, you are multiplying the training effect with quantum leaps. This is very intense and difficult to sustain, especially with a large group. So you chunk it down and do it at key points in the instructional flow.

Mental rehearsal or visualizing the possibilities are all good approaches. When working with weapons, visually rehearsing your draw, the continuous flow principle, all those are great – but what many people leave out with the visualization is the kinesthetic, or imagining what it feels like and feeding that back to themselves. For instance, you can sit in the chair with your eyes closed and visualize a perfect draw. That works. It works better if you stand up and go through the motions without a weapon with your eyes closed. It works even better if you go through the motions with visualization with the actual weapon (dry of course). But the ultimate results are when you visualize so vividly that you're getting an emotional response from yourself and you're going through the emotions with the weapon in your hand. And you can do this anywhere, anytime. This leads to the accelerated learning phenomenon I've seen with this stuff – people just make quantum leaps in terms of performance when you get the entire organism, emotions, mental imagery, and kinesthetic working together.

D: *This is all great stuff – how do you put it all together?*

M: You put it all together by spending the time and making the emotional investment in your training. Fighting for your life will be the most intense experience of your life, and in order to survive that emotional dump you have to put yourself through some intense experiences to be prepared. And understand you don't have to be a DELTA operator or Navy SEAL to do this – I've seen house-wives and rape survivors who did the emotional content exercises out shoot seasoned police officers in real world scenarios.

The ultimate responsibility lies with the individual and their approach to training. Anybody can do these exercises and make themselves better prepared for violence – the question is, will they take responsibility for it?

Chapter Three

LEGALITIES IN USING FORCE FOR PERSONAL DEFENSE

"Sue the Bastards!"

Author Unknown

A number of years ago I attended a defensive pistol course taught by one of the best-known firearms instructors in the world. While I found this training very worthwhile, one incident that occurred in the classroom portion has stayed with me all these years. The instructor was giving an excellent lecture on how to deliver deadly force in a crisis situation. During the lecture one student raised his hand and asked what should he expect from the criminal justice system after deadly force was used. The instructor, a highly knowledgeable and skilled individual, stopped and looked at this student as if he had just come in from another planet, and said, "I'm here to teach you how to shoot, how to defend yourself. If you have legal problems, hire a lawyer, that's what they're for."

I have never forgotten this incident and since that moment I continue to disagree with this instructor's thoughts on the matter. When dealing with the topic of personal security, I think it is essential to discuss what the student involved in such a situation can expect from the criminal justice system. This is especially true when it comes to a situation in which the taking of a life has occurred. While surviving the confrontation is the ultimate goal, personal liability cannot be ignored.

It has been told to me that taking a totally justifiable shooting case to a grand jury will cost an individual citizen $10,000.00 at a minimum. In order to go to trial in a contested shooting case, it will be upwards of $50,000.00 or more. This is something the student of personal security certainly needs to understand. It should not scare them away from personal defense, but I am a strong believer in feeling that being forewarned is forearmed. Defending oneself legally, even when you're totally in the right is going to be costly. At this point I feel that it is very important to state that I am not a lawyer. I am a retired police officer with 30 plus years experience. While I dealt with the law, I did not interpret it. At the same time I do not want the reader to become so liability phobic that they will be afraid to respond when it is appropriate. I have come to believe that the American Law Enforcement community has reached this point. Needless to say, this "liability first" trend bothers me more than just a little bit. Most law enforcement agencies have a use of force policy and contained in this policy is a diagram known as the Use of Force Continuum. This is a tool that is used nationwide by law enforcement agencies to train their personnel in the proper use and level of force. This continuum is basically a chart that says that if the bad guy does this, the good guy should do that. Whatever option is used is based on the number of circumstances such as the good guys level of training and skill, available equipment, the number of bad guys, etc. The underlying message is that the action must be reasonable based on the circumstances at hand. If the good guy continues to use force after the attack has stopped then he or she is facing some serious legal difficulties. In law enforcement circles this principle is called "the reasonableness doctrine." It is currently a growing trend to do away with force continuums as they can confuse an officer's response. A growing number of police agencies are using reasonableness as a model for response. This is a trend I agree with wholeheartedly.

This doctrine has evolved out of numerous court cases, most of all involving the use of force by law enforcement officers. While it is true that the law enforcement officers and agents of the government will be judged to a higher standard than the legally armed citizen, I feel it is safe to say that reasonableness will always be a factor anytime violence is used in self defense. I was recently contacted by a lawyer who feels that state by state "castle doctrine" laws will ultimately lead to a different reasonable standard for armed citizens and this may be true. Until then, I think it is safe to stick with the standards set by the courts. It makes no difference whether the person involved is a police officer or a legally armed citizen. Your actions, if you are defending yourself, will be judged on the basis of whether or not the action was reasonable based on the circumstances at the moment in question.

For example: The courts have ruled that deadly force should only be used when a person is facing a situation in which death or serious physical harm to himself or others could result if they do not act. Anything less than this is not considered reasonable. Generally for someone to place you in a position where you are in fear of death or bodily harm three things must be present:

1. **Ability.** Does the individual involved have the ability to cause serious physical harm or death? This usually means a weapon or some personal skill.

2. **Opportunity.** Is your assailant in a position to cause serious physical harm or death? This usually refers to distance based on the skill or weapon the person has available to them.

3. **Jeopardy.** Has your assailant given you reason to believe that you are in fear of death or serious physical harm? This usually refers to his/her actions and/or what the assailant says.

So what should you do if you are forced into a situation where deadly force is required? Well, quite frankly, expect to be treated like a criminal suspect. As a matter of fact, you *are* a suspect! You will be the center of a criminal investigation and you should think accordingly. You should do the following:

1. **Remain at the scene and await the arrival of the police.** Do not be in a threatening posture when they arrive.

2. **Do not try and change the physical evidence at the scene.** Trying to place a gun in the hands of an unarmed suspect will only get you into further trouble. The level of Forensic Science in the new millennium will uncover such an unsophisticated attempt to modify evidence. The courts will be more understanding of an individual who killed out of fear or panic than a person who tries to tamper with evidence.

3. **Say little.** The police may say they need your statement to proceed with the investigation, but this is not true. Homicides are investigated every day with the most important witness being deceased. It is best to make a short statement such as he tried to kill me and I had to shoot and then ask for a lawyer. There is nothing wrong with heading the police in the right direction, but don't

say anything you are likely to regret. You have the right
to remain silent. Use it.

4.   **Ask for a lawyer.** This is your right. Find a lawyer who
understands the dynamics of use of force cases. Find out
whom the police in your area use and have his/her card on
hand. Even if you are totally in the right, you will need to
talk to a lawyer, if for no other reason than to get the
facts straight about the incident. You must remember
that you will be coming down from an extreme adrenaline
rush. Remember in the first chapter when we talked
about body alarm reaction? You will not be thinking
clearly. Talking with a lawyer will help you get your story
straight as well as compose yourself before you give the
police a statement.

Remember, it is possible to amend a statement, but you cannot
change it. Once you have spoken it and it is written down, it will be
there forever. It will not go away. You have individual rights under
the Constitution of the United States. Use them. Do not let law
enforcement officials pressure you into doing something you are not
yet ready to do. I have been in the distressing situation of having my
Miranda rights read to me and I can tell you, it is *very* scary! Don't
panic, keep your cool and *think*. Remember, protect yourself. Just
like in the armed confrontation, no one will be there to protect you,
you must protect yourself. The aftermath is the same. Protect
yourself from prosecution, no one else will.

Chapter Four

PERSONAL FITNESS FOR COMBATIVES

"Donuts have already killed more cops than gunfire ever will!"
Sgt. Chuck Humes

T hose of us in law enforcement know what it is like to fight the "Red Man®." The Red Man® is usually an instructor dressed in a padded Red Man® or FIST suit, so they cannot be injured by the baton strikes or hand-to-hand blows delivered by their students. The padded suit gives the student an opportunity to fight with a living, breathing human versus a punching bag or a foam dummy. If you have never had the opportunity to fight the Red Man® for a minute, you are missing out on a very enlightening experience. It's always educational to see how even the youngest and fittest police academy student can become totally worn out by a one minute session of punching, kicking, fighting and rolling around with the padded instructor. After a minute or so, you come to realize very quickly how important physical fitness is for personal security. What did you say? You have a handgun? You will just shoot this attacker? Well, maybe, maybe not. What if the individual attacks you with nothing more than their fist. Is it going to be reasonable, based on the Reasonableness Doctrine, to draw your weapon and shoot this person? No... no, it's not. It is not, normally, a reasonable level of force to shoot an unarmed individual. That means in order to protect yourself you are going to have to go "mano-a-mano" with this attacker. Whether it be open hand or baton, you are still going to be using a great deal of swinging, punching, screaming, yelling, and kicking to defend yourself. This requires aerobic fitness. My question to the reader is, do you have it? Even if you don't have to fight man to man, or in some cases woman to woman, just the adrenaline rush of facing the hostile encounter can be physically taxing. I recently taught a carbine course where a rather large male had to go sit down between each relay of fire to catch his breath. Does anyone really think a gun will help this man if he gets into a real fight? I think he will be "toast" and I told him so!

There are documented cases where out of shape individuals have succumbed to a heart attack during a crisis situation because they were not in good enough physical condition to withstand the physiological "chemical dump" at the time of the altercation. Think about what your last thoughts would be as you succumb to a heart attack or you are physically incapable of defending your loved ones and seeing them fall prey to a predator, simply because you were not physically capable to defend them. It gives you pause, doesn't it? If not, it should! Without a doubt, there is a certain level of fitness needed to engage in personal defense. Carrying around a concealed handgun does not replace individual fitness. I'm not saying that you have to look like Arnold Schwartzenegger or Bruce Lee in order to be physically capable of fighting back. But you do have to have enough "wind" in order to stay upright for at least several minutes during a confrontation. Do you really think you will stand still when rounds are fired in your direction or punches are thrown at your face?

I'm not going to spend page after page in lecturing you on how to get physically fit. There are many books and magazines dedicated to the subject and let's face it – all of us reading this book know how to get ourselves in better physical condition. Essentially it comes down to *eating less and moving more*. It's a simple thing. It's like developing a Combative Mind. It is a life style choice. As a matter of fact, physical fitness should be considered part of developing the Combative Mind. Okay, so you have taken a look at yourself and you realize that maybe you could use a little help. How do you begin? First of all, go to your doctor and get a good physical. This is essential if you are derelict in seeing the doctor on a regular basis. An annual physical is an excellent way to begin any physical fitness program. In addition it gives you a good insight into exactly what your "state of body" is.

Once you have received a clean bill of health, or told how to get yourself healthier, the best way to begin is a good, hard walking program. Get your significant other to participate with you. Let's face it, they could probably use some good fitness time themselves and if they are already fit, then helping you out will be something that will be in their best interest. A good, hard 30-minute walk as many days of the week as possible is a good place to start. It doesn't cost very much. A good pair of walking shoes is the only real expense (running shoes if you opt for that). Don't skimp here. Good shoes are like any other piece of combative gear. Once you have developed this into your daily routine, then put in some common calisthenics; push ups, crunches, jumping jacks, squat thrusts, things like this that can be done without costly equipment and are extremely beneficial to help tone the body. If walking becomes boring, elevate to jogging and then running. It has been shown that running and jogging are the best aerobic exercises due to their lack of high costs and specialized facilities.

If you have access to a swimming pool or a bike, they are excellent physical fitness exercises. Swimming works the whole body; the chest, the legs, the abdominal muscles. Biking works mostly the lower muscles. So a biking program will require some type of weight lifting or calisthenics. The important thing here is to increase your aerobic capabilities as well as tone your body. Again, you don't have to look like Mr. Olympia, but trimming off some of that excess fat, and being able to do some push-ups, is a good way to begin a healthier lifestyle. And a healthier lifestyle certainly increases your ability to defend yourself, whether it is hand to hand or with a firearm. Get fit and stay fit. It's a daily routine. It's just as important as getting to the range. Mindset, physical fitness, combative skills; they are truly the Combative Triad.

Chapter Five

OTHER THINGS TO THINK ABOUT

"Preparation, not paranoia."
Dennis Anderson and Chuck Remsberg of Calibre Press

Before we move on to the realm of personal combat with pistols, there are a few other things that I would like to address. I'm not going to go in depth on any of these, but I do want you to understand there is more to personal security than just arming yourself with a handgun. As you are well aware, almost to the point of nausea, I feel the primary components of personal combat are awareness and willingness; part of awareness is readiness. A large part of readiness is being prepared to meet any level of threat. Not every attack is going to involve a deadly threat. Most will involve some lesser level of force. This being the case, it would be wise for any serious student of personal combatives to learn some type of hand-to-hand fighting system. This doesn't mean that you have to dedicate your life to a particular martial art, but understanding some basic techniques of open hand skills and then practicing them when appropriate would be a wise move.

Remember the chapter on legalities, when I discussed about the use of force continuum and the Reasonableness Doctrine? The vast majority of threats that you face **WILL NOT** be at a level in which using a firearm would be reasonable. Concentrating only on firearms skills is making oneself woefully unprepared as most confrontations will be lesser levels, which will have to be handled by either disengagement, avoidance, or hand-to-hand skills. There are a number of short duration, hand-to-hand combat courses available throughout the United States and Europe. These courses can be no more than several days and as long as a week. They build on the gross motor skills necessary for personal combat. Again, these courses are only designed to introduce skills. They do not introduce willingness. Without the desire to use them, the skills, themselves are worthless. A great deal of information is introduced during the short duration of these courses and the instructors make the assumption that once the skills are instilled in the student, the student will continue to practice them until they are mastered. There is no way that a skill can be mastered in the short duration of a single course. Listen, learn, and practice. It's amazing the level of skill that can be developed during a short duration personal defense course, if additional practice is dedicated to it once the class is over.

Two of the best **short term** hand to hand courses that I have seen are the "Close Quarter Personal Control" (CQPC) Course taught at the Tactical Defense Institute of West Union, Ohio. The other is the Dynamic Striking Techniques course taught by Chuck Humes of the Police Institute of Tactical Training in Toledo, Ohio. Chuck teaches techniques that are simple to use and easy to learn. Addresses for both of these schools are located at the end of the book. Both of these courses deal with simple to learn elbow, knee strikes, palm, heel strikes and kicks. They can be learned very quickly and have proven to be very effective in the street.

If you are fortunate enough to have been trained in Duane Dieter's Close Quarter Defense (CQD) training, then you may have very well received the best all-around defensive training ever developed. A result of a life time of study, Mr. Dieter has created a three tier system that has been embraced by high speed military and police units and has been *proven* in numerous encounters world-wide. Having been adopted as the *official* system of the US Navy SEAL teams his training schedule is filled with military and law enforcement personnel. The CQD system not only deals with physical skills, but also how to train the mind for combat. While I have not had the good fortune to be trained by Mr. Dieter, I have been exposed to his system via people who have been through it and it is most impressive. As good as CQPC, CQD and dynamic striking techniques are, the most proven system is Kelly McCann's "combatives" system. Based on the hand to hand system taught to S.O.E. and O.S.S. operatives in WWII, McCann has refined this fighting system into an effective and efficient training program that must be experienced to truly appreciate.

It has been my experience that street fights are never the closely choreographed encounters of the movies in which Steven Segal or Chuck Norris take on a number of armed suspects single-handedly as they attack the hero one at a time. They are wrestling, punching, pushing, grabbing, gouging and rolling on the ground situations that are very unlike the stylistic fights on television. As a matter of fact, fighting on the ground is an important part of any combative training program, whether it is hand-to-hand, baton, pepper spray or even firearms. Think about the fights that you have had in the schoolyard. Didn't the vast majority of them end up wrestling on the ground? It's a very disadvantageous location to be in because you do not have the stability of your feet to help plant your body so that you can use your upper body as in strikes and punches. Learning to grapple on the ground with handgun, baton, pepper spray or open hand is a very wise thing to master. Phil Messina and his Modern Warrior Training Center on Long Island, New York have long been recognized as the master of ground fighting techniques. Don't confuse ground fighting with the grappling you see in MMA matches. If there are rules, it's a sport, not a fight. If you are not cheating, you're not trying hard enough to win!

Other useful tools in the non-firearms realm are the use of OC sprays and expandable batons. OC Spray (or Oleoresin Capsicum) is a derivative of red peppers, which have long been known to sting the eyes, nasal passages and other orifices on the face creating a serious distraction. The good thing about OC Spray is that it works on most everything, including dogs. The bad thing is that the more the individual is introduced to OC, the less effect that it has. But in the world of what I like to call "Stun and Run" techniques, a shot of OC to the face may be just what is needed to give time to do a few quick elbow or knee strikes and leave the area. To me, OC spray can be compared to being the poor man's flash bang grenade or distraction device.

Expandable batons, like those from Armament Systems and Procedures (ASP) or the Monadnock Auto-lock batons, can add a degree of distance and enhanced striking capability that is not available from open hand techniques. Because the batons are expandable, they close to a relatively small size that can be concealed in a pocket or carried in the palm of the hand. However, they can be opened quickly or extended with just a flick of the wrist. Once extended to lengths varying between 16" and 26", they make a very affective striking tool that can be used against the large muscle masses of the body, primarily the arms, the legs and the mid-section. When closed, it can be used as a kubotan. The expandable baton should never be used against vital areas of the body such as the groin and the head, as they can result in death. If deadly force is justified, then so be it, but for the vast majority of situations in which an expandable baton will be used, it is unlikely that such force would be justified. However, I do realize that non-deadly force can turn into deadly force with a blink of an eye. Yes, surviving the confrontation is the paramount problem at hand, but one should never lose sight of the aftermath of any confrontation. A quality-training program with an expandable baton can last as little as four hours. Once again, it is up to the student, once the class is over, to continue to practice the techniques learned. But as far as the "simple is good" (SIG) type techniques go, the expandable baton meets this need like few other implements. Expandable batons and OC sprays are simple to use tools that can be learned very quickly and have been proven over and over again in actual street confrontations to be most effective.

Another area that should not be overlooked by the student of personal security is a defensive (or offensive?) driving course. A defensive driving course does not require the student to do James Bond-like "J" turns, such as those seen in the movies. The content of the course that I am speaking of requires a student to be able to quickly remove him or herself from a potentially hazardous situation. Such courses do a lot to heighten the awareness of the student when they are behind the wheel of the vehicle. The problem with driving in our cars is that we think of them much like our homes. When in our own personal space; we tend to forget what's going on around us other than the vehicle and traffic activity directly in front. The threat while driving usually comes at times when the vehicle is stopped in traffic. A solid defensive driving course will show the student how to not trap him or herself in the traffic flow. It will show them how to always leave avenues of escape, how to look for ambush, to develop counter-car-jacking techniques, how to use the vehicle as the ultimate weapon, if necessary. There are a number of schools offering this type of training including The Gryphon Group in Florida, BSR in West Virginia and U.S. Training Center in North Carolina, just to name a few. All of these schools have been training drivers in counter-terrorism techniques for many years. All offer excellent courses for the concerned citizen or law enforcement officer who feels they may face such a threat on the nation's highways. They will train the student in whatever type of vehicle they drive normally, whether that is a sports car, a mini van, an SUV or family sedan. Their techniques of defensive driving are simple but effective and cover a wide range of vehicle techniques in a short period of time.

Medical self-help treatment is essential. If you get involved in a fistfight, you should plan to be hit. If you get involved in a knife fight, you should plan to be cut. And heaven forbid if you ever get involved in a gunfight, you should expect to be shot. We will discuss later on, in the section on handgun ammunition, that handguns are not very effective man stoppers. Statistics have shown for many years that if you are shot with a handgun you don't die instantly unless a violation of a vital organ occurs or you bleed out in a couple of minutes due to the severing of a major artery. It's quite likely that you will not die of a handgun wound. Coupled with the fact that medical technology is better than ever before, it is likely that surviving a gunshot is what will occur. However, it is a priority that you be an active participant in your own survival, not only during the confrontation but also after the confrontation. If you are cut or wounded you must make an immediate overt act to treat that wound. These days, a number of firearm training schools offer wound treatment courses and you should consider attending one. As any combat veteran can tell you, it is a necessary skill to have. I am always amazed that when I talk to Vietnam, Afghanistan or Iraq vets who saw combat how, during the heat of battle when they were wounded, were capable of detaching themselves from the battle, deal with their wounds as best they could and then return to the fight. This is certainly the epitome of willingness.

While there are a number of courses now being offered across the country dealing with personal medical emergencies, I have had great success in taking the basic Red Cross First Aid Course and applying it to self-medical situations. The sections in the Red Cross First Aid Course book that apply with cuts, burns, abrasions and other wounds can easily be applied to treating oneself. While it is true that the course deals with treating another person's wounds, the same techniques can be used if one has the ability to detach themselves from the situation and actually treat themselves as if they are treating someone else. Certainly this will take a great deal of willingness, but combat veterans all over the world, as well as wounded police officers, have shown time and time again that it can be done. Closing the wound, stopping loss of blood and trying to keep from going into shock are the essential elements of treating any gunshot wound. Treatment is no different just because it is applied to oneself. Besides, the Red Cross First Aid Course, many of us know a paramedic or Emergency Medical Technician who works on the local fire department. Seek this person out and invite him over to the house on a slow Sunday afternoon or while having a few beers, create a basic self-help first aid course. Liability is not a concern. Are you going to sue yourself?

It is easier to be treated in such self-help medical techniques than one would believe. Once a basic level of knowledge is obtained, it is a good idea to develop a self-help medical kit to keep with you at all times. Now, I realize that you cannot carry a first aid kit around on your person at all times, but something as close as your office, your car, and your home would be a good idea. One of the best sources for such first aid kits is Adventure Medical Kits (1-800-324-3517). These kits are excellent additions to any combative "toolbox." Those of us who are involved or interested in personal defense should have one near or with us. If a situation arises, the self-help medical kit may very well be just as important as the firearm, ammunition, and the holster.

Last but not least, if you carry a gun, you should carry a knife. I'm not talking about this in the same vein as engaging in knife fighting. I have had a few knife fighting courses and I realize that when the blades come out the last place I want to be is nearby. I do not ridicule those that have engaged in an advance level of knife fighting skill. I, too, have sought such training, however, I have come to realize that the correct response for a knife is to use a firearm, if possible. If not, get the hell away! The thought of engaging in a knife slash duel is like running into a blender—the effect would be the same! For those that are interested in learning more about knife fighting techniques there is a large body of training courses, printed material and DVDs that cover this subject. Mike Janich of Martial Blade Concepts is a good place to start. They are not hard to locate. My feeling is that carrying a knife when you carry a gun is to have a tool, a cutting implement that can be used for a wide range of functions. Whether it be to cut various materials as you go about your daily life or to assist yourself in medical self-help is situationally dependent. But, having a cutting implement is a good idea. To me, a folding blade that can be opened with one hand and has a blade length of 2¼" to 3" allows the knife to be used for a wide range of functions, anything from a last ditch weapon to a cutting tool. It needs to be small enough so that when carried it is comfortable without undue burden. For those who wish to carry bigger knives, all the more power to you. But I feel that a knife length of 2½" to 3" may very well be ideal for a wide range of circumstances.

Figure 4

Good examples of daily carry knives:

Top to bottom:
Emerson Mach 1
Emerson CQC7
Masters of Defense Hornet
Spyderco Native
Columbia River SRT

It has been my personal experience to have some type of light with you at all times. It may be nothing more than a key ring size "MiniPhoton" LED light which is about the size of a nickel. Better yet, a compact white light like the Surefire back-up, executive or Luma-Max series. These lights offer 80 plus lumens of white LED light and are not much larger than the palm of your hand. Don't think you need a light because you work the day shift? Read the *911 Commission Report*—the people who had personal flashlights got out of the twin towers alive!

Think about more than just the gun and related accessories when thinking about personal security. For every plan there should be a contingency. Hopefully, such contingency will evolve around avoidance and evasion. At the same time don't become paranoid in your responses, you can't cover every possible situation you may face. Think about your daily life style, think about the environment in which you live and work and try to cover the situations that are most likely to occur. You can do this without burdening yourself with so much equipment that it is almost impossible to move without clanking.

Chapter Six

SELECTING THE PERSONAL CARRY HANDGUN

"Beware of the man who has but one gun, for he likely knows how to use it."

Origin unknown

hose of us who are firearms enthusiasts have a history of spending a great deal of money adding guns to our collections that we will probably never use, let alone fire more than once. Don't misunderstand, I am not making fun of those who are gun collectors as it is a wonderful hobby. I am not a gun collector, however. I am an individual who is concerned about personal security and I have firearms, which I think fill a void in my personal defensive plan. I do have handguns that I use for various teaching chores, handguns for various personal security chores and long guns that I feel are really the ultimate in small arms when the need arises, but I also realize that I am less likely to have a long gun than a handgun when trouble starts.

Over the last several years I have sold most of my gun "collection" in an effort to trim down to those guns that I feel have a particular task and have used the money to equip my remaining weapons so that they are set up just the way I want them. I will go into my thought process concerning this in Chapter Seven.

I greatly respect the gun collector, but I have equal respect for armed citizens who have the guns they need to solve perceived problems and nothing more. Instead of spending money owning ten different 1911 45's or six different M1 Garands, maybe it would be a better idea to have a primary and backup 1911 and M1 Garand and spend the remaining monies on ammunition and training time to become increasingly proficient with these weapons?! You don't have to be a "gun nut" (a term I hate) in order to be concerned about your personal security. As a matter of fact, the individual who picks one gun with related accessories, has that gun set up for them in such a way that it is easy to use and then practices with it, might very well be the wisest of all! No offense intended to those of you who are gun collectors. This message is intended for those who are interested in firearms for personal security only. Pick the gun that best suits your needs then go forward and be happy.

How do you pick this best gun for your needs? Well, a great deal of it depends on you as a person and the environment in which you live and work. Is the gun going to be kept in a night stand, or is it going to be carried on your person? Is it going to be concealed, or is it going to be carried out in the open? Such things would certainly be a factor when selecting the size and weight of your gun.

This book is dedicated to the combative use of the semi-automatic pistol because it is far and away the most popular choice for said purpose in the 21st Century. As I stated earlier, I was criticized after the first release of this book because I did not cover revolvers...after all, a revolver is a handgun, right? This would double the size of the book as revolvers have their own manual of arms. This being the case, I will focus on the gun that nine out of ten have selected for personal use. However, I do not dismiss revolvers. Short-barreled revolvers of 2" to 3" in length can be very handy and most effective tools for defense. For those who want the ultimate in simplicity and reliability in a personal weapon, a revolver is certainly an excellent choice. However, being a realist, I understand the majority of people in this day and age are going to select a semiautomatic pistol. If you want more information on the use of the combative revolver, read Ed Lovette's *The Snubby Revolver* available from Paladin Press.

Clint Smith says that the reason he carries a full size 1911 .45 "is because no one makes anything bigger." Well said. I understand Clint's thought process on this. However, it has been my experience that few people are going to be as committed to carrying a full size fighting weapon as Clint. Most people are going to want something a little more compact and easier to carry. At the same time we don't want to go too far in regard to compactness. A gun that is small and easy to carry around may be nothing more than a toy. Think about why you are carrying a personal firearm. Is it because you think that there is a possibility that you can be attacked by a criminal who may try to take your life? Think about the down, dirty and bloody aspects of a real gunfight. Is this the situation in which you really want a little "mouse gun" in your hand trying to defend your life or a handful of fighting handgun? It makes you better understand Clint's thought on the subject, doesn't it? It's important to be able to wrap all five of your fingers around the grip, don't you think? Or do you want a tiny, little gun in which your fingers are hanging off the edge, making it difficult to control recoil for rapid follow-up shots? Yes, the fighting handgun is certainly a compromise between too big and too small. You must be able to carry it with a certain amount of comfort and concealability but at the same time you want it large enough to take care of the problem.

Figure 5

A proper handgun grip length will be long enough to give a grip to all three lower fingers.

The first area to address is: Does the gun fit your hand? How do you determine this? First of all it is a good idea to make sure that the grip is long enough that you can get your whole hand wrapped around it—all five fingers. If the grip is so short that your pinky finger is hanging off the edge, you may wish to select something else. Many people do not understand the importance of the pinky finger in controlling recoil. When a projectile leaves the muzzle of a firearm, the equal and opposite reaction of that energy is for the pistol to move rearward in the hand. The hand trapping the gun is what makes the muzzle go up. Since the muzzle of the pistol is driving in an upward direction, it is the grip of the hand that will control recoil, primarily by the three lower fingers wrapped around the front of the grip. The middle finger, ring finger and pinky finger work in concert with one another to keep the muzzle pointed toward the target. Ask yourself; is it really wise to give up one third of this recoil control to make the grip a little shorter and a little easier to conceal?

Figure 6

A proper grip will result in a gap between the side of the frame and the extended trigger finger.

How much concealment are you gaining by giving up this one-half inch of grip surface? That's right, not a lot. Pick a gun in which the grip is long enough for you to get your entire hand around it without a lot of excess grip hanging out the bottom. If you have another ½" to 1" grip down below where your hand closes around the gun, then it is possible that the gun may be too big for you.

The gun needs to fit in the web of your hand straight down your forearm. When the arm is extended, the barrel of the gun should be an exact extension of your forearm. You should then be able to reach forward and engage the face of the trigger somewhere around the first joint. On a short stroke single action pistol, the center of the pad of the trigger finger may be all that is necessary to press the trigger to the rear. However, on longer double-action triggers, the finger is going to need a little more engagement space, closer to that first knuckle joint, in order to have the strength needed to press the trigger straight to the rear.

Try this exercise: With an empty hand, close the fingers and thumb as if they were wrapped around a gun grip. Extend the trigger finger as if it were reaching for the trigger. Try to make the spacing realistic for the pistol you normally carry. Look at where the pad of your trigger finger is exactly opposite from the web of your hand... Is it the middle of the pad? More than likely, it is. Now move it back and forth as if it is pressing the trigger. *The position on the pad that most stays in line with the web of your hand, while performing the pressing action, is probably a good place for the face of your pistol's trigger.*

If reaching this proper trigger engagement point requires you to roll your hand around the gun, breaking that forearm plane, the gun is too big for you. A gun that is too big will cause three problems:

1.   From a medical standpoint, all of the forces of recoil will be forced back on your thumb. Eventually this thumb will become damaged and cause a great deal of pain and future medical care.

2.   You will never be able to properly press the trigger straight to the rear without affecting the rest of your shooting grip. As you will see in a later chapter, the proper grip is essential for good, accurate combat shooting.

3.   You will not be able to use the body's natural pointing capability to get the gun on target.

There should be a slight gap between the frame and where the trigger finger extends down the side of the gun. The trigger finger should not be plastered against the side of the gun frame. This small gap will allow that finger to bend and press the trigger to the rear independently of the rest of the hand. If the trigger finger is flat against the side of the grip in order to reach the trigger, the gun is too big for you. At the same time, if the proper position on the trigger is found and the trigger finger goes too far beyond the trigger face, the gun is probably too small. If the gun is too small, it will affect the proper trigger press to the same extent as the gun that is too big.

Once you have gotten the proper grip and trigger reach dimensions, the gun should fit comfortably in your hand like a solid handshake. If the gun feels good in the hand, it is probably correct. If it doesn't feel right, it probably is not. Again, trust your instincts, if it doesn't feel right, it probably isn't. Don't let a gun store clerk push you into the gun they have in stock. Remember, they're interested in making sales. They are not as concerned with your personal security as you should be. Go from store to store until you find that correct gun. Adding after-market grip panels can modify some pistol grips and there is nothing wrong with this. Modifications, to make a gun more user-friendly for the individual owner, are certainly acceptable, if not downright smart, as long as they do not seriously modify the factory's specifications of the gun.

Another thing one has to deal with when selecting the proper pistol is caliber. For the most part, the larger the caliber the more felt recoil. Felt recoil can be tamed with proper technique, however, such technique is only developed and mastered with repeated practice. Be honest with yourself: How often are you going to practice? Monthly practice is probably best for those on a tight schedule and budget. The more practice the better. Remember the example about the professional football quarterback throwing the ball three times a year? Be honest with yourself, how often are you going to practice? If you can honestly say, not a lot, then a gun with lighter recoil may be a better selection for you. However, as we will discuss in the ammunition chapter, the rule of thumb is: The largest caliber you can control is normally better when we are talking about handguns.

It has been my experience over the years that personal defense calibers should start at the 38 special/9mm threshold. Again, this will be discussed to a greater extent to the ammunition chapter. It has been my experience over the last 30 years that calibers above this level tend to work pretty well, while calibers below this do not. Find a gun that is not too heavy for you to carry regularly, but not so light that you cannot control the recoil in rapid fire. Heavy guns are not the problem they once were, as the new generation of aluminum alloy and polymer frames can be extremely light while helping tame recoil impulse. Proper shooting technique and training can overcome recoil concerns, though some people will be better served with a gun of less recoil. The truth is, if you don't enjoy shooting your chosen

gun, you probably will not train and practice with it. Please understand that recoil does not cause cancer or does it cause serious health
problems. It is really a problem of the individual's psyche. Once you
have faced recoil, it is likely that it will no longer be a problem.
Recoil is generally only a problem when you do not expect it. In the
interest of "simple is good," my guidelines for selecting a proper
combat handgun are as follows:

1. A proper full-length grip that allows the whole hand to
    comfortably fit the gun.

2. Proper trigger reach that permits the finger to contact the
    trigger using no more than the first joint of the finger
    while keeping a little gap between the gun's frame and
    the outstretched finger.

3. A smooth trigger, not necessarily light, but smooth with
    no glitches that can be felt when the trigger is pressed. A
    smooth trigger is more important than people realize. If
    a glitch or a rough spot is felt when pressing the trigger,
    it might take the gun's muzzle off target, oftentimes
    without the shooter realizing it happened. Trigger control
    will be addressed in greater detail in later chapters, but
    a consistent trigger is usually an easier trigger to master.

4. A rust resistant finish is a good idea. Most guns come
    with such a finish these days. Even those guns that are
    what we used to call "blue" are really a black epoxy that
    will go a long way toward resisting the elements that can
    affect the gun's finish.

5. High visibility sights that can quickly be seen when
    needed but not so large that they will snag on clothing
    during a draw. Again we will deal with sights in greater
    detail later in the book.

6. Caliber .38 special, 9mm or larger.

Chapter Seven

INDIVIDUALIZING THE PERSONAL DEFENSE HANDGUN

"Strive to make something thy own...and it will be loyal"
Author Unknown

I am not a big fan of adding a lot of gadgets to any combative weapon, whether it be handgun, carbine, or shotgun. It has been my experience, while training law enforcement and military personnel, that these very interesting add on accessories quickly come off during the intense, rapid-fire regime of a solid combative weapon course. To my way of thinking, whether it is a long gun or handgun, a good defensive weapon should have a good trigger, a good set of high visibility sights. 100% reliability, proper hand fit and the capability of adding a lighting device quickly are necessary features to have in a combat

Figure 7

This Heckler & Koch USP Compact .40 has been converted into the author's version of the perfect carry gun.

weapon. Beyond that very little else is essential. At the same time I also realize that guns are never perfect for the individual user. Often safety levers are a little bit long, grips are either too tacky or they are not tacky enough, the sights could use some improvement, or possibly the trigger face is either too rough or not rough enough for individual preferences. Addressing these individual needs is, in my opinion, where modification or customizing of an individual weapon really comes into play. I wrote an article a while back for *Intermedia HANDGUNS* magazine entitled "Perfecting My Carry Gun." In this article, I detailed how I went about modifying my

Figure 8

This photo depicts the sight contrast between the bright orange front post and the flat black rear window permitting rapid front sight acquisition.

Heckler and Koch .40 caliber pistol to better fit my individual needs. Please understand that I am not trying to say the HK .40 is the best pistol for everyone, it is not. As a matter of fact, I have changed personal carry guns since the first edition of this book, which I discuss at the end of this chapter, but the *process* of how I modified the USP-C is still relevant in my view. It met MY individual needs at the time. As you review the following article, please think about your personal weapon and the modifications that may make it user-friendly for you. I am not advocating the same modifications for your gun, but trying to get you to understand the thought that went into the modifications in order to arrive at the gun I now have. Take the thought process I used and apply it to your individual handgun choice. I think that you will find that with very little modification and money, you can make your individual weapon truly your own!

Figure 9
An example of one of those simple modifications that make your carry gun more user-friendly. In this case, the rear corner of the slide stop was rounded so the author's thumb did not rest upon it when shooting.

PERFECTING MY CARRY GUN
(Intermedia HANDGUNS, October 2001)

Like many firearm aficionados, I owned more guns than I could shoot. I would see something that caught my eye and I would buy it with full intention of giving it a complete "wringing out" in the not too distant future. Due to life's many commitments (work, family, two "soccer" kids, etc.), the range time that I did have available was spent trying to stay sharp with my regular carry gun.

While gun collecting is an excellent hobby and pastime, it was never what I intended to do. I consider my guns tools to complete a given task. While some are purely recreational, most are for defense. Since I am currently assigned to a multi-jurisdictional narcotics task force, which makes forced entries on a weekly basis, I can honestly say that my personal environment is probably more hazardous than the norm. I want my personal defensive carry gun not only to be totally reliable, I want it to fit me and my personal needs like a glove!

Many custom pistol smiths offer an "XYZ" or "ABC" package gun, which is fine. But how many of these added features do you really **need**? I am a firm believer in the SIG principal (Simple Is Good) format of defensive firearms. It has been my experience that the more you change a factory handgun, the less reliable you make it. While total reliability is not as great a concern for a competition or sporting pistol, it is essential for a defense gun. If it ain't broke, don't fix it. And above all else, don't change the gun or add something to it just because it "looks cool." Ask yourself, "Does this modification make the gun more user-friendly for me in my given circumstance?" If the answer is not to the affirmative, then you probably should not do it.

What I would like to tell the reader about in the remainder of this article is the journey I took to arrive at my personal carry gun. Please keep in mind that this gun is perfection (or as close as I can get) in my eyes and probably not yours. What is important is the thought process I utilized to arrive at this final product, which I think is quite sound and will work for the reader. Another thing that should be understood is that not all gunsmiths will do individual work. Many offer their wares in package deals only. Robar and Chestnut Mountain Sports, the two gunsmiths that worked on my gun, are willing to undertake such tasks. The only thing they ask is that the modification is safe and does not affect the reliability of the firearm.

My basic carry pistol is the excellent Heckler & Koch USP Compact in caliber .40 Smith & Wesson. I selected the USP-C primarily for the way it fit my hand. All of us have picked up firearms that we just liked the fit and feel immediately, so it was for me with the USP-C. I also like the .40 caliber cartridge. Like many, when the .40 was first introduced in 1990, I thought it was an unnecessary cartridge. My feelings were that if you wanted high capacity, carry a 9mm. If you wanted a large caliber, get a .45. Like so many things, reality changed my mind.

The .40 proved to be a real life fight stopper, especially in the mid range 155-165 grain jacketed hollow point configuration. Some readers may not know that the .40 was one of the few cartridges in history that was designed, from the ground up, to be an expanding cartridge. For most others, hollow point designs came along after the original full metal-jacketed bullets. The mid-range .40 has proven to be one of the more reliable expanders currently available. If you think about it for a moment, it's really not hard to understand why.

The problem with 9mm bullets expanding is not velocity; it is the size of the nose cavity. To keep the 9mm feed reliable, the bullet nose needs to be rounded to a certain degree, which restricts the size of the cavity. The larger the cavity, the more tissue and fluid are permitted to enter to create expansion. The smaller the cavity, the more likely it is to be plugged. Just the opposite is true of the .45. The cavity is quite large, but the velocity is also slower, restricting the amount of forward momentum needed to make the cavity fold back.

The .40 splits the difference here better than any other handgun cartridge. The mid-weights offer a velocity in the 1150 to 1200 FPS region, certainly fast enough to start cavity rupture. At the same time, the cavity is sufficiently large enough to allow in fluids with less likelihood of being plugged. As a matter of fact, I have had several of the major ammo manufacturers tell me that the additional 1.2mm of diameter that the .40 has over the 9mm, allows them to do some terrific things with the cavity design. I have been fortunate to speak with law enforcement officers from all over the U.S., including agents of the Border Patrol, who have voiced a high level of satisfaction with their .40 caliber pistols. Selecting an effective cartridge is certainly part of selecting the perfect personal carry pistol.

Additionally, the .40 comes in a number of size efficient packages, much the same as the small 9mm.

The recoil of the .40 is also quite manageable as it relates to fast follow-up shots. The USP-C fills my hand like no other pistol. I don't want too small of a carry gun, as it is important to keep in perspective why you are carrying a defensive pistol. To my way of thinking, if I need a gun, I probably need it real bad! When I draw it, I want a HANDFUL of gun; I don't want some little pea shooter where my ring and pinky fingers are hanging off the end. I don't buy into this "carry a lot, shoot very little" concept of defensive handguns.

Once I took the USP-C to the range a few times (about 3,000 rounds), I then began to think about what I needed to do to make the gun work better for me. The first thing I needed to do was obtain a smoother action. The first long D.A. pull was heavy and the S.A. was not as crisp as I would like. A great deal of caution needs to be exercised when dealing with the current generation of polymer frame/component pistols. I went to Robbie Barrkman, owner of the Robar Companies, for his advice.

Robbie felt that the best course of action was to NP-3 the internal parts for the highest level of friction reduction. NP-3 is a surface treatment for steel and alloys that combines particles of P.T.F.E. (polytetrafluoroethylene) with elecroless nickel. NP-3 is very thin with a high level of even consistency in regard to thickness. Cleaning is minimal and no lubrication is needed on opposing surfaces. In short, NP-3 is a very slick surface that requires little maintenance and resists rust very well. It was decided that all metal parts, except the barrel and sights would be coated in NP-3. It was amazing how much this helped the action. It felt like a well-broken-in revolver after the NP-3 was applied.

To make the D.A. trigger smoother, a reduced power Wolff hammer spring was installed. I selected the lightest spring (10 pounds) for my gun. When combined with the NP-3, the D.A. trigger was a very smooth 8.5 pounds, while the S.A. was a crisp 4 pounds. In more than 10,000 rounds of shooting, I have had no missfires with the Wolff spring. Others I know have also used the 10-pound spring with excellent results, unless reloads are used. I have had reports where the 10-pound spring has failed to ignite the hard primers on some reloads, but do not worry. Wolff also offers a 12-pound spring, which solves this problem while adding about one pound of trigger weight. When you order, buy one of each and see which one works best for you.

Another problem that I noticed during my initial range sessions were problems with the slide stop. I shoot using a thumbs out grip. It works for me and I have no intention of changing due to the slide stop on any handgun. The two problems that developed were; One, my shooting hand thumb rested on the slide stop, keeping it from locking open the slide when the magazine was empty and two, the stud on the side of the slide stop wore a blister, due to constant friction, on the thumb of my support hand. Robbie rounded the rear corner of the slide stop which kept my shooting hand thumb from resting on it, while leaving it long enough to engage, if necessary. The slide stop stud was ground off, which loosened the two-part unit. The frame post was separated from the stop lever and was then re-attached with a high strength epoxy. The part was then coated with NP-3 to give it a consistent appearance.

The magazines also needed some attention from the good folks at Robar. The magazine bodies were treated with NP-3 to give them greater rust resistance as well as greater lubricity for the internal spring as well as sliding into place in the polymer magazine well. Metal magazines, coated with NP-3 insert much, much easier into a polymer frame than do polymer magazines in a polymer frame.

I also noticed that when the wide magazine floor plates went flush in the short USP-C grip, that the hand quite often got pinched. It hurts a lot and I really did not want it to happen during a speed load in the middle of a gunfight. The problem was solved by merely trimming the floor plates on each side so they could slide into place without trapping the skin on the shooting hand.

Once, the gun was returned from Robar, I headed to the range for another few thousand rounds of "self evaluation and soul searching" and discovered that I was far happier with my carry gun than I was before. Once the large problems were dispensed with, smaller problems then became visible. The first thing I noticed was that the three dot tritium sights were not as clear and fast as I would like. I have come to believe that sights on auto pistols are too "complicated" for the eye to use quickly. I feel that this is one of the primary reasons why point shooting techniques are making a strong comeback. Sights need to be robust and simple to see like, well, revolver sights.

Remember the sights on your first Smith & Wesson model 66 .357? The rear sight was a wide black blade with a big notch, while the front was a large plastic red insert. This set-up is hard not to see? It is my feeling that pistol sights need to be of this same simple, large and contrasting format.

Other changes I wanted involved modification of the trigger and magazine release button. The ambidextrous magazine release button that is standard on all HK USP pistols is an excellent design, but the right-hand side lever chafes my middle finger. The trigger was a little too wide and grooved for my liking. Also, due to the nicer action, I noticed that the trigger now had more over travel than I wanted for fast, follow-up shots.

To make this second round of modifications, I called Karl Sokol at Chestnut Mountain Sports. I discussed my desires with Karl who felt that they were well-thought-out modifications. The gun was boxed up and sent to Vermont. Karl addressed the magazine release button by cutting off the right side lever flush with the frame and then beveling the bottom edge. The polymer trigger was rounded and narrowed, which gave my small fingers a better reach. The grooves were removed during this process. To address the over travel, Karl drilled a hole in the trigger and inserted an Allen screw. Once the gun was returned to me, I set the proper elevation and then filled the hole in the trigger face with epoxy. This locked the screw in place so any future movement is now impossible. Shortening the screw can be done with a file, but making it longer is out of the question!

The sight system that Karl came up with was a work of art, in my humble opinion. His sights are reminiscent of the revolver sight discussed earlier. The rear sight is a Novak low mount sight with a wider sight window and a sight face cut so that it is a 45° angle from the eye. When combined with the face serrations and coal black color, this sight reflects no light whatsoever. The front sight is a Trijicon Tritium sight with an orange face attached. The orange face is a highly reflective piece of vinyl that cannot help but be seen. Even with my aging eyes, the front sight is quick into the field of vision.

When combined with a good holster, this USP Compact has become my perfect carry gun. I'm not saying that nothing will ever replace it, but I cannot imagine what it would be. The only thing I have done since I got it back from Karl Sokol, besides put about 10,000 rounds through it, is retro fit the new Heckler & Koch Law Enforcement Modification (LEM) trigger system into it. This new trigger system is the finest double action only (DAO) trigger I have ever used. It is very smooth and fast to manipulate and shows that a hammer fired DAO can be as easy to use as a striker-fired system. Unfortunately, this trigger system will only be made available to law enforcement agencies in new guns. The parts will not be available for retro-fitting. Don't be alarmed, however, the Wolff springs work great. I also added a set of the "sand" decal grips from GRUPO MERCARI (1605-B Pacific Rim Ct. Ste. 34-494 San Diego, CA. 92154 www.decalgrips.com). These grips add a more positive gripping surface without adding additional bulk.

This is the journey I took to obtain my perfect carry gun. I have begun to take a similar journey with a shotgun, battle rifle and bolt-action rifle I own. How am I going to pay for it? I'm going to sell all of those guns I never get the time to shoot!

As stated earlier, since the first edition of this book was published, I have changed my daily carry gun to a Glock 19 in 9mm. Like the USP Compact described above, this Glock is set up to fit *me* with most of the same features. The biggest reason I changed was I could never reload the USP with the level of speed and reliability I felt was necessary if I had to do so in the middle of a fight. The ambidextrous push down magazine release button was difficult for me to manipulate regardless of whether I used my thumb or index finger. The push button magazine release found on the Glock helped me cut a second off my reload time while allowing me to NOT have to flip the gun in my hand.

What I did like about the USP-C was the grip configuration. It fit me well and I wanted the same feel on my Glock. My personal carry Glock 19 was built by David Bowie of Bowie Tactical Concepts to fit and feel like my USP-C with the same features that I discussed in the HANDGUNS article. The USP Compact is still a great gun, but the Bowie Glock just works better for me at this stage of my life. I call this gun my "Heckler & Glock" as the gun feels like a combination of the two.

Figure 10

This custom built Glock 19 9mm is set-up to the author's personal specifications. It is his current idea of a perfect gun.

Others have asked why I would "step down" to a 9mm over the .40? Economy and ease of use is the answer. I no longer have the millions of rounds that were available to me in my department's armory. Like most of you, I now buy my practice ammo which is expensive. I have discovered that .40 can cost as much as six dollars a box of 50 rounds more than 9mm. Since my normal practice regime is three hundred rounds or more a week, this can really add up. I believe a bigger bullet is a better bullet, but only if you can hit reliably with it under real world conditions. This requires practice...nothing more, nothing less.

I also have found that the 9mm is easier on me when used in a long practice session. As I have aged (the older I get, the better I used to be!) I have found that the things (stupid and otherwise) I did as a young man are now catching up with me. Carpal tunnel, ulnar nerve compression and rotator cuff repair are all part of my world now and 300 rounds of .40 just beats me up, plain and simple. At this stage of my life, I would rather be able to train as I want without lasting pain, than have a "major caliber" in my gun. After all, it's only "major" if I hit with it and that requires practice...nothing more, nothing less.

Chapter Eight

WHAT IS THIS THING CALLED "STOPPING POWER?"

"It's not important that you hit something, it is important that you hit something important!"
Ed Sanow from his book *Handgun Stopping Power.*

Y ou want to try something interesting? Go to your local gun shop or to the next gun show in your area. Watch the individuals who gravitate to the counters that sell handguns intended for personal carry. It won't take long for you to realize these people tend toward high capacity 9mm pistols or low capacity, large caliber pistols, primarily those of the 1911 design. Walk up to one of the people who are fans of the high capacity 9mm and make the comment, nodding your head toward the other group, "you know, those guys over there say these little tiny pipsqueak cartridges won't stop a squirrel in his tracks and that the reason you have to have a lot of bullets is because you plan on shooting a lot." Then drift over to the other group and tell them, "Hey, those guys over there say the only reason you rely on these large bullets is because you are not capable of placing your shots accurately and you need all the help you can get." Then step back and watch these two groups get together and start arguing. During a very heated exchange, the only thing that will be accomplished is additional carbon monoxide being released into our atmosphere, because neither side is going to be able to convince the other that they are wrong.

It's a controversy that will probably go on forever...at least until we can get phaser guns that we can put on stun. Quite frankly, it is a controversy that those who publish gun magazines just love because magazines that contain articles with the word "versus" in them; such as 9mm versus 45, 40 vs. 357 Sig, 45 vs. 44 magnum; sell magazines. People follow the stopping power controversy like no other in the firearms' realm. It's a controversy that is unique to handguns because handguns and long guns really have nothing in common in regard to ammunition effectiveness. Long guns have long barrels, they have a long sight radius, they have an overall length that allows the shooter to have four contact points on them, thus making them more stable for accurate fire. They permit a rear grip, a forward grip, a shoulder weld and a cheek weld, which goes a long way toward stabilizing the gun and enhancing accuracy. The increased sight radius allows for a more precise shot and higher velocity rifle bullets create a true level of hydrostatic shock that common pistol velocities will never attain. Shotguns fire either a large slug or a multiple projectile shot that induces what is known as "sensory overload," in which the body is penetrated by so many projectiles at once that it tends to shut down far more reliably than getting hit by an individual projectile.

Handguns on the other hand, are quite small. As a matter of fact, we don't carry handguns because they are particularly effective, we carry them because they are portable. The handgun has a short barrel regardless of model, with a sight radius that is also short, making sight alignment unreliable, if not unremarkable. A fraction of an inch on the front sight, in relationship to the target, can mean inches off the intended area to be hit. Unlike the long gun, with the handgun there is really only one point of contact with the body and that is the gun's grip. Once the shooting hand is wrapped around the grip, the only additional point of contact is the remaining open space on the off side of the grip. This requires the wrapping of the support hand fingers around the shooting hand. Unlike a long gun, in which the forward hand can help stabilize the movement of the rear hand, when the shooting hand on the handgun pushes the gun in one direction or another, the support hand can only do so much to help hold the muzzle in place. Shooting a handgun, whether it is in competition or a lifesaving event under stress, is a most difficult proposition. When it comes to using handguns for personal security, it is truly a matter of accuracy as to whether a hostile target will stop quickly. Unlike the pinpoint accuracy that is needed to win a handgun competition, the type of accuracy that is essential for defense is to be able to hit a paper plate-sized target at a room size distance. As a matter of fact there is a great argument to be made for not placing one's shot on top of another when engaging a human target. Everyone agrees that the best way for a handgun projectile to work is to destroy any tissue in its path. One bullet on top of another tends to destroy the same tissue area, however, two bullets that are four inches apart certainly destroy more and different tissue; thus a double or triple shot with handgun rounds that are three, four or five inches apart would appear to be more effective than a cluster of bullets. Just a thought!

Much of the controversy these days involving handgun ammunition effectiveness has to do with the individual bullet's performance, which for the most part, tends to be measured in blocks of 10% ballistic gelatin. I do not profess to be a ballistic expert, however, I have seen more than my fair share of autopsies. My big concern with ballistic gelatin is that it is a totally homogeneous substance that has no variance whatsoever. Anyone who has ever seen an autopsy, or even seen photographs of autopsies or surgeries, is well aware that the human body is by no means consistent and homogeneous. What ballistic gelatin represents is an indication of potential performance. It is not exact performance in itself. Tests in ballistic gelatin compare one bullet against another in this particular substance. They are not a comparison of one bullet against another in human tissue. Such a test will never happen. The problem with the human body is it is inconsistent. It is hard bone, it is non-stretching muscle, it is wet areas, it is dry areas, it is fatty areas; all of which contribute to a bullet path that is not likely to be consistent. One bullet fired into a person can enter into the chest cavity and travel upward and go out the shoulder while the following bullet can enter the same general area, travel downward and end up in the knee. It is unlikely, at least from the many gunshot wounds I have seen in the last 30 years, that a bullet will travel a straight path with no variance whatsoever. As a matter of fact, the one consistent thing that you can count on with bullet performance is that it will *not* be consistent. I have no problems with testing ammunition, I think it is a wise idea. But the testers, whether they are using ballistic gelatin or a water tank or rolls of wet cotton, need to understand that the test is nothing more than an indicator of what the bullet might do when it strikes actual tissue. It should not, and I repeat, it should not be thought to be exactly what the bullet will do when fired into human tissue.

I remember watching an autopsy several years ago in which a suspect was shot three times with 9mm hollow-point ammunition. Once the three bullets were removed and cleaned up, you would have never known that they had come from the same gun. One bullet was fully expanded and looked like the mushroom seen in many gun magazines. Another bullet was a little less mushroomed, but it had peeled back its jacket. The third bullet not only did not expand but it looks like it caved into its own cavity. The interesting thing about these three bullets is the bullet that did not expand at all was the fatal bullet. Why was this? Because that bullet was fired into the head and upon impact with the very hard skull, the bullet actually caved into itself. Once it passed through the skull bone, it entered a vital organ instantly killing the subject. The bullet that expanded completely was fired into the pelvic area where there is a lot of wet material (urine, fecal matter and blood). The bullet that expanded to a medium level was fired high into the chest where it impacted on a rib bone and muscle. Shot placement, when it comes to handgun effectiveness is everything.

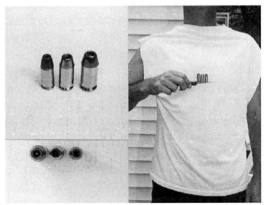

Figure 11
The top left photograph is a typical gun magazine view of three popular defense cartridges. Left to right: The 9mm, .40 S&W and .45 ACP. Notice that what defines the size of each cartridge is the cartridge case, which never strikes the target. A view from the end of these bullets shows a less dramatic difference and when compared to the size of the human chest cavity, all are quite small.

Let's take a look at three common pistol bullets, the .45 ACP, the .40 Smith & Wesson and the 9mm Parabellum. If you look at them from the side, there is a dramatic difference. This is the typical view that you will see in most gun magazines. As you look at this view, you will note that the .45 cartridge looks much, much bigger than the 9mm. It would tend to make the uninformed think that .45 cartridge would just rip your arm right off, where the 9mm is a pipsqueak cartridge. But, what are you really seeing in this photograph? If you think about it, what you are really seeing is the side of the cartridge case and where does the cartridge case go? It is ejected from the gun when the bullet is fired. The projectile that really goes downrange is nothing like the size of the entire cartridge when it is together. If you take a look at another view, which is the end view of the bullet, you will notice that the cross-sectional diameter doesn't look near as large as it does when it is contained in the cartridge case. If you put these bullets into real perspective, which is to place them against the size of the human chest cavity, you quickly realize that all of these bullets are pretty small. A 9mm bullet high in the chest cavity is truly going to be more effective than a 45-caliber bullet that impacts the shin. What is of greater importance when we are talking about ammunition effectiveness is firepower versus control. Without a doubt the .44 Magnum is a very powerful cartridge. But how well can a moderately to minimally trained shooter, such as a police officer or legally armed citizen, control this weapon in rapid fire?

A number of years ago, a very well known Federal law enforcement agency was in transition from their 357 revolvers to a semi-automatic pistol. This agency took into account, very wisely I might add, that the momentary recoil force of an individual round fired is something that should be taken into consideration. They looked at a cross section of their general enforcement population and decided that they needed to pick a gun that would fit not only the largest male but also the smallest female. Through research they determined that 1600 pounds of momentary recoil force was about the most that the "average agent" could control in rapid fire. They found that most .38 special cartridges met this momentary recoil force. At the same time, the 357 magnum carried in the short barrel revolvers issued at that time, were far more powerful than what the average agent could handle. On the other hand the 9mm cartridge, whether it be the high velocity 115-grain +P+ rounds or the slower, heavier 147-grain jacketed hollowpoint rounds, all fell underneath the 1600 pounds momentary recoil force. The 10mm cartridge that was becoming quite popular at that time, due to interest shown by the FBI, only met their momentary recoil force option when using the light FBI load. This agency wisely selected the 9mm cartridge and went on to have a great deal of success with it.

This is a perfect example of looking at the entire picture, not only the most powerful bullet that they could find. At the same time, looking for a round that could be put into a package (individual firearm) that their agents could carry easily concealed. This well thought out package is what any individual or law enforcement agency should do when adopting a particular gun and caliber. After all if the cartridge is so powerful that you can't fire two or three fast shots and keep them in say, an eight inch circle at twenty feet, then the gun's power is going to be wasted, because you're going to miss.

Bullet effectiveness truly comes down to shot placement. Hitting areas vital on the body with complete functional reliability. It is my feeling that much of this "lack" of stopping power comes down to training. Let's take for example, a look at the B-27 target, which has served law enforcement agencies very well for a long period of time. Even though this target is on a human silhouette, you'll notice the X-ring scoring area, which is the area most people try to shoot for, when compared to actual human anatomy it is too low for the stopping hits that are required. The area high in the chest, not in the center of the torso, is the area that contains the vital organs that will be most affected by handgun rounds. That is the heart, the lungs, the major arteries, major blood vessels and other related vital organs. The other areas of the body that are most likely to be affected by handgun rounds are a small portion of the head and the pelvic girdle.

Please keep in mind that the head can be a difficult target to hit because it is round, it is well armored and it moves a lot. Watch

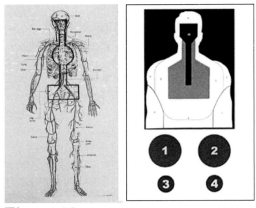

people. Notice the head very seldom sits still. People are not going to be like the silhouette target at the range where they stand upright and serve you their frontal area. The head is going to be moving, bobbing and weaving, thus the head shot is not going to be the panacea that many believe. But if you can hit that small area of the head, which is basically represented by the eye sockets and nose cavity, then a very rapidly incapacitating wound can be obtained.

Figure 12
Targets used for defensive handgun training should be representative of the vital areas of the body. Shown on the right is the DST-5 target designed by the author. It permits scoring of those areas that are most likely to result in rapid incapacitation.

Moving down from the head is an eight-inch semi-square high in the chest, where the vital organs that are susceptible to handgun bullets are located. Down through the center of the torso in about three inches in diameter are the spinal column and many of the major blood vessels that then feed down to the pelvic area. While it is not likely that one or two handgun rounds will break the pelvic bone (it is actually quite *unlikely*), it is possible. And if the pelvic bone is broken, the upper part of the body cannot stand because it will not be able to support the weight. Yes, the person may still be able to shoot, but they are not going to be very mobile...what is known as a "mobility kill." An even faster mobility kill would be to shoot the ball joints that connect the leg bones to the pelvic girdle. During my SWAT days, we used to call this "shooting pockets." At the same time the pelvic area houses a lot of wet, urine and fecal filled materials as well as blood vessels and major arteries, that can bring about incapacitation when violated. Thus, it is essential that, when training for personal defense, we use a target that only score hits that are susceptible to handgun fire. Using a silhouette style target and allowing any hit to be counted is counterproductive, let's face it, a hit to the upper shoulder is not likely to be incapacitating unless the individual shot is predisposed to stop movement anytime they are struck. While it is true that people can be psychologically incapacitated by handgun rounds, i.e., anytime they are shot anywhere with any cartridge they're inclined to collapse to the ground and stop, it should not be counted on. Anyone who has ever gone deer hunting can tell you stories of how they shot a deer through and through with 12 gauge slugs and then had to track it for another two to three hundred yards because the animal didn't understand that once it was shot it should fall down. There are many adrenaline filled criminal suspects who will take two, three, four or five hits from a handgun and continue to be mobile. During the battle of Fallujah, Marines found empty syringes that had been used to inject adrenaline and other narcotics into insurgents making them *very* hard to kill! There are numerous documented cases in which an individual is actually shot through the heart and be clinically dead, but there is enough blood still flowing to the brain that they are still functioning for 20, 30 or 40 seconds. This phenomenon has come to be known as "ambulation after death." Developing targets and target systems that will only be scored after vital areas are hit is an essential factor for combative handgun training. The fact of the matter is, anyone who carries a handgun knowingly to a gunfight is not very wise. If you have any warning that an armed confrontation may occur, I would strongly suggest that you take a carbine, a rifle, a shotgun, or possibly a LAWS rocket, if available, anything but a handgun. Unfortunately, I also realize that it is likely you will have a handgun when the fight starts, as carrying a long gun is impractical. So, let's be frank, practice with your chosen handgun, as it is probably the weapon you will have. Of all of the firearms available, the handgun is the hardest to shoot for the very reasons that I discussed earlier in this chapter. But, if you have confidence in your selected ammunition, shoot your gun well and you are switched on to your environment, it is likely that you will win a confrontation regardless of the caliber used.

While I intended to stay away from recommending any particular ammunition, I have discovered since the first edition that *many* readers wanted such recommendations. I belong to a group of law enforcement officers who are scattered across the country who regularly exchange information on ammo effectiveness from actual shootings.

Based on the input that I have received from this group, my ammunition recommendations would be as follows (June 2010):

9mm:
1. Winchester 127 grain +P+ SXT HP
2. CCI/Speer 124 grain Gold Dot HP +P
3. Federal 124 grain or 147 grain HST HP +P

.40 S&W:
1. Winchester 165 grain SXT HP
2. CCI/Speer 155 or 165 grain GOLD DOT HP
3. Federal 165 grain or 180 grain HST HP

.357 SIG
1. Federal 125 grain HP
2. CCI/Speer 125 grain Gold Dot HP

.45 Auto
1. Federal 230 grain Hydra-Shok HP
2. Federal 230 grain HST HP
3. Winchester 230 grain SXT HP

Note: I like Corbon's DPX Ammo, but have few actual street
shootings. Still, the DPX load seems to have all the necessary
features for a superior load.

The truth is that any good hollow point design above and including 38 special and 9mm, traveling at the fastest velocity that the
shooter can control will likely work well. Is a larger bullet necessarily a better bullet? Yes, I believe common sense shows that it is,
however, the only way to truly quantify this belief is testing in
ballistic gelatin, which I have already stated is *not* human tissue.
Setting this aside, if we look at the wound cavities of the various
calibers, we will see that the best .45 has a 15 to 20 percent larger
wound cavity over the best 9mm. This is the good news and would
seem to answer the question: "Is a bigger bullet a better bullet?" The
bad news is that this 15 to 20 percent larger capacity *is not enough*
to make up for poor shot placement.

This being said, if the larger bullet cannot be controlled, then a
smaller, easier to control bullet should be adopted. Select what works
best for you... as they say, to each his own!

In conclusion, handgun stopping power can be summed up in the
words of noted ballistic and gunshot wound researcher Dr. Vincent
DiMaio, "Stopping power is a direct result of where you shoot
someone and how many times you can shoot them."

Pretty simple, eh?

Chapter Nine

SAFETY

"There is no such thing as a 'safe' weapon, only safe people"
Author Unknown

S afety is a function of the brain. Fingertip manipulation or mechanical devices will not make up for a loss of brainpower. No matter where you are, whether it be the range, the street or in your home, there are four basic safety rules that will always serve you well. However, simply reading them will not make them habitual. There is no substitute for hands on training to develop good safety habits and the necessary gun handling skills that are the mark of the responsible gun owner or the armed professional. Weapon safety is truly a function of the brain. It requires concentration, it requires being switched on whenever handling a weapon.

An interesting phenomenon has occurred over the last decade or so, primarily with the striker fired Glock pistol. There have been a number of accidental "shootings" involving the Glock, which occur at the time the pistol is being disassembled for cleaning. Anyone who owns a Glock or has read the Glock owner's manual knows that it is required to dry fire the Glock in order to release the action so the slide can be removed. This means that it is absolutely essential to remove the magazine from the pistol, work the slide making sure the chamber is empty and then on an empty chamber, pointing the gun in a safe direction, pressing the trigger to release the action. Unfortunately a large number of these "accidental" shootings occur when individuals remove the magazine, do not take the time to check the chamber, then press the trigger and the gun goes off. Or they eject the round from the chamber before they remove the magazine, which just chambers another round. Is this a design flaw? Absolutely not! The individual user should know that the Glock functions in this way before they ever handle it. The problem is lack of concentration; people not being switched on to what they are doing prior to field stripping the Glock for cleaning. Any gun is working as intended when the trigger is pressed and it goes off. It is the user and their lack of "brain power" that is making the gun discharge. The fact is that very few modern firearms will fire "accidentally." They fire because the handler manipulated them in such a way that the gun fired as it was designed to do. This being the case, besides the four normal rules of gun safety, there probably should be a fifth added which is "concentrate on what you are doing!" Don't let your mind wander when manipulating a firearm. Beyond that, the four basic rules of gun handling safety, what Defensive Tactics Guru, and my good friend, Chuck Humes calls "The Flawless Four," are:

1. All guns are always loaded.
2. Never let the muzzle cover anything that you are not willing to destroy.
3. Keep your finger off the trigger until your sights are on the target.
4. Be sure of your target and what is beyond it.

Very straightforward, very simple rules to live by. If you are cognizant about what you're doing, and you use these four rules without fail, safety while using a weapon will never be a problem.

Chapter Ten

TECHNIQUE, PHYSIOLOGY, AND THE CONTINUOUS MOTION PRINCIPLE

"Simple is Good"

The Author

As stated earlier, there is a path that must be followed to become a good combative shooter. The beginning of this path, after mindset, is correct fundamentals. From correct fundamentals we move to concentration, then consistency, then accuracy and finally speed. This path must be followed in this order, because without the correct fundamentals you will never "run the gun" with skill. But to master the fundamentals, you must concentrate on what you are doing in order to perform them correctly. Without concentration on the fundamentals, consistency will never be achieved and without concentration on the correct fundamentals being performed consistently, accuracy will never be obtained. If accuracy is never obtained then speed is a waste (refer to the "Combative Pistol Skill Building Pyramid" in Chapter Two). A mouthful, I know...but it is the reality of combative shooting. Correct fundamentals are the basics of proper shooting. Such things as stance (body position), grip, alignment of the weapon on the target, consistent trigger press are the things that will be dealt with in subsequent chapters. Consistency comes through practice, essentially correct repetition, like the old saying of "perfect practice makes perfect." While it is unlikely that practice will ever be totally perfect any practice is better than no practice at all. If the correct fundamentals are practiced consistently over and over again, accuracy will come....it can't help but come! And if accuracy is achieved consistently while removing all unnecessary motion, speed will result. This is the path you must follow to hit what you are shooting at, as quickly as possible, without complicating the process.

We also need to know how to draw the weapon quickly, while keeping a good shooting grip. We need to learn to look for, recognize and make use of available cover and if cover is not available, moving in such a way that we can remove ourselves from incoming fire. Yes, armed confrontations are not simple affairs. But you will become "simple," as your motor skills deteriorate. So it is essential that we make things as uncomplicated as possible so that we can perform to our highest level while under stress. Remember the 3 S Test? Techniques must be simple in the training environment, if they're not simple in the training environment there is no way you will accomplish them under the stress of someone trying to kill you. Simplicity during practice will equate to rapid mastery. And mastery of the technique can lead to performing said technique without conscious thought, which will certainly go a long way to improving your skill on the field of battle.

For many years, firearm trainers have relied on the "Pattern of Encounters" that were developed from the annual FBI Officer Killed Summaries. These patterns revealed the following:

1. The "average" distance for a police gunfight was a distance of four to twelve feet.
2. A time factor of 2.5 seconds per encounter.
3. The number of rounds exchanged was 2.8 per encounter. (It should be noted that with the onslaught of semi-automatic pistol use this number of rounds exchanged has moved into the area of 7 to 9 rounds.)
4. More than 40% of the encounters involved more than one gunman.
5. 2 out of 3 situations occur at night or in reduced light.

The one concern I have with these statistics is that they come from situations where the officer lost, i.e., died. Remember they come from the FBI Officers **KILLED** Summaries, so we know what occurs when the police officer loses. Wouldn't it be great to know what happened when they won?

In 1993 the Police Marksman Association conducted a study trying to determine what happened in situations where the officer won, where the officer was the victor in the confrontation. They studied 180 shooting incidents and they determined the following:

1. The average distance was 20 feet. Makes sense, because in close quarter confrontations you don't have to be good, you just have to be lucky. The farther an individual can get from their opponent the more likely their superior training will kick in making their hits more accurate.
2. They found the average number of rounds to be fired was 3.5. However, this broke down to the type of weapon you used. 38 special revolvers were 3.6 rounds per incident, 9mm pistols were 5.5 rounds per incident, the 357 mag-

num was 2.3 rounds per incident and the 45 ACP was 2.7 rounds per incident. This total equates to 3.5 rounds per confrontation. (It is very clear to those of us who study armed confrontations that an individual being attacked will shoot until the subject in front of their gun is no longer a threat.)

3. It's interesting to note that for many years, shooting statistics stated that officers missed as much as 86% of the time which translated to a hit ratio in the area of 14%, sometimes as high as 20%. Again, these were situations when the officer lost. The police marksman study showed that the average number of hits was 61.5%. This makes a great deal of sense since the officer who hits their opponent is likely to win the confrontation in which they are involved.

Since the first edition was released, the FBI released an excellent study entitled *Violent Encounters,* which looks at both cops and criminals and what they do to win gun fights. If you haven't read it—DO! It's very enlightening.

The lesson is train, move to create distance or get to cover, continue to fire until the adversary is no longer a threat and the person that hits what they are shooting at first is most likely to be the victor. *Hitting what you're shooting at is the key to winning an armed confrontation!* Unfortunately there are many people out there carrying guns (military, police service and legally armed citizens) that feel such a situation will never actually happen to them. Thus, they are not prepared to engage in combat. When the situation arises they will be delayed by startle effect and they won't rely on the training that have received, because they have received very little training. With minimal training and a mindset that is not set for engaging in combat, it is not surprising that they will not hit what they are shooting at, which is everything in a gunfight.

In my mind, it comes down to three things that are necessary to develop a repertoire of combat handgun skills. They must be *simple,* the techniques need to be as *consistent* as possible and they must *flow together* with one technique meeting the needs of multiple situations. Hick's Law states that lag time increases significantly with the greater number of techniques or skills that are introduced. In 1952, Hicks discovered that response time increased 58% when the number of responses increased from one to two. During my classes I have conducted a little experiment with students to reinforce this concept. I make a motion to poke them in the eyes. Now I don't actually make contact with their facial area, but movement toward the face or eyes is something that creates a great deal of startle in most people. So what I'll do is explain to the student that I am going to poke toward their eyes and then I'll have them do a sideways swipe motion. Going from left to right knocking my hand out of the way, we then practice this a few times. I will then tell them to do it again but have them go from right to left and knock my hand out of the way. We then practice that several times. Then I will have them go from top to bottom, smacking my hand out of the way. After these three techniques are practiced, I will then ask the student if they are ready to defend their eyes. When they say they are, I try to poke them and, without fail, there is a hesitation as they try to decide which technique is best to move my hand out of the way, when any of the three are very capable of doing so. What has occurred by inducing more than one technique, is I have actually created lag time as they try to decide which of these techniques they should use in this situation.

Along this same line is the story of the fox and the cat. It goes something like this: The fox and the cat were standing on a hill talking about how many ways they know of escaping a pack of dogs. The cat, feeling rather inadequate said, "I only know one way. I run up the nearest tree." The fox gave the cat a sardonic smile and said, "well actually I know fifty different ways of escaping a pack of dogs." As fate would have it just then a pack of dogs appeared on the horizon and started toward the fox and the cat. The cat, utilizing his only escape technique found sanctuary very quickly up a nearby tree. While the fox was busy deciding which of his fifty escape techniques he should use, he was pounced upon and eaten by the dogs. The SIG Principle certainly correlates quite well with Hick's Law!

It makes sense to pick a technique that works and get good at it. While there should also be room for a contingency in the event that something goes wrong, trying to develop multiple ways to do one function is likely to slow reaction time. When I "packaged" the techniques that I am going to present in this book, I tried to make these techniques move from one to another with very little need to adapt. The more I could make singular movements blend from one to another, and make singular techniques apply to multiple functions, the more likely it is you are going to remember how to perform a particular technique and it's going to be consistent, thus increasing accuracy and speed. I have come to call this the Continuous Motion Principle (CMP). CMP simply means all motions needed to complete an action flow into one another without having to throw a particular muscle group into reverse. Let's take for example, the controversy over shooting stances, what I prefer to call "body position."

Without a doubt, the best way to shoot a handgun is to use two hands. As we discussed earlier, trying to stabilize the handgun is much more difficult than trying to stabilize the long gun. Thus, being able to do a 360° grip around a handgun is the preferred way to do it. No one disagrees here. Where the controversy starts is what to do with the arms. Those who choose what is known as the bent arm or "Weaver" position, have the shooting arm pushing the gun out away from the body with the support arm engaging the grip and the elbow bent, actually pushing and pulling against one another. The "Isosceles" or the straight-armed method requires both arms to be straight out in front of the body, basically locking the gun out in front as if one is stabbing a spear. The fact is, I could care less which stance or which arm position my student's use. The only thing that I insist upon is that the shooting arm be locked. Why would I insist on this? Some think it's weapon or recoil control. Actually it's not. It has to do with the Continuous Motion Principle. We all realize there are going to be situations where you will have to return fire with one hand. It's very unlikely that you will be able to control the weapon, for rapid follow up shots if your shooting arm is bent as Weaver shooters insist. In reality, you're going to lock the gun arm straight in front of you. Now if you are going to teach this technique for shooting one handed, why would you teach a different technique, i.e., having a bent shooting arm, when shooting two-handed? It's not a consistent motion.

The Continuous Motion Principle requires that techniques blend into one another. Thus, if you are going to use a locked armed when shooting with one hand, would it not make sense to use a locked arm when shooting with two hands? Whether the support arm is locked or bent, I really don't care, as long as the shooting arm is used consistently. The Continuous Motion Principle blends into other areas such as ready position, drawing the weapon, reloading, using flashlight techniques, as well as one handed shooting techniques. Whenever we can make these things blend together to feel consistent, less time will be spent on training multiple techniques and more time will be spent shooting from positions that already feel comfortable and familiar. As you're going to see throughout the book, "feeling the shot" is very important. As we move forward, we will continue to refer back to the Continuous Motion Principle. You will see how CMP makes things easier to recall at a moment's notice, because they are consistent. Consistency makes things simple. Simplicity is easier to learn, master, anchor, practice and recall, when needed. Simplicity translates to victory and when fighting, victory is everything!

Chapter Eleven

GETTING A GRIP

*"I've never understood all this concern about
malfunction drills and the like. Hell, I'm just afraid,
at the moment of truth, that I won't be able
to hold on to the damn thing!"*
Unknown U.S. Customs Agent to the author at the
IALEFI Annual Training Conference in 1997

S hooting a handgun with precision is the most difficult of firearms skills to master. The reasons for this have already been stated. The only place to put your hands on the pistol is on the grip. It is a rather small surface in which to try and wrap two hands around. One hand will always get in the way of the other when trying to cover as much of the grip surface as possible. The human body also works "in sympathy," meaning when one side of the body does something, the other side will also do it to a lesser degree. This means that if the shooting hand moves, the support hand will too, which makes pistol stability a challenge. In order to get as much neutrality as possible, the firing grip must wrap all the way around the available grip surface and it must be consistently tight, without being so tight that the trigger finger cannot work independently of the rest of the hand. As you will see, trigger finger independence is the difference between the championship shooter and the novice.

The shooting grip must be as high on the back strap as possible. There should be no gap between the web of the shooting hand and the tang of the pistol's grip. Trigger finger placement should be as discussed in Chapter Six. The grip should be firm like a solid handshake. Much is made about how tight the grip should be...60% vs. 40%, etc. But, I think it is best to just grab it as tight as possible.

Here's why—Make a tight fist with your shooting hand and hold it. Now, without loosening your grip, separate the trigger finger and move it back and forth, as if working a trigger. Did you note how the other fingers loosened a bit to allow this? That's right, the hand will find the right pressure, so just grip the gun as tight as possible.

The shooting hand thumb should extend straight out, down the side of the frame. Some advise to bend the shooting hand thumb to obtain a more solid hold, however, I have found this position interferes with the support hand making solid contact and creating a gap. This gap interferes with a solid two hand hold and inhibits weapon control as it gives recoil a path of travel.

Try this experiment: Make a tight fist with the thumb locked down. Now straighten the thumb and see if the grip is any less snug. You will note that whether the thumb is locked down or straight out, it has very little impact on the grip. When shooting a semi-auto pistol place the thumb straight out along the frame. It is interesting to note that the grip is often described by the thumb position; thumbs out, thumbs up, thumbs down, etc. But the thumbs have little impact on the grip. The shooting hand should apply pressure front to back as if gripping a pair of pliers. The thumb merely supplies a "hook" that holds the gun in place. The fingers on the front strap compress the backstrap into the web of the hand with the base of the thumb offering a pocket to lock the gun in. The support hand provides side to side pressure as if squeezing a rubber ball. The supporting hand thumb does nothing.

This thumbs forward grip provides an open space on the opposite side of the gun. To properly fill this void, take the large muscle below the support hand thumb and force it into this space. Make it a tight fit with the off hand thumb extending down the gun's frame underneath the shooting hand thumb. Some instructors will advise their students to cam the off hand down in order to help control

Figure 13
To achieve a proper 360-degree grip, the shooting hand must engage the grip like a firm handshake with the thumb extended straight down the frame.

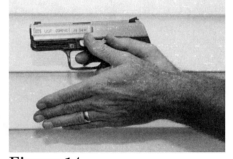

Figure 14
This will leave a gap on the off side that must be filled with the support hand. To do this efficiently, the muscle below the thumb will be inserted into this void.

recoil. I have no problem with this, but I have found that when the support arm is extended in a solid isosceles stance, the support hand locks the gun down on its own. Naturally, if you choose to shoot with a bent support arm, it is the bending of the arm that locks the gun on target. The four lower fingers of the support hand will then lock around the three lower fingers of the shooting hand. Once this is completed, the hands will form a 360-degree wrap around the gun grip. By doing this, you limit the gun's ability to move around during recoil. Additionally, when combined with locked wrists and an aggressive position, this grip helps bring the gun back on target without conscious effort.

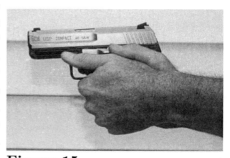

Figure 15

The support hand thumb will lie underneath the shooting hand thumb and will extend straight down the frame. The four lower fingers of the support hand will then wrap around the shooting hand below the trigger guard.

The extended thumbs also do double duty as a sighting tool. By squaring the upper body with the target and pointing, then pushing

Figure 16

The author has found to achieve a consistent combat shooting grip time after time is what he calls the "peak-to-peak" technique.

the thumbs in the same direction, the gun will go on target with little effort. You will find that where your eyes are looking is where the thumbs tend to go, when extended. Try it for yourself. Look at an object and then extend your thumbs (with the gun in your hands) and you will find that the gun's front sight will land very close to where you are looking. While I believe in using the front sight to ensure accurate fire, it's nice to know that I can put the gun on target with accuracy using other methods. Consider this: When does the front sight become important? Right before the shot "breaks." Getting the gun on target is necessary so the front sight can be used.

Getting the hands to come together consistently is also important. Since any inconsistency of the shooting grip can throw off the shot, the hands must be joined the same way each and every time. This is one component of what I call "feeling the shot." Once the shooting grip is established and practiced, the shooter will be able to "feel" when it is not right instantly. There are two ways to bring the hands together on the way to the target, so that they will be the same every time. The first is to deliver the muscle below the thumb to the open area first and then close the support hand around the shooting hand. This is done in a "clapping hands" fashion. Some people like this as they can sink that muscle into the open space on the grip with surprising consistency. I have found that this technique does not work well for me. Since my shooting hand is moving forward (toward the target) at the time the two hands come together, I have found that the "peak-to-peak" technique works better for me. Your fingers bend around the gun grip creating two peaks (like mountain peaks) where the knuckles bend. By placing the peak of the second knuckles of the support hand over the second knuckles of the shooting hand (thus, peak-to-peak), you will find the support hand folds around with the thumb muscle and heel of the hand filling the void on the grip without searching for it. The index finger of the support hand should fit snugly against the lower edge of the trigger guard.

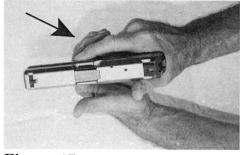

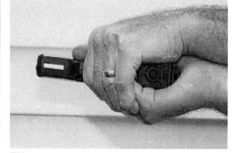

Figure 17
When the shooting hand fingers wrap around the gun's grip, the lower knuckles will create points that resemble a mountain peak.

Figure 18
This will result in a grip that is a 360-degree wrap all around with no gaps.

When the shooting hand and gun clear the holster and move toward the target, the support hand will move in from the side and the hands will come together. You will notice that this position (where the hands join) is similar as the third eye ready position, to be discussed later, thus being consistent with another technique (remember CMP?!). When the hands come together, they will first meet with the two peaks attaching first. By doing this, you have created a situation so the hands will fold together in the same position every time, increasing your chances for a more accurate shot. Try to join the hands as early as possible in the process. The support hand makes a wonderful "windage adjustment" when trying to deliver the gun to the target.

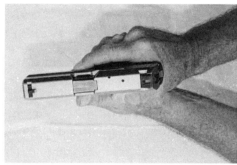

Figure 19

As the support hand moves to rest upon the shooting hand, these same knuckles will engage the shooting hand knuckles in a peak-to-peak format. This will allow the support hand to fold into the grip void without effort.

The other part of the grip that makes for accurate shooting is the trigger finger press. Note that I have called it a press and not a squeeze. As I stated previously, I believe in being as verbally descriptive as possible so that the mind can better visualize what you want the body to do. The word squeeze is something that is done with the entire hand, like squeezing a tennis ball or a lemon. A press is something that is done with an individual finger, like pressing a doorbell. Since the trigger needs to be moved with one finger, I feel the term press is more appropriate. In addition, the word press is short for depress which is defined as "a consistent, applied pressure to a breaking point" which I feel is exactly what is being accomplished. The trigger must be pressed straight to the rear in a movement that is independent from the rest of the hand. This is a tall order when you take the time to think about how the human hand operates as it functions normally. The fingers of the hand are designed to work in concert with one another, with the thumb opposing the four fingers in a gripping action. The thumb and its opposing pressure, a full 50% partner in the grip process, makes us unique in the animal kingdom. You use this action to grip the steering wheel, open door knobs, shake hands as well as thousands of other functions every day. Then, a gun is placed in your hand and you are told to use the trigger finger separately of the rest. After thousands of repetitions (daily) to the contrary, is it any wonder why people have difficulty shooting a pistol accurately?

I actually think that this is the reason many people cannot shoot a handgun well. While "flinching," "anticipating recoil" and "pre-ignition push" may be the reasons it is difficult for a new shooter, I feel that once recoil is felt, that trigger finger separation is the reason the muzzle strays from the target. Trigger finger separation can only be mastered with much practice, concentration and dry firing will help. This is the difference, in my opinion, between the pistol champion and the basic shooter. The champion has learned to separate the trigger finger at all times, including under competitive stress. This is the result of practice, discipline and a high level of concentration. These are things that few will take the time to develop as it takes considerable commitment to separate the trigger finger from the rest of the hand. The question is, will you take the time to practice and develop your personal skill and concentration to this level? It's up to you. Most of us will never get to the master level, but we can get to a level where we can shoot well enough to save our own life! But like the master, it takes time, effort, practice and concentration.

Another important aspect of trigger control is called follow through. Follow through allows you to prepare the trigger for any additional shots needed without losing muzzle alignment. There are two preferred ways of doing this; the first is to press the trigger for the first shot and then hold it back against the frame until the gun comes back on target. Then release just enough pressure for the trigger and sear to reset itself and no more. The more pressure you have to apply to the rear, the greater the likelihood you will take the muzzle off the target. By just resetting the trigger, only the minimal amount of trigger pressure will be needed to fire the gun. The second method is to press the trigger for the first shot and as the gun is coming back on target from recoil, reset the trigger so that it is prepped and ready to fire as the gun comes back in alignment with the target. Trigger control and follow through are the most difficult aspect of combat shooting with a handgun.

A recent trend has been introduced by a number of the high end competition shooters to "slap" the trigger. They advocate the finger comes all of the way off the trigger and then re-contact is quickly made with the slack taken out and the trigger/sear connection (what we have called re-set) being caught what has been called "catching the link." At this point, a smooth press is initiated. This eliminates the trigger re-set motion described above. Those who advocate this say it will allow you to shoot any gun well and not just the one you carry regularly. I guess if this works for you its OK, but it seems to me to defy everything that has been previously taught to control the trigger's movement. I have tried this and have found that all it does for me is make me push the gun off to the left. Control is about contact. You can't have one without the other. Think about driving down a winding country road. As you steer your way through each curve, you grip the steering wheel and "feel" the car turn until it is on the correct path and then repeat in the opposite direction. You could slap the wheel and make the car turn, but it wouldn't be very efficient. Like the steering wheel, the trigger is better controlled by staying in contact regardless of its length of travel.

To further complicate the trigger action, it is imperative that the finger not be on the trigger unless a shot is imminent. This means that the finger must be placed on the trigger face with authority, but not so hard as to set the gun off prematurely. Certainly a tall order! For many years it has been common for firearms instructors to teach the position of having the trigger finger laying down the side of the frame until the target is engaged. I have found over the years that this position does not work as well as many believe. Unload your gun, double and triple check it, and then place it in your hand. Put your finger down the side of the frame as you have been taught. Now, convulsively tighten your whole hand around the grip. You will notice that it takes very little effort for your finger to slide off the frame and enter the trigger guard. If you have long fingers and a small trigger guard, the trigger guard may stop it, but that's unlikely with large trigger guards being the current design on most combat pistols for gloved hands.

Figure 20

Indexing the trigger finger means to place the tip of the finger in a specific location so the shooter can feel where it is.

I have taught a position that I feel is superior in terms of weapon handling safety. I call it the trigger finger "index point." It is important to feel what is going on. Indexing the trigger finger means you find a location on the side of the gun that you actually engage with the tip of your finger. On a Glock pistol, it may be the serrated edge of the take down lever. On the Colt or HK it may be the rounded tip of the slide stop lever, though one well known instructor has advised against this as the inward pressure could disassemble the gun. I guess this is possible, but the slide and lever would have to be aligned just so to permit it. On a double stack gun like a SIG-Sauer P226 or Beretta 92, it may be the step in the frame where the grip starts to widen for the double column magazine. If you don't have an obvious location, a piece of skate board tape could suffice. It really doesn't matter, find a location above the trigger and touch it with the tip of your finger. Your finger should either be feeling this location or feeling the face of the trigger, no place else! When the finger is in this bent position, it is more likely the finger will not engage the trigger in the event of an involuntary muscle contraction involving the whole hand. It is not absolute, but I have several documented cases where police officers have slipped with their guns in their hands and due to the bent position of their trigger fingers, the gun did not go off as the finger traveled back above the trigger.

Again, it is important to feel what is going on. Since it is very unlikely you will be looking at your gun as you search, or engaging in whatever function that has you in a ready position, it is good to know where your finger is located. Thus, trigger finger indexing and feeling what is going on is a sound idea.

Don't dismiss trigger finger indexing as insignificant. There have been several cases where police officers and legally armed citizens have actually had their trigger finger on the side of the frame, but in a tense, fast evolving situation they convulsed on the grip and their trigger finger impacted the trigger. One such case involved a police officer that approached a car with his 9mm Glock in his hand and his finger along the frame. When the suspect attempted to drive away from the officer, the officer tried to open the car door and his hand convulsed on the pistol grip, firing and killing the suspect. According to newspaper accounts, this resulted in the police department in question retraining all their officers to hold their finger under the trigger guard to prevent accidental shootings. This position certainly is not conducive to being what we think of as "ready."

Another advantage of indexing the trigger finger is it permits the shooter to place their finger on the trigger in the desired location instead of "slapping" it. Slapping usually occurs when the finger is straight down the side because of the route it travels in order to reach the trigger face and it usually moves quickly, making control more difficult. By having the finger bent above the trigger, it is easier to bring it down and *place* it into position.

My trigger finger philosophy is: If you are off target, you are off the trigger. If you are on target (a target is anything that you are willing to shoot), you are on the trigger. At what point does this happen? As the gun comes out in front of your body toward a hostile threat and the elbows lock into a firing platform, you should be engaged and the shot taken, if necessary. If the gun is held back in a close quarter position, then the finger should be clear of the trigger until such time as YOU DECIDE to take the shot. Taking a shot is a conscious effort. It should not be something that is done without prior thought. Whether you are a military officer, police officer, or legally armed citizen, you are responsible for each and every round you fire. Make sure that you are firing because you want to, not because of an involuntary muscle contraction or startle response.

Chapter Twelve

READY POSITIONS, RANGE SAFETY AND GETTING THE GUN ON TARGET FAST!

"The secret to winning a gunfight is taking your time in a hurry"
Wyatt Earp

Webster's Dictionary defines the word "ready" as "prepared to act or be used immediately; willing; available at once." The word "position" is defined as "the way in which a person is placed or arranged." This being the case, the phrase "ready position" would lead one to believe that "it is a way a person is positioned to be prepared to act or be used immediately." Makes sense, doesn't it? But how many of the classic ready positions being taught really are used to prepare for armed conflict and how many are just used for range safety?

Every instructor or school I have experienced has a signature ready position they build their doctrine around. The problem is, no single ready position will handle all situations. The fact is, ready positions are situationally dependent. The position used should offer the operator maximum effective response capability for the situation at hand.

The two most common positions are the high ready and the classic low ready, or "guard" position. The high ready has no tactical applicability that I can see. This position originally had the front sight in line with eyes on target. Once it was discovered that this position blocked one's view below the gun, it was moved up next to the head. Other than putting the handgun in the same film frame as an actor's face in a movie, I see no reason to use this position. I was involved in a building search years ago with a deputy who was using the tactical high ready (though I admit to not knowing what is "tactical" about this position...that is what I have heard it called). Several times during the search, this deputy craned his head and neck around a corner (yes, too close to cover) to look for any threats.

Figure 21
The low ready position when used improperly during actual building searches has resulted in situations that are dangerous.

Figure 22
Such things as trapping the gun against the wall while the searcher is attempting to look around the corner or pointing the gun at their own feet in similar circumstances is common.

Figure 23
During a building search involving the author he saw a fellow deputy sheriff point his gun at his own head when trying to look around a corner.

As he did this, due to his high ready position, he pointed his loaded revolver at his own head! Not good, but it looks great in the movies and on TV! The low ready position is actually a good one when used properly. Low ready is normally defined as holding the gun straight out from the body and down at a 45-degree angle between the target and the ground. Some people define it as lowering the gun just enough to see your adversary's hands. When used properly, it gets the gun on target very quickly. Unfortunately, it is not utilized as well as many believe. If you attend any firearms training program, whether it be police, military, or a private course, as the day wears on and the gun gets heavy you will quickly see the low ready position degrades into a position in which the gun is pointed at the ground, allowing the elbows to rest against the body supporting its weight—the gun is pointing directly at the shooter's feet! If this isn't corrected during training, something that many firearm instructors ignore, over a short period of time this down at the ground position becomes their ready position. While this position is safe on the range, it is dangerous on the street. I have seen officers searching buildings for armed - criminal suspects, supposedly in a position that will keep them ready to engage, pointing their gun at their feet or trapping the gun against the wall as they look around the corner. It is very frightening to see when the stakes are so high.

As I became increasingly knowledgeable about handgun combat, I began to look at the low ready position and to reevaluate its effectiveness for real world situations. Exploring other options, I settled on what I began to call the "third eye position." I now wish that I had called it "compressed low

Ready Positions, Range Safety and
Getting the Gun on Target Fast!

97

ready" as third eye has become confusing due to other "chest ready" positions that have become increasingly popular. They are not the same.

The "chest" or "air marshal" ready offers the gun's muzzle straight forward which is why "third eye" fits this position better. However, chest ready can point the muzzle in directions that are not

Figure 24

The third eye ready position places the gun below the shooter's chest with the wrists locked and the muzzle canted slightly downward. To get the gun on target quickly, the shooter merely straightens the elbows bringing the gun up in front of the face taking the gun to the target in a straight line.

appropriate, while at the same time, is the fastest of all the common ready positions. The third eye, or compressed low ready, is a position in which the gun is held in front of the body with the upper arms down to the side and bent at the elbows that are locked against the torso with the forearms parallel with the ground. The wrists are locked, which cants the pistol down keeping the muzzle depressed toward the ground. Think about lowering the gun as if you were using a low ready, but once the gun's muzzle starts to travel beyond the groin line of your adversary, the elbows are bent and the gun is allowed to rest against the torso. If the gun is needed, it can be brought into action quickly by straightening the elbows and pushing the gun straight to the target instead of trying to lift and stop. The shortest distance between two points is a straight line, not an upward angle. An additional problem I have seen with low ready over the years is shooters, in an attempt to fire fast, either under or over travel the target. With the third eye, this doesn't happen as often. Since the shooter's eye will be locked on the target in a life-threatening situation, all that needs to be done is straighten the arms, following the thumbs which are pointed at the target and bring the gun to the eye-target line offering a quick response time. When in this ready position, the elbows are held tight against the torso and the gun is out from the body six to eight inches. Wherever the upper body turns, the muzzle turns, thus the name the "third eye" position. Though, again, I regret this name. Shots on target from this position can be accomplished in less than one second with practice, and I am not talking about hits anywhere on a full size silhouette. I am talking about twenty foot hits on an eight-inch plate in less than one second, which includes the 1/4-second lag time that occurs after the beep of an electronic timer. Third eye is an excellent "bridge position" between low and chest ready.

I have heard some concerns about this position in regard to getting the gun straight to the target. Some are concerned that the gun will dip once it comes on the target, while others are concerned that the gun will go too high, but this is not the case. Try the position for yourself. Get into a solid stance and bring your arms down to your sides and let them hang. Your handgun should be held in your shooting hand in the grip you want when you shoot. Bend at the elbows, bringing your hands up in front and join the hands together in a good 360-degree grip. At this time you will notice the gun is held out away from your torso about a six to eight inches. With this gap, the gun could be fired allowing the slide to fully cycle, chambering

Figure 25
When looking at the third eye weapon presentation from the front, you will notice that all the shooter does is take his/her thumbs straight to the target.

the next round without interfering with the gun's functioning. This is certainly a strong consideration when involved in close quarter combat. Now point the thumbs to the target down the frame of the gun and lock the wrist. You will notice that the muzzle takes a slight downward cant. This cant is enough that the bullet will impact the ground about seven feet in front of you. The wrists should stay locked. If a close quarter shot is necessary, bend at the elbows, raising the pistol straight toward the target in what is called a "chest ready" position. Don't break the locked wrists. If the gun needs to be depressed to go around a teammate or some other object you do not wish to "muzzle," the gun should be lowered at the elbows keeping the wrists locked and bringing the heel of the hands to the torso, thus depressing the muzzle.

Figure 26
The third eye ready position follows the continuous motion principle in that multiple functions can be accomplished in the same basic location. Such things as reloading, searching with a flashlight, and one hand close quarter shooting are performed in this same basic location.

From the third eye, take the gun very slowly toward the target. As it moves out, you will notice the gun's muzzle will go on target by itself. As the gun is straight out from your shoulders at a ninety degree angle, the gun's muzzle will be a bit depressed, but not very much. As it travels past the ninety degree angle and comes up in front of your eyes, you will notice the muzzle is right on target without any concentrated effort. Being able to straighten your arms and go directly to the target without hesitation or problems will result in a quick and accurate shot. This may take some tweaking, as it will not be spot on each and every time without practice, but you will notice that the body dynamics are such that the gun will come straight up in front of your eyes and go to the spot you are looking at with few problems. This is the case whether you are facing the target or you must pivot toward it. If you can turn your upper body, the process is the same. Remember shooting is done from the waist up. If you turn your upper body and can point toward the target, then straighten your elbows taking your thumbs to the target. Again, driving your thumbs to the target will take the gun to the target without having to "chase it down..." the sight will arrive on its own.

Another thing I like about the third eye position is it works well with the Continuous Motion Principal. If you stand in the third eye position, the finger off the trigger, wrists and thumbs locked toward the target, you'll notice you're in a similar position needed for a number of other functions. For example, searching a building with a flashlight, you'll notice the gun will go straight out to the target with the flashlight engaged and straight back. This way you can see up over top of the gun and the flashlight beam and again presenting the gun and the flashlight to the possible threat in a straight line. It also works well from what we call a close quarter retention shooting position. If you merely drop your support hand away from the gun, you'll notice that the gun is locked into your side in what is known as a "full hip" position. The upper arm is solidly locked against your body, the gun is directed toward the target, and is quite accurate out to ten feet. Additionally, as you will see later when we discuss holster skills, when the gun is drawn from the holster and the hands come together on the way to the target, they meet in the same general location as the third eye. These motions add to consistency in that they are similar and can easily be practiced. The third eye ready position goes well with holster skills, reloading, flashlight positions and one-hand shooting. It also goes well with "feeling" the shot and the felt aspects of shooting are grossly underrated.

Please, do not misunderstand, I don't dismiss the low ready position as I think it works. I think it is the best threat management position available. When confronting a suspect, low ready keeps the gun, well...ready to use better than any other. Low ready is best used when you are covering a suspect and you only drop the gun low enough to see their hands and no further. To me, this position makes

Ready Positions, Range Safety and Getting the Gun on Target Fast!

101

a great deal of sense but at the same time it is unlikely you will have to hold this position for an extended period. If the gun needs to be lowered more than groin level in a threat management situation, I would recommend that you begin to bring the gun back into the body instead of continuing to lower it. A gun pointed at the ground cannot be used in close combat and as stated earlier, can be a real bad position in a search. The muzzle must *always be directed towards the potential threat.* Not always pointed at it, but somewhere in its direction.

Figure 27

For those shooters who are advocates of the Weaver/Low Ready position, the third eye can be used if thought of as an "at rest" position.

For those who are fans of the Modern Technique of the Pistol, do not despair. I like the Modern Technique and I think you can resolve this discrepancy in your own mind by considering the third eye/compressed low ready as an "at rest" position. Think about it, when you are in the low ready position and the gun begins to get heavy, instead of dropping the gun down so it points to the ground, merely bend at the elbows and bring them back until they rest against your torso. They can immediately go into a low ready position, if necessary, but without the tiring effects of trying to stay at a 45-degree angle. It really doesn't matter to me, but the position is valid, fast and it works well under stress. It is also consistent with other motions you are going to make.

I feel that a true ready position prepares you for combat. A range safety position keeps you, other students and the range officer safe from accidental gunfire. Ask yourself, which are you using on the street? Recently, a new group of positions have become popular that I think of as "preparatory" positions instead of ready positions. Prepare is defined as "to make ready" versus ready's "prepared to act." Positions like Sul and the Safety Circle, to me, are preparatory positions. Sul, which means

Figure 28

One hand shooting as taught by many instructors is to step forward with the gun canted inward to lock it in place. The author questions this as he feels that rotating the shooting arm elbow straight down better locks the gun in place. Additionally, there is no "combat logic" to stepping towards the target.

"south" in Portugese, created by several, true "high speed" trainers, who came from and still work in/around the special operations community. In one instance, these trainers noted a number of shooters pointing guns at each other during live fire dynamic entry training. In an attempt to keep an unfortunate situation from occurring, they developed Sul, which holds the gun flat against the chest, with the support hand acting as a spacer to keep the muzzle from pointing at the user. The knuckle of the middle finger on the shooting hand rests on the knuckle of the index finger of the support hand. The thumbs of the two hands touch in a pyramid formation above the gun. When the gun is deployed to a target, the hands collapse around the gun with the thumbs and knuckles acting as pivot points. If the body leans forward, the spacer hand moves outward and clears the muzzle. For its intended purpose, Sul is brilliant! Hell, I show it to my students during building search classes, but Sul is NOT a ready position. It is to be used when armed people are within close contact with one another. If space allows, why would you not want to have both hands wrapped around the gun in a shooting grip? You can depress the muzzle of the gun AND keep both hands wrapped around it, if not in close confines. But is you are in a "butt to nuts" stack prior to making a forced entry, then Sul is a good way to go, but not the only way. Much of this controversy has developed due to a small number of firearms instructors, in an attempt to raise their profile, started showing Sul as the new "spec. ops. ready position." After all, it is new and it looks cool and we have already discussed this phenomenon. As Kelly McCann has said, "the muzzle leads to danger"...be ready, don't be cool. I feel the safety circle falls into this same category...used to make ready.

While it would be nice to always shoot with two hands on the gun, reality tells us that this will not always be possible. The biggest disadvantage of shooting with one hand comes from the lack of stability placed on the pistol. One hand just cannot hold it as still as two! Other than that, nothing really changes. The gun is held in the same grip with the thumb straight out toward the target, though the shooting hand will grasp it more firmly than when using two hands. It is a common technique to cant the gun inward when shooting with one hand as it is felt that this helps lock the shooting arm, though I have never personally felt this "locking" action. I have had greater success locking my shooting arm by rotating the elbow down toward the ground and keeping the pistol upright. This is also consistent with how I hold the gun when I shoot with two hands. By adding a forward lean, I have found this arm rotation technique to lock the gun on target as well as can be expected. As with a two-hand hold, the forward lean will control recoil and bring the gun back on target without conscious effort.

Another common practice is to step into the shot with the strong side foot when shooting with one hand. I question this practice for combative applications as I'm not sure time and space will allow this. Think about when a one-hand shot is normally required. It is either due to an injury or one hand being occupied with some other function or because of an extreme close quarter engagement. If this is the case, is it wise to try and step into your opponent? If you do this in training, what is the chance that you will do it, without thought, in a real fight? It has happened, which is why I discourage it. Also, if the gun is brought back to a close quarter retention position and the shooting side leg is in front of the body, what will be to the rear to stabilize the body for fighting and shooting? That's right, nothing. Your body will be off balance. When I need to shoot with one hand, I just drop my support hand and rotate my elbow down, shooting from whatever stance I happen to be in. I know that you are tired of hearing this, but, by doing this I am shooting in the same position, as I am when I am using two hands. It's that CMP thing again.

Being able to get on target quickly is important in a gunfight. It could literally mean the difference between life and death. But at the same time, not shooting accurately can lead to just as serious a consequence. The fast shot that doesn't hit anything is the same as the shot that was never fired, as far as protecting your life is concerned. Without a doubt, speed must be tempered with accuracy.

This brings us to the debate of point shooting vs. sighted fire. Let's try to set aside our emotions for a moment and take a good look at exactly what is being accomplished here. First of all we need to establish the fact that **EVERYBODY POINT SHOOTS!** Before you throw this book down, let me explain.

Figure 29
One-hand shooting is usually done for two reasons, a hand is injured/occupied or the engagement is quite close. If a close encounter were the case then stepping into your opponent would be a serious mistake. If the gun is brought back to a close quarter shooting position the forward gun side foot will now place the shooter in a position that is too off balance to fight. By shooting one handed in a conventional strong side foot back stance, the gun can be brought back into a weapons retention position or fired from any position in between without a loss of balance.

What I mean is everyone directs the gun to the target using the upper body and arms. Anyone who thinks they can just thrust the gun out in front of them, chase down the front sight, hoping for a fast and accurate shot is only kidding him or herself. From the moment the gun leaves the holster and starts toward the target, your upper body and arms are directing that gun to its intended end point. Whether you want to or not, you are looking at your adversary to keep track of his (or her) whereabouts. You have to! How else will you be able to see if they are about to kill you? Hopefully, as the gun comes up in front of your face, you will be able to focus on the front sight. Research over the years has gone back and forth on this. Some say you can and some say you cannot. Quite frankly, I have interviewed more than my fair share of gunfight veterans over the years and I have found that some people say they can remember and some say they can't remember seeing their front sight. But the fact remains they directed the gun to the target using body motion and movement. If the front sight was seen, it was in the last nanoseconds prior to pressing the trigger when the gun came up in front of the eyes. The gun was already on target. The front sight was merely used to *reconfirm the location* of the pistol. Isn't the upper body direction of the gun toward the target a form of point shooting? If not, what is? If you think about it, if you use the front sight to train yourself to deliver the gun to the target consistently, but then fail to "view" it in a fight—what difference does it make? Isn't the gun still on target? At this point, it is more likely that you will miss due to poor trigger control than due to lack of front sight focus.

As stated earlier, the third eye position, with a solid grip and thumbs pointed straight to the target, can result in very accurate shooting out to distances of 25 to 30 feet. I can point shoot, i.e., not look at the front sight and hit an 8-inch plate as far back as 25 feet with boring regularity. How about skipping empty shotgun hulls at 10 feet? I have students doing this in just a few minutes. It's nothing more than "feeling the shot," making sure every time you present the gun *it feels the same way as before,* which requires concentration, but it can be done. It will become comfortable and you will be able to "see" it in your mind's eye, hitting that target over and over again. Will you get the precision pinpoint accuracy needed to win a PPC match? Nope, but you will be able to hit someone in the upper chest, reliably, over and over again without conscious thought and very little movement. The interesting thing about delivering the gun to the target from the third eye ready is that if you feel like your hardly moving, you're probably doing it right.

This being said, I admit that I am a believer in using the front sight. If I can use the front sight to confirm the location of my pistol, I will use it. What is this likely to depend on? Distance, and distance equals time. If you are so close to your adversary that you can't get the gun up in front of your face, you're not going to be able to use your sights. Thus, some type of body direction shooting is appropriate, especially from just above the holster. Extreme close-quarter engagements (discussed in depth in a later chapter) are possible and, in many of these engagements, the gun will not be the answer. Frankly, if your opponent is so close you cannot bring your gun up to eye level, it is probably too close to use a gun at all! The answer will be hand-to-hand combat until you create enough distance to use your gun.

Why do I like to use the front sight when I can feel my shot to the target with such accuracy? Well, I keep coming back to that old saying, "You can't miss fast enough to win." Or how about another quote by noted instructor Dennis Tueller, "If you don't think you have enough time to aim, then you certainly don't have enough time to miss." Accuracy is everything. I will do everything I can to assure the accuracy of my shot, period! At the same time, I am the first to admit that trying to find the front sight under the stress of an armed confrontation will be difficult at best. Over the last three decades, I can safely say that I have interviewed more than 250 individuals who have prevailed in armed conflict. These have included soldiers, law enforcement officers, legally armed citizens and yes, felons! While I do not profess to say that my study is "scientific" (I admit to being a bit of a skeptic to things done in the lab), I have seen some interesting trends, which I continue to see to this day. First, individuals who use some type of long gun during their confrontation, remember seeing their sights. This isn't remarkable considering how people are trained to use the long gun. The long gun is "welded" to the shoulder, brought up to meet the cheek and the front sight, barrel and receiver assemblies are forced in front of the face. The sights on shotguns and rifles tend to be large and quite bold, so it is not unusual for people who are involved in confrontations using long guns to remember using their sights.

From those using handguns, I discovered that more people using revolvers remember seeing their sights than those using semiautomatic pistols. I think there is an obvious reason for this...the majority of people who used revolvers, and remember seeing their front sight, described to me they remember "that large red insert" or "that orange spot at the front of the gun" coming up in front of their face and helping them direct the gun to the target. These were not always clear...sometimes they were just a blurry blob, but they did see the color in their visual plain. Think about the Smith & Wesson, Ruger and Colt revolvers that were popular when revolvers ruled in law enforcement. Many of them had large ramp front sights with red, white, orange, or lime green inserts and large, bold black rear sights. It was not unusual to paint the front sight with Liquid Paper or fingernail polish. These are the types of sights that you couldn't help notice, or at least are likely to see. Now think about what occurred with the adoption of semiautomatic pistols. The manufacturers made the sights smaller so that they were more snag-resistant. Then they complicated them (at least for the human eye to pick up quickly) by putting three dots on them and bars that require the shooter to put the dots on top of the bars; this causes complications when trying to focus. We've lost the simplicity of the revolver sight when the semi-automatic pistol was adopted. What revolvers have, that pistols do not, is a bold, easy to see contrasting front sight. This contrasting color, I believe, allows the eyes to see it, at least reference it, as it moves toward the target, intentionally interrupting the field of vision. The complicated pistol sights that are common, I believe, are too complex for the eyes to use quickly.

I ran this idea past my eye doctor during one of my annual visits. After listening to my thoughts and admitting that he knew nothing about shooting, he advised me that it made a great deal of sense in regard to contrasting color and eye reception. He used this example: He asked me if I had ever driven at high speed to which I said that I had. He asked if I was able to see how fast I was driving and how that was possible. I said that I would quickly cast my eyes down, take a look at the speedometer and then look up again. He asked me what I remembered most about the speedometer. I said that I remembered the bright bold colors, usually the arm that comes up and indicates the speed is some kind of a bright yellow or orange, and the numbers themselves, are a bright white color against a black background. He said, "Do you think the contrasting color helped you quickly read your speedometer?" I said yes, it did. He then said that I answered my own question. I guess the folks in Detroit understood the contrasting color idea long before those of us in the shooting community.

There are a number of ways to develop a contrasting sight on a semiautomatic pistol. The easiest is to merely black out the white dots or bars on the rear sights with a black magic marker. This will leave the white dot on the front allowing the shooter to quickly differentiate the front sight from the rear. The rear sight is only used as a window to line the gun up with the target, in combat situations precise sight alignment is not necessary. By merely noting the front sight through the rear sight in a fight, the amount of sight alignment necessary for good combat shooting will be available. Another way to develop a contrasting front sight on pistols that have tritium sights is to black out the white rings on the rear sight globes. Sights like Ameriglo, Mepro-Light and Trijicon will have a white/ green combination housed in a black rear sight. Take a fine tip marker and black out those white rings which will leave the green globes for low light, but will also leave a large black/white/green front sight that can be easily seen. Sights that are commercially available from XS Sight Systems offer a large white dot or a white dot with a green tritium insert that lines up with an express rear sight. Essentially, the XS sight picture looks like a lollipop. These sights are *very* popular with combat shooters as quick sight alignment is amazingly simple with these after market sights. A new sight system was recently introduced, called Diamond Speed Sights, which use a diamond-shaped front in conjunction with two diamond-shaped rear sights. To align the sights, the side points on the diamonds touch with the front diamond being a bright contrasting color.

I have found that the best sights for my aging eyes are to color the front sights with orange and then totally black out the rear sights. I leave the tritium globe at the front for reduced light use. To accomplish this, I buy a bright orange friction tape which is available from any auto supply store. This tape is designed to be held in place under extreme circumstances including greasy and oily environments. This flourescent orange tape is used as a warning device on the edges of lawn mowers, steps, etc., so it has a high degree of sticking power. I clean the front sight and then apply this tape and hold it in place for 30 seconds while it adheres. I then take a sharp craft knife and trim away the excess around the edges of the sight. To bring out the green front globe, I poke the tape around and around the sight globe until I perforate it and can pop out that centerpiece. This allows me to see a large orange front sight with a green globe for reduced light situations. No, I don't get precise sight alignment, but what I do get is a flash of orange as the gun comes on target. Remember Jeff Cooper's "flash front" sight picture concept? This just enhances it. As a matter of fact, Cooper told his students in the 1980s, "if you are going to use a contrasting front sight, use a color that it not normally found in nature." I can see the orange dot in my lower peripheral vision as it comes on target. Thus, not only do I have the best of point shooting, i.e., feeling my shot, I also have a sighted index to know that my gun is where I want it to be. I have found this contrasting sight picture to be most effective, both in practice and in real street situations. Another reason I like orange is, it is a color society reserved for things we want seen like traffic cones and hunters' vests.

I have been able to document several cases involving my students who have prevailed in fights and can remember their contrasting front sight. Give it a try. Whatever contrasting front sight arrangement you come up with, I think you will find it to be most satisfactory.

Kelly McCann pioneered the use of the mini-red dot sight on combative pistols when others thought them to be a novelty. The red dot sight on a pistol allows the shooter to superimpose the sight dot on whatever the shooter is looking at without the "eye sprint" traditional pistol sights require. It is my feeling that these sights will soon be as common on pistols as they are on carbines.

When looking at your sights, it is important to keep both eyes open. During a high risk situation, it is quite likely that your vision will "tunnel" on the threat, limiting your peripheral vision and ability to see secondary threats. By closing one eye to better focus on the sights, you further inhibit your combat vision. I realize that as you age, using both eyes and focusing can be difficult, but by "cranking down" your off-side eye, vision can be shifted to your primary eye without having to totally close it. Some vision on your off-side is better than none, but, if possible, keep both eyes up and open.

Chapter Thirteen

THE COMBAT STANCE OR HOW TO AVOID FALLING DOWN DURING A GUNFIGHT!

"So he says, 'yea, I'm good! I shoot, I move, I communicate.'
But can you do it on the ground? Because that's where
you're probably going to end up!"
Clint Smith, Director, Thunder Ranch

I n every shooting class I have ever attended, whether it is for handgun, shotgun or rifle, a large amount of time is spent on the "proper" shooting stance. Instructors will have you put your feet so far apart, spread so wide or canted just so, but the fact of the matter is, it's really not going to matter. Your feet are going to be where they are when the fight starts and it is quite likely they will not be in that "proper stance." These days, I prefer to use the term body position as this is more important then the position of your feet. Whereas I am sure there may be a perfect shooting platform, the fact remains that there is no perfect fighting stance. This is because you are not going to be able to achieve it in the midst of shooting, moving, communicating (screaming, yelling, running?!), and all the other things that are essential to prevail in armed conflict. The most ridiculous thing(s) that I have ever witnessed are instructors who require all of their students to be standing in the same exact position, down the firing line, before they are allowed to fire the first shot. I am not built exactly the same as you and you are not exactly the same as one of your friends. No two human beings are exactly alike. So why would we expect everyone to stand the same when shooting a handgun?

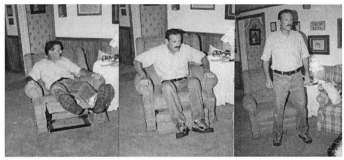

Figure 30
A good shooting stance is one in which the shooter will assume naturally. Such a stance would be similar to that which occurs when you are rocking forward from a recliner.

The best foot position would be one that an individual assumes automatically, a placement used without artificial positioning or conscious thought. That is how anyone will perform, it's how individual motor function works as we go throughout daily life. A number of years ago I was laying back in my favorite recliner, enjoying one of my favorite television programs, when my then 14-year-old daughter got into an argument with her mother. For those of you who have or have had teenagers in the past, you will appreciate this. Anyway, sometime during this argument, my daughter pushed my "last button" and I rocked out of that recliner and I took a step toward her. At this moment she very smartly backed off from what she was doing (and I admit I can't remember it now years later) and I stopped with that one foot stepping forward toward her. It was then that I realized that I was in a pretty good fighting stance and it was totally natural!

Adopting a natural foot position, such as the one described above, is probably the best fighting stance. Instead of trying to determine how many inches apart your feet should be or how many inches wide, it is best to use a position that you can just walk into. This is the stance that, during an armed confrontation where you are bopping, weaving and moving around, that you will probably end up in anyway. Trying to adopt an artificial position in the heat of battle is not likely to work and more than likely will result in you being in a position that is not upright, i.e., laying on your back. Anyone who has ever had to engage in ground fighting can distinctly remember that it is the most disadvantageous position to be in when trying to prevail. The lack of mobility when bullets are flying is possibly the ultimate terror.

While it is a good idea to adopt a fighting stance based on your own stride, it is essential to practice with your feet in varying positions: climbing steps, straddling an object, getting up from a kneeling position, and shooting on the move, which will be addressed in a later chapter. In the event you must shoot from the ground, it is not good to use that particular moment to try and determine what is the best way to fight back. Practice shooting from your back, while laying on your side, in a kneeling position and stomach down. Try to think of every crazy way possible to be involved in a gunfight and shoot a few rounds in that position. You will realize that shooting is really done from the waist up and that placement of the feet is not important. Yes, it's great if you can get your feet in the "perfect stance," but don't count on it. Again, practice shooting from the waist up, where your feet are located really doesn't matter.

What I think is important about any upright shooting position (standing, sitting, kneeling, moving, etc.) is getting your upper body "behind" the gun. By having your upper body and arms canted forward into the gun, recoil is less of a problem. An aggressive forward position, where the shoulders forward of the waist, will bring the gun back on target without effort, providing that your arms are "locked" in behind the gun. Try this; stand up and place your feet in a natural position, something comfortable that you would assume if you were going to be standing for a long period of time. Bend at the ankles and lean forward until you are just about to fall (a position that should place your shoulders above your toes), un-lock your knees and lower your center of gravity. You will likely find this position to be quite stable and natural. Now extend your arms into the preferred shooting position and have a friend push against your hands with a level of force that would mirror recoil. You will find that the aggressive lean will return your hands to their original position without effort on your part. Any stance that will allow you to do this is a "proper" combative shooting stance regardless of where your feet are.

Figure 31
What is more important than a proper stance is to have the upper body in behind the gun. A good way to find this forward balance is stand with the feet in a natural position and then lean forward at the ankles as far as possible without falling forward. Once in this position, bend at the knees and your center of gravity should be in a good position for combat shooting.

Once we start to consider shooting as something done from the waist up, how you position your arms really makes no difference to me. If a person decides to adopt a straight arm or an isosceles stance, that's fine. If they adopt a bent support arm, or Weaver-like position, that's fine too. The only thing I try to correct with a bent arm stance is keeping the elbow down toward the ground instead of bent outwards. An elbow that is bent out away from the shooter actually pulls the support hand away from the gun's grip, pulling the gun off target, instead of helping hold the shooting arm on target. The best way to support the shooting arm, when using a bent arm stance, is to keep the elbow pointed toward the ground, thus helping pull the straight shooting arm back into the shoulder like a rifle stock. A solid argument can be made for the straight arm isosceles stance and the ability to transition *to either arm for one hand shooting* which jives well with the Continuous Motion Principal. However, if I have a student that shoots in the classic Weaver stance and they are hitting what they are shooting at, I LEAVE THEM ALONE! Never mess with success.

Make sure that you adopt an arm position that will allow you complete mobility, especially when wearing body armor. For many years, I shot in a very canted Weaver position until I became a member of my department's SWAT team. Once I started wearing heavy body armor with a load-bearing vest on top (this was before they had combined the two), I realized that the Weaver position was no longer feasible for me because the chest mounted equipment got in the way. It was then that I adopted an isosceles shooting position because it better fit the environment I was operating in at that time. I'm not critical of those who adopt the Weaver position. I have seen some excellent shooters use the bent arm position, it's just I have found that taking the gun directly to the target in a straight line, until my elbows lock into position works very well for me and gives me the accuracy I need at close range.

The key is to try both positions and find out which one works best for you but don't dismiss either one as there has been some research that has shown that in startle response people draw their gun and stab it straight out. At the same time, when trying to maintain a position of cover, such as behind a wall or telephone pole, canting the body back and adopting a Weaver stance often keeps the body better protected from incoming rounds. Thus, it is a good idea to have a working knowledge of both positions, although it is wise to pick one as your primary shooting stance and give it the most attention during practice.

To recap, to develop the proper foot position for combat, adopt a position that you can naturally walk into, something that you're going to do anyway. Remember to shoot from the waist up, pivoting, directing the arms and chest to the target, and getting the gun where it needs to go. Arm position should be comfortable and feel natural to you. Whether it is a straight arm or a bent arm method really makes no difference provided the shooting arm is straight. Though shooting does occur from the waist up, one thing that needs to be taken into account is recoil control. This is easily accomplished by leaning the upper torso and shoulders into the gun. By doing so, and having the shooting arm locked, the gun will come back on target for you without effort. An easy way to find this position is to get into a good stance and lean forward as far as possible without falling on your face, generally the shoulders over the toes. Once in this position unlock the knees and you will have a "proper" fighting position regardless of where you place your feet.

Chapter Fourteen

CARRYING THE HANDGUN: HOLSTER SKILLS AND HOLSTER SELECTION

"Make no mistake about it, that handgun jutting out so jauntily from his hip is not there as an ornament designed to give a swashbuckling air. If he has to use it he will be playing for keeps!"
Bill Jordan

T he highest level of ready possible is to have the gun in your hand. However, this is not reality for the vast majority of us, unless we live in some sort of combat zone. Quite frankly, if our environment were that hostile, we would not be relying on a handgun, we would be carrying a rifle! No, most of us who rely on handguns for defense, rely on them because of their portability. Thus, they are secured in a holster of some sort. For the majority of people who carry a handgun, they are usually carried concealed unless you serve in some sort of uniformed capacity. Selecting a holster can be a truly overwhelming experience due to the large number of styles available. As your skill and experience grows, you may find that you will end up with several holster types based on specific situational requirements. These requirements can include weather conditions, styles of clothing, the locations that you are intending to visit, etc. Although I am a firm believer in carrying the same gun and holster at all times (which is best to increase the transfer of a familiar task and the "feeling the shot" capability), I also realize that there are certain environmental factors that may interfere with the same holster/ gun for all situations. For example, a while back I was asked to chaperone my daughter's after-prom festivities. It would have been nice to carry my regular gun in this particular environment, but it was of great importance for me to be as discreet as possible. For this event only, I opted to carry a small 380-caliber pistol in an ankle holster. While the threat of violence is always there, I felt since this event was going to be behind locked doors, the threat level was reasonably low, so I felt comfortable going dressed in this mode on this particular occasion. What I had to do is take a few moments before I left the house and make sure my mind "understood" that my gun was now in a different location! A few practice draws and a bit of mental "war gaming" potential scenarios helped temporarily anchor (remember NLP?) this different carry mode.

In an effort to conform to the SIG principle, I feel the best holster selection (at least for most of us) will be a strong side belt holster. This holster style, whether belt-mounted or inside the waistband, will probably best facilitate your learning process as it is the easiest to access. After all, it is the closest location to your hand when it is unoccupied or at rest. Take a few moments and let your strong hand hang at your side or rest in front of you at belt buckle level as if you are in a conversation. Note how little distance the hand must travel to acquire the gun. Less distance equals greater speed...its as simple as that. Some may gravitate to a belt mounted cross draw holster and this is fine, however, the majority of people will limit the cross draw to specific circumstances such as driving or working in surveillance operations. It should be noted that when I say strong side, I am talking about your dominant or shooting hand side. The strong side belt holster, while being the easiest to access, is also one of the easiest holsters to conceal. Where and how you wear this holster is going to depend on a number of factors such as your body type, your girth, your flexibility... basically the movements permitted by your upper body and shoulders. Some people are capable of easily reaching around to their backside to draw from a kidney position holster, however, some people do not have this flexibility and can only draw to the front portion of their body, such as an appendix position. A great deal of thought should be put into this and it should be determined by how well you can draw from a given location based on your anatomy. Naturally, males and females are different and should be taken into account. In direct contradiction to many of the gun experts I feel there is no one best location to carry a gun for everyone. It's going to depend on how well you function from a given location.

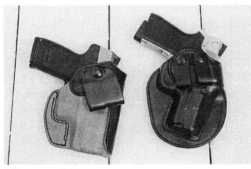

Figure 32
The Inside the Waistband (IWB) holster is a good choice for concealment. These two are excellent examples. The holster on the left is from Mitch Rosen while the model on the right is the EX from Milt Sparks.

Uniformed duty holsters are unique in their requirements. These guns/holsters are worn out in the open by uniformed personnel and must have characteristics that will resist attempts to forcibly remove the gun. The selection of such a holster will be up to each agency and individual officer and should be selected with care. Security holsters are fine, but they DO require additional practice to master so the gun can be drawn quickly. If you are not going to spend this extra time, DO NOT use a security holster...go with something a bit more conventional. However, this does mean that you will need to spend time working on weapon retention. Regardless of which path you take, you must *spend time practicing* or you are resting your fate in the hands of someone else. This said, the vast majority of the people reading this book are going to have a gun that is worn concealed, so we will deal with concealment holsters for the remainder of this chapter. There is quite a large selection of concealment holsters that will hide a handgun in almost every location on your body including ankle holsters, pocket holsters, belt holsters, inside the waistband holsters, cross-draw holsters, and shoulder holsters. There are even holsters that will mount a gun in the small of your back, but these holsters should be looked at with a jaundiced eye as they do not allow the rapid access that is necessary for a gun that is intended for combat. Shoulder holsters do have some utility for people who are carrying a secondary handgun for hunting or for individuals who are bodyguards/chauffeurs or individuals seated in

cars that are involved in surveillance operations. It is my personal feeling that the advantages gained in these situations by using a shoulder holster can also be gained by using a belt mounted cross draw holster. Pocket holsters and ankle holsters do have some practical applicability

Figure 33

The strong side belt-mounted holster is the best all around selection for defensive handgun use. These two holsters are both the same excellent design with one being made from leather and the other from Kydex. The holster on the left is the CQC-S from Alessi while the one on the right is the DS model from FIST.

for deep concealment or a secondary gun. I have a great appreciation for the ankle holster for back up gun purposes, whether I am wearing a uniform or operating in plain clothes. The gun is out of the way when worn in a quality holster and it rides quite well. However, due to the location, it requires a gun of relatively small size, which limits its effectiveness as a true combat handgun. The same can be said for guns worn in pocket holsters. Even though pants with pleated fronts and large pockets, including cargo pockets, are in style, carrying a gun in the pocket limits it to a relatively small size or it will print badly against the fabric and make the pocket sag. Almost everyone I know has some sort of small frame snub-nose revolver or 380-caliber pistol. These armed professionals relegate these guns to backup and secondary roles, which is certainly a wise decision. If circumstances require, being armed with a lesser caliber gun is certainly better than not being armed not at all. A gun will always beat open hands or a knife, if you see the threat coming.

I prefer belt-mounted holsters because they fit the need with as little material as possible and with as much simplicity as is available. I don't like high levels of security on concealment holsters as their highest level of security should come from the fact that they are hidden. Having to manipulate retaining straps, twisting the gun in an effort to remove it from the holster and other such motions only slows the drawing process—at least in my experience. Drawing a weapon from concealment will slow your draw a bit as it is. Anyone who says that it does not is only kidding themselves. It will slow your draw, even if only for a quarter of a second, because it requires a separate movement in order to remove the garment from over the gun. When in the stress of combat, clearing the covering garment, accessing the grip and trying to get the gun on target will be even more complicated if security devices must be released before drawing.

My recommendations for a belt-mounted concealment holsters are as follows:

1. Dual slots or loops (the so-called pancake design) holsters or an inside the waistband style, either of which should hold the gun close to the body while keeping the grip in one stable location. I do feel that there are a number of single loop, pouch type holsters available that are very good, but these holsters should have a wide tunnel belt loop that is molded exactly for the width of belt that it is intended to be carried on. This long molded single belt loop will stabilize the gun and hold it in place. Paddle holsters that meet this same snug fit requirement are also a good choice, but they should lock onto the belt and waistband in such a way that the holster is not too easily removed.

2.   A holster that will stay open at the top as the gun is with-
      drawn so that it can be re-holstered without having to use
      the support hand to help replace it or the gun's muzzle to
      "wiggle" it into place. Looking at the holster when re-
      holstering is not good, as taking your eyes off a threat can
      invite attack.

3.   A traditional thumb-break or open top design. I think
      many of the open top holsters that use a muzzle retention
      or trigger guard screws to tighten the holster are very
      good. A number of today's holsters also use a trigger
      guard indent, which holds the gun in the holster's pouch
      with a high level of security. The new Blackhawk SERPA
      push button concealment holster is a simple and function-
      al choice for the person who wants a concealed security
      type holster. When using the SERPA, depress the release
      button with the pad off the finger and *not* the tip to make
      sure the finger stays clear of the trigger as the gun is
      drawn.

4.   A holster which is designed to fit the exact gun that it is
      intended for. Multi-fit holsters should be avoided for the
      most part. There are a few multi-fit holsters that are
      good, but they are in the minority.

As previously stated, the type of holster you select should be
based on how your draw stroke interacts with your body style. If you
can't comfortably reach around your back, then carrying a canted
FBI holster above your kidney would be a mistake, while wearing it
close to your body in the front, in an appendix position, will allow
rapid access as well as a more fluid motion. I have discovered that I
(as well as many of my students) perform best when carrying the gun
at the center of the strong side or slightly to the rear of the pants
seam in a straight upright position. There is a way to determine the
best holster location and gun cant for you as an individual. This can
be accomplished by standing in front of a mirror with your strong
side toward the mirror. Perform the following steps in slow motion
and take the time to look and see exactly where your hand, wrist and
shoulders are as you complete a slow motion draw stroke.

1. Let your hand hang down at your side or toward the front of your body, what I call the "common hand position", whichever is a natural location for you as you go throughout your daily routine. Try not to lean forward or do anything unnatural.

2. Bend the strong side elbow straight back. It is essential that you take it straight back and not out. If the elbow travels out away from the body, the wrist will be in an unnatural position to access the pistol's grip. Remember the pistol's grip will be pointing to the rear of your body and that is the direction you want the palm of your hand to be in to properly grasp it without having to search for it. Take the elbow straight back until your hand reaches the elevation of your belt. This "path" can be achieved with great consistency which speeds your draw stroke.

3. Look at the hand position, see which way the wrist is cocked. Is the hand in a position where the gun's grip would be best served straight up and down? Is it canted forward? Or maybe is it canted a little bit to the back? It will be different for each and every one of us.

Whatever position the hand is in at the end of this self-test is the best position in which to carry your holstered firearm. Whatever angle your hand is at is the proper cant for your gun's grip. By placing it in this position...by merely bending your elbow straight to the rear your shooting hand will engage the gun's grip all by itself *the same way every time.* You won't have to seek it out. It will just be there. It is amazing by using proper gun placement and taking the elbow straight back how much faster your draw will be versus trying to seek out the gun's grip in some artificial "concealment" location. Now, I realize you may have to adjust this position somewhat in order to make your weapon more concealable, this is understandable. However, try to adjust this position as little as possible. Weapon concealment is important, but, it is not as important as accessibility. Try to remember why you are carrying the holstered handgun in the first place. Is it because you think there may be a situation in which you may need it? If you need it, will you need it very badly and very quickly? Don't put your gun in a position where you are going to have to search for it. Place it in a position that your natural body movement will allow you to access the gun without thought. Draw it by feel, by merely bending your elbow straight to the rear and landing on the grip surface. Like many things in life, handgun concealment is a compromise.

There are a large number of holster designs and styles from a wide range of holster makers. It is impossible to keep track of all the new designs. At the end of this book you will find a list of holster makers that I feel deserve your business. All of these people make topnotch equipment and if one of them doesn't make the holster that works just perfect for you, I would be surprised. All of them have web sights; take the time to shop around for holsters and find the one that best suits your needs.

It is my recommendation that you pick one gun for defense, one holster for carry and use these two continuously. After repetitive practice with this gun and holster, learn exactly what motion is needed to bring the gun up and out of the holster (and nothing more) and drive it to the target. The type of familiar task transference can be developed by carrying the same gun and holster at all times and will translate into a very fast draw. I have many students who are able to draw from concealment while moving laterally and hit an eight-inch plate at 20 feet in less than 1.5 seconds consistently. This type of standard is easy to meet with just a little bit of practice and eliminating unnecessary movement

Figure 34
Kydex is quickly becoming the material of choice for many knowledgeable students of pistol craft. The left holster is the Speed Pro from Hoffner's while the one on the right is the speed slide paddle from Comp-Tac.

from the draw. I have been able to get 20-foot hits on eight-inch plates from concealment in less than one second, but, admittedly, not always. Getting old sucks! Like many of you, I do not get the practice time I would like, but I practice whenever I can, even if it is nothing more than dry skills in my bedroom.

While discussing holsters, I would be remiss if I didn't discuss holster selection as a system. The holster needs to be supported by a proper belt. This belt should be at least 1¼" wide and probably no more than 1¾" wide. Belts wider than this, if not worn in environments such as the southwestern United States, will call attention to the wearer. For most of us, a belt of 1¼" to 1½" in width will match the wide majority of the clothing that is worn regularly. Pick a nice looking belt in black and brown. These two belts will match the majority of clothing that you wear; whether you wear suits and ties, or jeans and T-shirts. A proper gun belt should be made of two pieces of leather that are stitched together in opposing grain formats. By turning the belt so the grain opposes one another, the belt actually becomes stronger and more rigid and will better support the weight of the holster. Some holster companies are actually putting strips of plastic or Kydex in between the two belt pieces, which give greater rigidity and weight supporting structure. Belts that are designed to carry guns are far superior to heavy leather belts that are sold in local clothing or western shops. An eight ounce strap of leather is not as good at carrying the weight of a gun as two four ounce pieces of leather that have been split, turned in opposing grain directions and stitched together. Another good choice is the instructor and frequent flyer belts from the Wilderness. These nylon belts are strong and support the weight of a gun very well.

The final piece of this holster system is a magazine pouch. While it is quite likely that any armed confrontation you may face will be resolved before your gun is empty, you cannot count on this. In addition, the number one malfunction in semiautomatic pistols is due to faulty magazines. If you happen to have a magazine that is bad and keeps the gun from functioning properly, the only solution to your problem is to insert another magazine. Mr. Murphy is alive and well and you should have a contingency in place if your gun malfunctions. The best way to clear that gun and get it running again (which will be addressed in a later chapter) is to have a spare magazine. A magazine pouch is a relatively simple piece of equipment. It can be made from leather or Kydex, though I have to admit I prefer Kydex material for magazine pouches, and they are essentially all the same. The one feature that you want to look for in a proper magazine pouch is to make sure that the pouch material *does not cover more than one half of the magazine body*. In order to grasp the magazine quickly, you must be able to get your support hand around it in a good solid hold before it's removed and directed toward the bottom of the gun's grip. This will require at least half of the magazine be exposed so that you can get a good grip on it. If most of the magazine body is covered by the pouch, it will require you to use fingertip dexterity to remove it from the pouch, which is not likely to be at its best during the stress and duress of a fight. I have found the best magazine pouches to be made of Kydex that covers half and have a retention screw that will allow for a level of tightness based on the user's own desires. I also like magazine pouches that can be canted forward or back depending on the location in which they will be worn. Like the holster, you need to determine the best location for your magazine pouch. This should be done the same way as when you selected your holster. If your body allows you to reach only so far around your body, then the magazine pouch should be worn toward the front and probably canted a bit to the rear. If you like wearing your magazine around the back of your body for added concealment, then the magazine should probably be canted a bit forward. Take a look at the location of your hand and wrist as your elbow travels to the rear. You'll notice that when it is in the front of the body the hand is canted back a little bit, as it travels around to the rear of the body the hand actually cants a little bit forward. By having the magazine canted in the same position that gives you natural access, you can actually speed up your reloading time by as much as ½ a second versus trying to adjust the cant of your wrist to whatever position the magazine happens to be in. Work with your body's natural motion to eliminate unnecessary movement.

Take the time to select the best combat accessories. Yes, holster, belt and magazine pouches can be as expensive as the gun, but not necessarily. With today's plastic and Kydex materials it is possible to get a good quality holster for as little as $30.00. But don't pick your holster just based on cost. Pick your holster based on your individual body and needs. If you take care of your holster, belt and magazine pouch, it will last your entire life. Pick your handgun with care, pick your combat accessories with care and use them over and over again. Vary as little as possible and you will become very proficient very quickly with those pieces of equipment.

Being able to draw your gun the same way each and every time, with a solid combat grip before it ever leaves the holster, is essential. I can remember when I was a cadet in the police academy, I was on the line for my first day of firearms training and our instructor was up in a booth above the class looking down. He said, "Okay class, we're going to begin holster skills. Now it's absolutely essential that you get your combat grip before it ever leaves the holster so you don't have to fumble with it when you get it out in front of you. Are you ready?" I can remember thinking, "yeah, okay, now is the time that he is going to tell how to do this." But the next thing I heard was the whistle, which was our signal to draw and fire. We were pretty much left to our own devices on how to get that combat grip before it ever left the holster. This is just not acceptable. Proper training requires instruction on how to draw so that it can be done over and over again. This brings us back to using index points so that we can "feel" our way through our draw stroke. Remember, feeling the shot, from draw to follow-through, is important. It has to feel the same way each and every time because we can't watch ourselves in the middle of a confrontation.

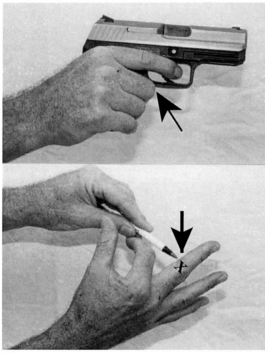

When working on your draw stroke, it makes good sense to watch yourself in the mirror making sure you also feel what is going on. The use of a video camera is also advised. Know how it looks and know how it feels to accomplish a proper draw. Over the last twenty-plus years, I have used a system of index points to teach the draw so a level of consistency can be developed. This system has been used time and again in actual armed confrontations and I have had students report back to me that their draw stroke remains good even with low levels of practice. If you have a good draw, then by no means change it just because you're reading this

Figure 35

The shooting hand must engage the gun the same way during each draw. This will ensure the gun goes directly to the target without having to fumble with it. To begin, get the gun in the shooting grip you wish to use when the gun is fired. Force the middle finger into the juncture of the trigger guard and the grip, this will create an index point. If this position can be anchored to the grip/trigger guard juncture, the shooter will be sure of a proper grip before the hand ever wraps around the gun.

book. But maybe you're an instructor and looking for a good way to teach others how to draw. Keep an open mind. Remember it is A way, not THE way. The draw stroke should be tacked onto the ready positions that were discussed earlier. Remember all combative skills are a pyramid. You must build on top of things that you have already learned. Don't disregard something previously learned just because you have moved on to something else. The draw starts with the arms in whatever position is normal for daily routine and ends when your hands come together and travel to the target. To make it one continuous, smooth motion, your hand should move upward from the side of the leg, or back from the front of the body, with the elbow bending straight to the rear. For years I have encouraged my students to make an effort to keep their hands at the front of their body near the belt buckle as they go about

Figure 36

The common hands position is a natural position in front of the body that will help create a consistent path to the holster for the shooting hand.

their daily routine. This "common hands position" is good for not only drawing the gun, but for garment removal (discussed in depth later), open hand techniques and other potential uses. Hands left hanging at the side of the body or pushed into pants pockets will be of little use in an attack. Keep them in front of your body. Frankly, if you are startled, your hands will move up near your head, your shoulders will shrug and your knees will bend. This natural startle position is also a good position from which you should practice your draw as well as other combative skills. If a covering garment is concealing the holstered weapon, the hand will remove this garment as the elbow is moving to the rear. The hand wraps around the grip the same way each and every time, which should be a proper firing grip. Adjusting the grip as the gun travels to the target is not only unacceptable, it's down right dangerous!

How do you determine what this grip position is? You must find the index point that best suits your grip on the middle finger of your shooting hand. To do this, grip the unloaded gun in a proper firing grip and push your middle finger into the junction of the trigger guard and the grip. This will leave a mark on the middle finger, which should be considered your draw stroke index point. This is the position you will seek when your hand moves to the holstered gun. Once acquired, you will know that your firing grip is correct before the hand ever wraps around the pistol. By understanding that your grip will be the same each and every time, it will result in greater on target speed from the holster. The range commands I use during basic holster work may help you better visualize this process.

1. **Index** – bring your hand to the grip by bending the elbow straight back, sinking the middle finger index point into the grip/trigger guard junction. Wrap the three lower fingers around the grip. This three-finger wrap is very important to weapon control.

2. **Wrap** – the shooting hand wraps over the top of the gun releasing the thumb break (if your holster has one) on the way to the proper shooting grip. Releasing the retention snap is not a separate motion, it is done while obtaining a shooting grip. If no retention strap is used, the hand can grasp the gun in a "C" clamp configuration. This position has the hand engage the grip with the middle finger at the same time the thumb and web of the hand close on the grip tang.

3. **Draw** – draw the handgun from the holster with the desired grip. Draw up until the arm will not bend at the elbow any further. By doing this, you will be able to recreate the draw by feel. Once the arm is bent to its extent, the gun must be oriented towards the target by bending the wrist or lower the elbow, either of which will point the muzzle towards the target. Once accomplished, it is pushed/driven straight to the target along the eye/target line. Do not "dig a ditch" by bringing the gun down as it travels to the target. At the same time, do not "cast a fishing reel" by bringing the gun over head as it travels forward. It is important to orient the gun to the target while the gun is still close to the body for a close retention shot. It also gets the gun pointed at your opponent's chest for the best shot possible. If there is room to drive the gun to the target, the elevation is right below the shooting side eye so a straight line is more likely versus the "ditch digging" and "fishing" actions described above. Your

support hand should move up in front of your body. Allow the support hand to move up in front of your breast bone, as this will put it in a proper position to receive the shooting hand as it goes to the target. As the gun clears the body the support hand should come over to the front and collect the shooting hand in the "peak-to-peak" method previously discussed. Collect the gun hand as soon as possible as the support arm makes a wonderful

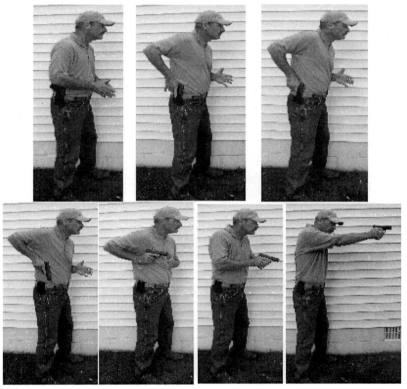

Figure 37

The draw begins with the hands in the common position. To reach for the gun, the shooting side elbow should bend straight to the rear bringing the hand to the gun in a consistent path that can be re-created. The index point on the middle finger seeks the juncture of the trigger guard and grip ensuring a consistent grip. Once in this position, the thumb travels over the pistol and releases any retention straps. The gun is drawn up and out of the holster pouch until the elbow is fully bent. The gun is then rotated toward the target in one of two ways; the wrist points the muzzle straight ahead or the wrist locks and the elbow is rotated downward which will point the gun toward the target. The hands come together using the "peak to peak" method in front of the body as early as possible and the gun is driven straight to the target. The secret to speed of draw is lack of unnecessary motion."

"windage adjustment" when driving the gun toward an attacker. Do not be surprised to discover that this will occur in the same general area as the third eye position, making it consistent reinforcing the Continuous Motion Principle. The gun is then driven to the target in a straight line, coming up in front of your eyes allowing you to see the contrasting front sight, pressing the trigger independently to the rear and getting an accurate combat shot. If a second or third shot is needed, the forward lean of your upper torso will control the recoil for you. Follow through, being ready for any follow-up shots is important.

When you believe the hostilities are over, take time to check your 360-degree environment or what I call "checking your world." If you believe the situation is over and it is time to put the gun away, it should be replaced in the holster with your finger off the trigger and properly indexed. In essence, to replace the gun in the holster, you merely do in reverse what you did to get the gun on target. Bring the gun back to a close retention position, separating your hands,

Figure 38
To re-holster the pistol, the opposite motions are made. The arms return to the third eye position and the hands separate. The gun goes back past the holster pouch and the muzzle is inserted from the rear. This eliminates any possible entanglement with any retention straps. The gun is then rocked forward into the holster pouch. The thumb holds the slide down (the thumb check) to make sure the pistol does not go out of battery.

making sure that the muzzle of the gun does not cover your support hand. Take the pistol back past the body and over top the holster mouth. Keep the muzzle clear of your torso and bring the gun back past the holster and down into holster mouth, pivoting the muzzle down and in. This action will make sure the thumb break snap is not in the way as you re-holster your gun. If you don't have a thumb break snap, it is still a good way to re-holster your gun consistently. A "thumb check" should be performed on both semi-autos and revolvers to ensure that the gun's hammer is not cocked when pushed back into the holster. A thumb check is nothing more than placing the shooting hand thumb on the gun's hammer and holding it in place as you push the gun into the pouch. The motion of drawing, firing and holstering should require very little upper body movement. Most of the movement will be accomplished by your shooting arm and shoulder. While it is common for many people to dip down a little bit in a crisis situation, due to startle response, don't make the motion so exaggerated that your hand comes up to the gun, your upper body sinks down and you miss the gun's grip. It is easy to see that acquiring a combat grip on the first attempt is critical when trying to save your own life.

Garment removal is critical for concealed carry applications, but should not complicate the draw greatly. Yes, it will slow the draw some as you do have to get the garment out of the way, but it won't make it as complex as you might think. We will deal with garment removal techniques with open front garments, closed front garments (such as sweatshirts), and will also review a few garment removal techniques for ankle holsters due to popularity.

Figure 39
The concealed draw will always begin from a natural arm/body position or startle.

Figure 40
The open hand technique uses the whole surface area of the open hand to push the garment out of the way.

Figure 41
The Gaylord Technique takes the hand to the rear in a karate chop fashion between the garment and the torso.

Figure 42
The Lapel Technique requires the shooter to insert their hand
behind the lapel and then slide down to the holstered gun.

Figure 44
The hook technique has
the hand hook the garment
as the elbow travels to the
rear at gun level.

Figure 43
The HK Technique places the hand on the abdomen, which
then slides around to the holstered pistol, removing the
garment on the way.

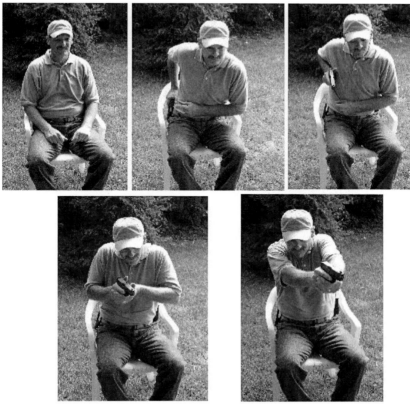

Figure 45

Drawing from a seated position is no different than standing up. Obtain the pistol by
bending the elbow straight to the rear and accessing the gun's grip. The only space
you have control over when seated is what you can create behind you, so use it
effectively to draw. Make sure that the gun is rotated toward the target, close to the
body, so that it will clear any obstruction like a table or dash board.

Garment removal techniques for open front garments involve the
position of the shooting hand as it moves back to the pistol. The
easiest technique to use is what I call the open hand or impact
technique. When using this, the hand is open to its full extent, giving
it a large impact area to engage the front edge of the garment. As the
elbow bends and the hand moves back toward the pistol, the hand is
spread open wide pushing the garment back past the pistol. Once the
garment is pushed back past the pistol, the hand is turned into the
grip engaging the middle finger index point. The second method is
what I call the Gaylord technique – as holster master Chic Gaylord
was the first person I ever saw use this particular technique. Bill

Jordan also demonstrated this technique in his book *NO SECOND PLACE WINNER*. When using the Gaylord technique, the hand comes back toward the grip and stiffens up similar to a karate chop. The stiffened hand is then inserted between the torso and the open garment. The lower forearm then pushes the garment out of the way and the hand can access the grip at the index point. The third technique I call the lapel slide technique – because it requires the hand to move to the upper area of the chest, inserting the fingers back behind the lapel of an open front garment. The hand then slides down the lapel pulling it back as it moves downward to the gun. The HK technique, which I named after the Heckler and Koch International Training Division where I first saw this technique taught, requires the shooting hand to lay flat against the belly at the opening of the garment. The hand then stays in contact with the torso and slides around, clearing the garment, and allowing the hand to engage the grip.

The final technique is what I call the hook technique – and it is my preferred technique. This technique merely requires the hand to hook the fingers around the garment's forward edge. As the elbow bends and the hand travels back, the fingers hook inward, trapping the open front garment and as the arm moves back pulling the garment out of the way. The hand can then rotate down acquiring a shooting grip quickly.

There are advantages and disadvantages to all of these techniques. The techniques that seem to be superior for garment removal offer the hand in an improper position to access the grip quickly. Those techniques, that have the hand open and ready to engage the grip, tend to be lacking in garment control. Which technique you decide on will depend on your body, hand size and ability to move the arm.

There are two closed front garment techniques that I happen to like. The first one is called the Hackathorn Rip. This technique is named for master weapon craft instructor Ken Hackathorn. It requires the support hand to reach across the body in a cross-draw motion, grab the bottom of the garment and pull it up and out of the way, uncovering the pistol on the strong side of the body. The shooting hand can then access the grip as if drawing from a normal belt holster. As the gun clears the body, the support hand lets go of the garment and collects the shooting hand. The second closed front garment technique I like is called the Bowie Sweep. This technique was named after David Bowie, lead instructor at the Tactical

Defense Institute in Southern Ohio. This technique requires the shooting hand to grab the garment in the center of the body at the belt buckle level. The shooting hand then pulls the garment upward and to the rear until it's above the holstered handgun. The hand then lets go of the garment and immediately slides down onto the grip, drawing it up and out and driving it to the target. Another advantage of the Bowie sweep is, it works quite well when two layers of clothing are worn, such is the case in areas that have very cold winters. It is quite common for people to wear a sweater or sweatshirt underneath a heavy winter coat, intending to take the winter coat off to sit in a restaurant or some other location. This allows the closed front garment to conceal their holstered pistol. By using the Bowie sweep, both garments can be removed at the same time allowing access to the holstered pistol.

There are two primary ankle holster techniques that I like and both require a similar action for garment removal. The first technique – kneeling – requires the shooter to grab the pants' leg just near the crotch area. By trapping the garment here, any other motion will lift the pants' leg. In this case, the shooter will step forward with the ankle-holstered leg and go into a kneeling position. It should be noted that both of these techniques are making the assumption that the ankle holstered weapon is on the leg opposite the shooting hand. Once the shooter has reached a kneeling position, the pants' leg will have been pulled back exposing the gun to the shooting hand and fire can be returned from a kneeling position. The kneeling position for ankle carry is excellent for situations in which low cover is available.

The step out technique – or what is better known as the Ayoob technique (named after famed weapon craft instructor Massad Ayoob) is very similar in that it requires the pant leg to be trapped near the groin area. The shooter then steps out in the direction of the ankle-holstered pistol, clearing the pant leg along the way. The upper body then leans over and draws the exposed weapon and comes up into a shooting position. While it is true the stance will be quite wide, it is still more mobile to be on both feet in an upright position than to be kneeling.

Both techniques should be practiced as either could come in handy in a fight depending on the environment and obstacles in the immediate area.

Holster skills are a critical part of handgun combatives. As a matter of fact, they are probably just as important as being a good shot. The concealed draw technique doesn't have to be complicated if the shooter will practice their normal holster techniques in the same format as they do when the gun is covered. By this I mean use a technique that will access the holstered handgun in the same motion that is necessary to remove the garment prior to drawing. By doing so, adding the little bit of additional effort needed to remove the garment will not cause undue delay. The gun that is not in the hand when the hostilities begin is a gun that may never come into play. Practice holster skills and master them...they may be what keep you alive!

Chapter Fifteen

KEEP IT RUNNING

"If there are rules, it's a sport, not a fight. In a fight, if you are not cheating, you are not trying hard enough to win!"
The Author

Reliability is the number one priority when selecting any combative firearm. The gun has to be 100% reliable in order for you to have the confidence to use this weapon for defense of life. But let's be honest, how many human designed and engineered items are 100% reliable? Do you really think your firearm can be expected to perform to a higher standard than any other manmade mechanical device? There are going to be times when it will malfunction and you must be able to clear it quickly and get back on target or you will be on the losing end of the confrontation.

I have heard it said that the revolver is more reliable than the semiautomatic pistol. In years gone by I would have agreed, as I have seen Smith & Wesson Model 10 revolvers thrown across a parking lot, picked up and fired, something that semiauto pistols of an earlier generation were incapable of doing. However, as we continue into the new millennium, I'm afraid I have to disagree as the current generation of semiautomatic pistols are about as reliable as any human designed mechanical device can be. The one advantage the current semiauto has over the revolver is malfunctions can be cleared quickly getting the gun back in operation. The majority of the time, if a revolver fails, it requires a trip to the gunsmith to repair. Trying to clear a revolver malfunction in the heat of battle can be quite complex, whereas many semi-auto problems can be cleared in seconds. Though I like the double-action revolver, it's very unlikely that I will select one for personal security at any future date. From what I have seen from my students (both police and citizens) this will be the case for most of the readers of this book.

The first thing that needs to be understood, and for many of you this is going to be somewhat remedial, is loading the semiautomatic pistol. In order to put the pistol into a loaded condition what is required is to fill the magazine (not the "clip") to its full capacity with ammunition. Care should be taken to ensure that the bullets are forward in the magazine and the primers are to the rear, otherwise the gun is not going to function correctly (this happens more than many would believe). Once the magazine is full, it is then inserted into the grip until it clicks into place and will not fall out. The slide is pulled to the rear and let go in a sling shot fashion. DO NOT ride the slide home. Pull it back, let it go and let the spring(s) do their job. To interfere with the spring action is to invite malfunctions in a modern semiautomatic pistol. Once a round is loaded into the chamber, it will then be a matter of placing it into a proper carry mode and this will differ from gun to gun. On pistols that are double-action only the hammer (or striker) will follow the slide home, the trigger will go forward and the gun is ready to be put in the holster. On guns that are double-action on the first shot and single action on remaining shots, the hammer will need to be lowered. This will usually be done with some form of de-cocking lever, which will be located on either the frame or toward the rear of the slide. By pressing down on that de-cock lever, the hammer will safely go to an at-rest position. You do not have to lower the hammer with your thumb, let the spring loaded de-cocker do its job. It will safely lower the hammer onto a chambered round without igniting the primer.

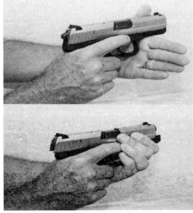

Figure 46
The press check begins with the off hand staying clear of the muzzle, this can be done by indexing the palm of the hand against the face of the trigger guard. The fingers and thumb then wrap around the slide and press it to the rear just enough to see in the chamber.

On single-action semiautomatics, like the Browning High Power and the 1911, the gun should be carried in what is called a "cocked and locked" mode. This will require you to push the safety lever upward, locking the hammer into a cocked position. This will render the gun inoperable unless the thumb safety is moved downward prior to pressing the trigger. Any and all of these weapons are good choices for personal combat. Which gun is selected is completely up to the individual with one being no more reliable than another. The biggest difference is the action of the trigger and how easy it is to press it to the rear. This trigger weight is going to be up to the individual shooter and their individual operational parameters (Chapter Six).

At this stage, it is a good idea to make sure the gun is loaded. It is possible that the magazine was not completely seated at the time the slide was cycled, thus a round was not stripped from the magazine and loaded into the chamber. This can be accomplished in several different ways, all using the support hand. For many years, the "pinch check" was taught. The pinch check required the thumb to go in the front of the trigger guard with the index finger engaging the face of the slide just below the gun's muzzle. The slide was then "pinched" to the rear allowing the operator to see into the chamber. It works quite well with 1911 style pistols with short recoil guide rods, however, with the full-length guide rods that are current in most pistols, this technique is all but impossible to do due to the guide rod pushing the finger out of the way. What is a more common technique today is known as the "press check." In order to do a good press check, the support hand should be open to its full size, approaching the live pistol from underneath. The palm of the hand should be pressed back against the face of the trigger guard wrapping the thumb and fingers around the slide. At no time does the hand go forward of the muzzle. Once the hand is cammed against the trigger guard, the fingers can merely press back slightly on the slide allowing a brief glimpse of the chamber making sure that the round is in place. For those who are nervous about the press check because of its close proximity to the muzzle, there is the "rear press check." In order to do this, the thumb is placed under the grip tang just above the shooting hand. The index and middle fingers then wrap around the rear sight and can pinch back against the sight camming the thumb against the grip tang pulling the slide back just enough to look into the chamber.

Figure 47

A rear press check can be done by placing the thumb of the off hand under the grip tang and the trigger and middle fingers against the rear sight. The slide can then be pressed to the rear to see into the chamber.

A different rear press check requires the support hand to actually grasp the top of the rear of the slide, with the palm and fingers engaging the rear serrations. The shooting hand can then push forward a little bit on the gun's grip (finger off trigger!) allowing the slide to move slightly to the rear and making sure a round is in place. Any of these techniques work quite well and which is chosen is up to the individual shooter. I strongly suggest using the same technique all the time and to grasp the gun in a different way than what you do when vigorously working the slide such as chambering a round. Quite often, I have seen students attempt a press/chamber check only to pull the slide all the way to the rear and eject a live round.

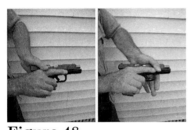

Figure 48
Two additional methods of press checking a semi-automatic pistol are turning the gun sideways and "saddle gripping" either the rear or front of the slide and pressing to the rear.

DO NOT make the two actions feel the same. By chamber checking it the same way each and every time a step will never be missed and safety will be commonplace.

On DA/SA pistols, the press check can be accomplished with greater ease if the hammer is manually cocked before press checking the slide. This will reduce tension on the slide making it easier to do. Once the check is completed, the gun should be de-cocked using the appropriate lever.

There is no reason to be in a hurry when doing a chamber check, so it can be done with a great deal of care and safety. But remember always make sure your gun is loaded before you hit the street. Don't take it for granted that everything is fine just because you worked the slide before you put the gun in the holster. Check and double check. An empty gun is a gun that will not run and a gun that will not run is no fun, as well as being hazardous to your health. Make sure it's loaded before you put yourself in harm's way.

Become smooth when you check the chamber using a press check technique. There is nothing more unsettling than watching an individual leave the range and go on duty and look like they're fumbling around with their gun and have no idea how the thing functions. The person that fumbles with their gun and looks inept is going to be the individual that all of us are going to be wary of. At the same time the person that looks like they know what they are doing instills confidence in all of us. This is the type of professional I want to hit the street with. The one that knows their weapon, knows how to use their weapon and will back me up when the situation requires.

Figure 49

The fast reload is begun by bringing the shooting side elbow back against the torso, in a position similar to the third eye. This accomplishes two things; first it stabilizes the gun to hold it in place and second the gun will be in the same place every time a reload is needed, making it easier to do without looking at the gun. The magazine in the pistol is released when the spare magazine is removed from the pouch and brought up near the gun.

Figure 50

Once the magazine has left the pistol's grip, the new magazine is immediately inserted with the flat back of the magazine engaging the flat back of the magazine well. The finger held straight down the face of the magazine will help guide it in place. The magazine is then forcefully seated with the heel of the hand.

Just as loading the pistol should be done with great care, unloading the pistol should probably be done with even greater care. There is no greater potential tragedy than mistaking a loaded gun for an unloaded one. When the gun is unloaded, double, triple, and quadruple check that it is unloaded. Unloading the handgun is easily done. The FIRST step is to remove the source of ammunition from the pistol, i.e., the magazine is withdrawn. Don't try to take the round out of the chamber until the magazine is free of the pistol as you will just reload another round. Turn the gun to the side and work the slide vigorously several times, then lock the slide to the rear using the slide stop. Check the chamber visually and by feel to make sure that there are no rounds in it. At this time you now have a safe weapon. It is more common than people realize for individuals to unload their gun by first working the slide and then removing the magazine. Not good...

Loading and reloading is a fairly simple process, unless it needs to be done in a hurry or under great stress, which is the case in a fight. There are two basic reloads that are taught in the majority of shooting schools. They are generally known as a speed load and a tactical reload. To simplify this, a speed load is essentially getting the magazine out of the grip as fast as possible and getting a new magazine in place so the fight can be continued. What happens to the spent magazine is not a major concern. A tactical reload is done when there is more time available and you wish to secure the magazine coming out of the gun. Being a firm believer in simplicity, I have come to call these two reloads the fast reload and the slow reload. Simplicity is a good thing, unfortunately neither one of these reload techniques is simple to perform under any type of stress. Quite frankly they are difficult to execute on the range, but knowing how to do them is a real good idea.

By this time, hopefully, you have selected a location to carry your spare magazine in a similar fashion to how you selected a position for your holster, one that is advantageous for you and your body style. Like learning to acquire your handgun's grip, take the time with your support hand to practice locating your spare magazine. This should be done without conscious thought and you need to do it by feel. During a gunfight it is going to be important to keep your eyes on your adversary so that if they move you can keep track of where they are. Remember—They are trying to kill you!

Completing the following steps by feel will keep you from having to look down to locate your magazine. Keep your holster and spare magazine in the same location all the time so you can access them without thought. The fast reload requires the shooting hand and the support hand to do different functions at the same time. Yes, this is a complex action, but it is a skill that must be learned and mastered. Once it is decided that a fast reload is necessary, normally because the gun is empty, the shooting hand thumb must push the magazine release button. For those who are left handed, this may be the trigger finger. It really doesn't matter which one. Both work just as well in all truthfulness.

Figure 51
The "McCann" technique has the shooter turn the gun in the hand as the off hand leaves the pistol to travel to the spare magazine.

For those, like me, who have small hands, a certain amount of shifting is going to be required so that the thumb can reach the release button. Many people have been taught to flip the gun around. I have no real problems with this because I have seen this done with a great deal of skill, however, it does raise a certain amount of concern due to fine motor skills being lost during a confrontation, meaning the gun could be dropped while doing this. Kelly McCann, one of the sharpest writer/trainers currently in the business, teaches a technique in which he turns the gun in the shooting hand as the support hand leaves the weapon to go to the magazine. He merely takes the support hand fingers, turns them upward and pulls the gun toward the thumb as it leaves to travel to the spare magazine. By doing so the gun turns into the shooting hand thumb putting it into an excellent position to drop the magazine. This is an excellent technique, and in my opinion, unless you just have an incredible amount of motor skill already dedicated to the flip, it is a good technique to adopt for fast reloads.

Once the thumb/finger is on the release button, do not release the magazine in the pistol until the support hand has gained a solid grip on the spare magazine. As a matter of fact, pull the spare magazine up and out of the pouch and have it near the bottom of the gun *before the magazine is ejected.* Think about this for a moment... the reason that a reload is missed is because the magazine and magazine well are not in alignment when insertion is attempted. This is due to one or the other...or both...are in action which makes insertion impossible. The gun must be held in place, without movement, momentarily so that the magazine can be inserted. Hold the gun in your hand and push on the magazine release button with your thumb and note how your whole forearm stiffens and how still the gun is when the thumb applies pressure. *Make use of this! Release the spent magazine and immediately insert the new one while the gun, hand, arm is still.* Just make sure to release pressure on the release button BEFORE you insert the new magazine.

It is also a good idea to make sure you have something to put in the gun before you eject the magazine you have. Yes, it's true that this magazine may be empty, but what if you are able to find additional ammunition you will need a magazine to load. Never trade a known for an unknown. Get your support hand solidly on the spare magazine and then dump the magazine from the pistol. Before pulling the magazine out of the pouch, make sure that you have a solid grip on it before removing. If not, two things can happen:

1.   When you violently jerk the magazine up and out of the pouch and turn it toward the pistol, it is possible that you could throw it at your opponent instead of inserting it in the bottom of your gun.
2.   As stated above, getting the magazine into that relatively small hole in the bottom of the grip, requires a certain amount of accuracy. You don't want the magazine flipping around when you are trying to insert it into a specific location.

How you grip the magazine will depend a great deal on the size of your hand. The generally accepted technique, one with which I agree, is that the thumb is on one side and the middle, ring and pinky fingers are on the opposing side of the magazine with the index finger down the face of the magazine toward the point of the top round. This grip will allow you to remove the magazine and guide it into the magazine well, using the index finger as a felt index to get it in place. The index finger will also allow you to deal with any rounds at the top of the magazine that have moved forward during strenuous activity. Where a variation of this preferred method may come into play is when the support hand is too large or too small to grasp the magazine as described. If the magazine cannot be firmly seated or the size of the hand seems to interfere with the reloading process, then the magazine may have to be adjusted in the hand to allow for positive insertion.

The magazine should be inserted into the magazine well with the flat back of the magazine flush against the flat back of the magazine well. This action will help guide the magazine up and into the gun grip. Trying to insert the magazine straight in, like threading a needle, will likely meet with failure, especially with single column magazines. Some advocate laying the side of the magazine against the side of the magazine well, which is actually a decent technique.

Look at a loaded magazine and you will note that it is rounded on the sides, allowing it to slide into place. Use something to give a felt index so you know the magazine is ready to be inserted. Once the magazine is in the correct position, use the heel of the hand to push the magazine up into the well until it locks in place. The support hand should then slide up the side of the grip and seat itself in the open space and shoot as needed. While this sounds easy enough, it can be difficult when trying to do it quickly. Fast reloads are a weak spot for me and I practice them regularly.

Some instructors teach their students to bring the gun up in front of their face to reload. The thought here is that the shooter will be less likely to miss the magazine well if it is right in front of their eyes. Good idea for competitors who KNOW that the target is not shooting back. Bad idea for someone who wants to keep track of the person trying to kill them!

It is a better idea to keep the eyes on the threat when trying to reload and if looking at the magazine is necessary, only look for a brief moment to ensure alignment and then return to the threat. This is where another of the CMP lessons will come into play. I have found that by using a variation of the third eye position for the fast load, it can be accomplished most of the time without looking. The reason for this is the handgun will be located in the same position every time the reload is executed. Since your forearm will always be the same length, the location of the gun will be the same. We are back to "shooting by feel" by doing this. The elbow comes back to the same place every time, and is FELT in the same location. Once the arm/hand/gun are stable in one location, the magazine can be inserted as previously described and the gun brought back into the fight. The gun can be elevated to satisfy the user (a little more elevation will help get the eyes back on target if a quick peek is needed), as long as the elbow indexes against the torso in the same location.

The slow reload is done in the same basic way with the exception of allowing the magazine to fall free to the ground. In this instance, for whatever reason, the magazine will be retained. Maybe it is only partially spent, but it needs to be kept. The support hand will grab the spare magazine and bring it up under the gun BEFORE the magazine is ejected from the pistol. The support hand will make room to catch this magazine so that it can be retained. There are

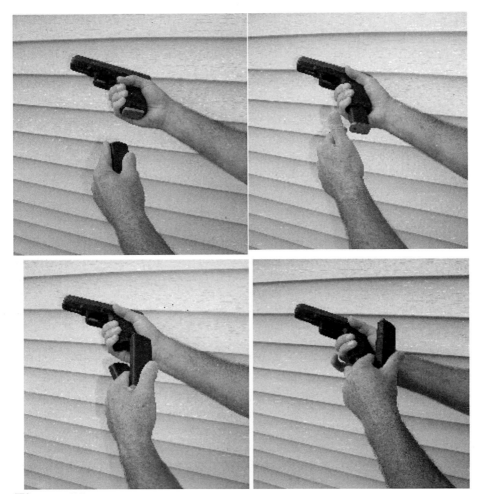

Figure 52

The slow reload requires the spare magazine to be brought up under the pistol in the same fashion as the fast reload. The difference being the magazine removed from the pistol will be retained for possible use. The magazine is released and caught between the thumb and trigger finger of the support hand. The magazine is then removed from the gun with the support hand tilting over far enough to insert the new magazine, which is being held between the trigger and middle fingers. The heel of the hand pushes it in place.

several ways currently taught to catch the old magazine, none of which are good when fine motor skills are lacking. Some instructors call for using the ring and pinky fingers so the three primary fingers can retain the same hold on the magazine. Sounds like a good idea at face value, but let's take a closer look. For whatever reason, you have decided that keeping the magazine is a good idea. You will want to make sure that it does not fall to the ground or doing a fast reload would have been the best move. Think about which of your fingers have the most gripping power. That's right, the thumb and index finger. The thumb and index fingers are designed to oppose one another and offer the most positive grip...use this! Once the support hand with magazine is brought up under the pistol grip, take the index finger and slide it down the thumb side of the magazine. This will allow you to retain the magazine between the index and middle fingers while opening the space between the thumb and index fingers to catch the expended magazine. Once the expended magazine is secure, pivot the hand over slightly and push the new magazine into place with the heel of the hand. Do this from the third eye ready position and it will feel like and similar to other physical skills.

Another method to change and retain the partially spent magazine is to eject the magazine into the support hand and put it in a pocket or other location and then reload the gun as described in the fast reload. The chief advantage of this is the hand handles one magazine at a time instead of filling the support hand with two magazines. Try each technique and see which works best for you. It is my suggestion to be familiar with a slow reload technique, but do not spend a great deal of valuable practice time on it. How does one know that they have enough time to perform a "reload with retention" in the middle of a fight? When in doubt, there is no doubt...perform a fast reload and KNOW you are ready.

The majority of malfunctions with semiautomatic pistols are due to either operator error, faulty ammo or defective magazines. What many people do not realize is magazines are manufactured to very strict tolerances. The curvature at the top of the magazine, or what is known as the feed lips, are precisely set to work within the individual model of handgun they accompany. If these feed lips are off just a fraction of an inch, failure to properly feed the next round into the chamber can occur. Think about the number of times during practice that your magazine drops to the ground or gets banged around during storage. It's not hard to see how the feed lips can be damaged without the user being aware of it. Quality magazines are a must for any combative pistol. While there are some excellent quality after market magazines (Mec-Gar, Metalform, Wilson,

McCormick), the shooter should stay with the magazines that are supplied for that pistol by the manufacturer.

Operator error usually occurs in the form of the limp-wrist. The majority of semi-autos are recoil operated, meaning the recoil of the pistol and the cycling of the slide makes the gun function properly. A solid grip and leaning forward into the gun not only assists in control of recoil, it also increases the reliability and functioning of the semiautomatic pistol. Limp wristing of the gun is the primary malfunction in my experience. I have seen this over and over again in the thousands of students I have taught over the years. I'm even willing to go so far to say that as many as 80% of the malfunctions that I see during pistol training are operator induced. If such operator-induced malfunctions can happen in the training environment, then it is not hard to see how they can happen in the street when an individual is fighting for their life and will not be operating at their best level.

Being able to quickly clear malfunctions in a pistol is not only good pistol craft, it is an effort in life saving. You must be an active participant in your own rescue! No one else can be counted on to do it for you. Thus, practicing malfunction clearance drills is a necessary function for winning the fight.

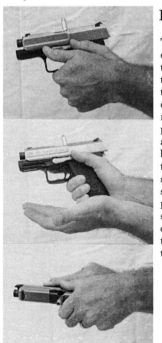

Figure 53

The "Tap – Rack – Target" drill can clear all malfunctions with the exception of the double feed. This includes the "stovepipe" malfunction if done as described. When the malfunction occurs, the support hand releases its grip and immediately taps the bottom of the magazine with the heel of the hand to make sure it is firmly seated. The shooting hand then turns the pistol sideways allowing the support hand to grab the rear of the slide with all fingers, thumb, and the muscle below the thumb.

(Continue to Figure 53.)

All but one type of malfunction can be cleared with what I call the "Tap, Rack, Target" drill. This drill is nothing more than tapping the bottom of the magazine hard to make sure it is firmly seated in the grip. If the magazine is loose, it is possible that the next round in the magazine will not be stripped free and inserted into the chamber. Then rack the slide to make sure that a fresh round is loaded into the chamber and drive the pistol back to the target and prepare to shoot. For years this drill was taught as "tap, rack, bang," however, it is possible that every time you clear a pistol malfunction, you won't go back to the target and shoot. Thus I have changed it to Tap, Rack, Target, as I feel that it is more verbally/visually descriptive. Get back on target, be prepared to

Figure 54

This gives as much hand contact as possible to the slide. DO NOT use just the fingertips and thumb. The hand works the slide allowing gravity to clear any malfunctions from the chamber. The support hand releases the gun, which allows the gun hand to bring it upright and back into the normal shooting grip.

shoot, but do not develop a familiar task requiring every time you clear the gun you also shoot it. This could result in a use of force that is not reasonable under the circumstances.

The way I teach Tap, Rack, Target, is somewhat different from many instructors. Since I am a firm believer in keeping it simple and consistent, I have changed some of the hand positions to keep them simple to perform. When a malfunction occurs, it is likely that both of your hands will be in a shooting grip. For my version of Tap, Rack, Target, release the support hand from the grip, tap the magazine and turn the gun to the side so the slide assembly is turned into the open support hand. Grab the slide with the support hand using all of the available hand

Figure 55
The author's concern with bringing the support hand up and over the slide is that the strongest part of the hand (the thumb, trigger and middle fingers) can possibly slide off the end when the hand tries to stay clear of the ejection port.

and **NOT** just the fingertips! The fingertips do not offer the level of strength necessary to clear some malfunctions. By getting as much of the fingers, palm and the large muscle mass underneath the thumb onto the slide as possible, it will allow a more firm grip without covering the ejection port. Once the grip is obtained, rack the slide to the rear. If the slide is hard to pull back, use the shooting hand to push forward on the grip of the pistol as this will offer more leverage.

Many instructors teach a different clearance drill for what is known as the stovepipe malfunction. When a gun has a stovepipe, the expended round has failed to clear the top of the slide being trapped between the rear of the barrel and breach face, resembling a stovepipe. Many teach a swiping method in which the support hand comes up over top of the gun, engages the spent casing sticking up and swiping it off. I have found that by merely turning the gun to the side and racking it, the stovepipe round will clear the pistol, along with the round that was destined for the chamber but not fully inserted (due to the pull of gravity) allowing the slide to cycle, stripping a new round from the magazine. Yes, you will loose a live round, but I think the simplicity of the action and the elimination of an additional technique, more than makes up for this. Make sure that you turn the gun and allow gravity to do its work, otherwise you could create a double feed which is an even greater problem.

Figure 56

The double feed is the most serious of all malfunctions. If it occurs, draw a second gun or run! To clear it, lock the slide to the rear to release any pressure on the magazine. Once this is done, merely unload and reload the gun as you have many times before. A simpler way to reload and retain a partially spent magazine (slow reload) is to remove the magazine from the gun, insert it into a pocket (note how the index finger is used to assist insertion) and then reload as you would when executing a fast reload.

Remember, Simple is Good!

Another reason I like to turn the pistol sideways and grab it as described, is that with many stovepipe malfunctions, the spent casing will not always be up from the top of the slide but will be sticking out the side of the pistol. I have seen individuals try to swipe off the sideways stovepipe and not actually be able to get the casing clear from the slide, but merely glancing off of it with their fingertips. I have also seen shooters cut their hand on sharp cases or burn their hand on hot cases when this action is not performed quickly.

The more common way to rack the slide, which requires the support hand to come up/over and trap the rear of the slide in the palm of the hand, oftentimes covers the ejection port interfering with the extraction of the spent casing. I have come to call this a "saddle" grip, as it resembles a saddle being placed on a horse's back. To avoid covering the ejection port, large hand shooters will slide the hand back, meaning they are attempting to work the slide with their ring, pinkie fingers and the lower part of the palm of the hand. Anyone that understands ergonomics knows that the strongest part of the hand is the thumb, the muscle below the thumb and the index and middle fingers, which quite often are hanging off the back of the slide when using a saddle grip and negating their superior grip capability. By turning the gun sideways, not only do you allow for the clearance of most malfunctions, but it also puts more of the stronger portion of the hand onto the slide making for a more positive grip in general.

Some will be skeptical of this technique as it is not "mainstream," but let me ask a question: *How would you clear a malfunction on a small pistol like a Walther PPK, KAHR, Ruger LCP or Kel-Tec?* There is not enough slide surface to saddle grip and stay clear of the ejection port. The "Tap-Rack" method I discuss here works for *all* pistols regardless of size. Consistency is part of efficiency. Clearing malfunctions with the gun in an upright position, pointed toward the target, creates a risk of dropping any malfunctioning ammunition back into the gun due to gravity. So allow gravity to work for you by turning the gun sideways and working the slide.

As previously stated, the Tap, Rack, Target drill will clear all malfunctions except one. What is known as the "double feed" (in reality is an in-line failure to extract) is the biggest nightmare for anyone using a semiautomatic pistol. There is just no way it can be cleared quickly. The double feed is easy to diagnose because when you tap, rack, to clear a malfunction, you will notice (read that feel!) the slide will not move. It is locked in place. A double feed is a round that has been stripped from the magazine and loaded in the chamber, but the chamber is full with a spent cartridge casing that was not extracted. This locks up the gun tight making it useless. If this occurs, the best thing to do is run for cover, draw a second gun, do something because you are not, I repeat, not going to be able to stand there and clear it in the heat of battle quickly. It is also possible the extractor is broken, so even if you do get it cleared as soon as it is fired again, the same thing will occur. If the double feed is experienced, GET GONE!

There seems to be a disturbing trend across the country to teach one malfunction clearance drill for all malfunctions. Essentially what this entails is students are taught to clear a double feed malfunction no matter what happens to the pistol. I think this trend is a HUGE mistake as the tap, rack, target drill can clear all malfunctions except one in just a few seconds. Even the best pistol craft student cannot clear a double feed malfunction in less than five seconds. For almost a century, statistics have shown that gunfights are generally over in this time frame, it seems somewhat ludicrous, if not dangerous, to teach people to stand in the open and clear even the most minor malfunctions with the most cataclysmic malfunction clearance technique. My concern is that we are training individuals to be targets, standing out in the open, fiddling with their pistol, when they should either be doing the tap, rack, drill or running for their lives!

Think about this for a minute: Does it make sense to teach a student to clear even the most minor malfunction with a clearance drill that can take six-plus seconds, maybe as long as ten or twelve seconds for the unskilled? A clearance drill that takes a great deal of time and motor skill versus a drill that is simpler to execute and can be done quickly and easily and will suffice for all but one malfunction? I hope this is something that is short lived for I fear we are going to have individuals shot standing out in the open trying to clear pistols with a technique that is not required for the task at hand.

To clear the double feed, you will have to unload and reload your gun. There is a very popular technique being taught these days that starts by ripping the magazine from the pistol. While this does work with some pistols such as the Glock and HK USP, when the slide is locked forward on a double feed, ripping the magazine from the grip is tough to do with some semiautomatics. This problem is compounded by the flush fitting magazines and floor plates that are common place. If the technique works for you, it does save time and effort, but for many guns, the first thing that needs to be done is to lock the slide to the rear. Locking the slide will take the pressure off the magazine and the round stuck in the slide will most often fall from the ejection port. When the magazine is removed, the round in the chamber may fall out of the magazine well, but anytime you unload your pistol, including clearing a double feed, you should check the chamber and make sure there are no rounds in it. If there is, you will have to work the slide to remove the round that is stuck. If the extractor on your pistol is broken, working the slide will not remove it. But then again, if the extractor on your pistol is broken, you have a one shot gun that should not be relied on to save your life. However, if it is the only gun you have, having that one round is better than none. Talk about a time when deliberation is essential...

Once you have locked the slide open, it is a matter of reloading it with a new magazine. I have found that since most students unload and reload their pistols with great frequency during initial training once they have locked the slide to the rear, they clear that double feed quickly using this felt commonality. They do this by doing what they have done so many times, unloading the gun and then reloading it with a fresh ammunition. Once the gun is reloaded, then find your adversary and prepare to engage. But again, clearing the double feed is not something to be done while standing in the open. If you tap, rack, and feel the slide locked in place, then it is a really good idea to "get out of Dodge!" An even better solution to the double feed is a second gun.

Chapter Sixteen

GOING TACTICAL

"The difference between practical and tactical shooting is – that practical isn't and tactical is."
Dennis Martin
CQB Services Limited, Liverpool, England.

U p to this point we have dealt with developing the proper mindset to engage someone in combat with a handgun. We have also dealt with the fundamentals on how to shoot including body position, grip, holster skills, getting on target quickly and aligning the gun to the target. Unfortunately these things are not enough. You are going to have to communicate, you're going to have to move and you're going to have to shoot in an environment that is probably not going to be to your liking. Additionally, it is not going to be like the range where you're doing all the shooting. There is going to be someone shooting back at you and it is very possible that innocent people, who will be scared, will get in your way and confuse a situation that is already a mess. The primary tactic for any gunfight is the use of cover, as incoming rounds have the right of way. Proper cover offers a number of things. It buys time to evaluate the situation, as time can be everything. It buys time to determine the identity of the person shooting at you, the people who are not a threat to you, responding police officers or other non-hostiles, or additional hostiles other than the one who first shot at you. And finally it allows safe, return fire from a position that will keep you from getting shot.

The biggest problem is recognizing what is true cover. There is a distinct difference between cover and concealment. Concealment can be anything that can hide you from view. However, very few things that are concealing are true cover, because cover will stop whatever bullet is headed in your direction. Another problem is there are different degrees of cover. What may be cover for a .22 handgun round may not be cover for a full metal-jacketed 9 mm pistol bullet. And what may be cover for that 9 mm may not be cover from a round fired from a 7.62 caliber AK or SKS. Certainly knowing what you are *being shot at with* will have an impact on what you select as cover. Without a doubt, looking for and being able to recognize cover is a primary combative skill... Too bad you won't know what cover is until you are taking rounds.

There has been a great deal of misinformation about cover in the past. One of the biggest misconceptions (in my opinion) that has been shown repeatedly over the years is the use of the mailbox. True, a mailbox is a metal receptacle. But you must remember that it is a hollow receptacle. Most small arms ammunition can go through one side of a mailbox and out the other. If the mailbox is full from top to bottom with mail, i.e., paper; then it may have some limited cover from handgun rounds. However, as a general rule, the mailbox is not good cover. Anything made of metal and is hollow is probably not as good as many think. Another example would be an automobile. With the exception of the engine block, the drive train and the rims/tires, an automobile is basically hollow and most bullets can travel from one side to the other. Unless, of course, they hit a large metal area, such as a window gearbox, door opening assembly or other impediment. The best thing that anyone can do is to settle in their own mind what is cover. First, determine the possible threats in the environment in which you live. Then take the time to look around you and see what is the likely cover in your area. Collect some samples of these things and shoot them with the ammo threat you are likely to face. You may be somewhat concerned when you realize that very few things are as good as previously thought.

I can remember watching in amazement as both .223 and 7.62 caliber rifle bullets shot a cinder block to pieces in very short order. Cinder blocks are made of concrete but they are also hollow and crumble very quickly. A solid concrete block of the same size makes for excellent cover, however, the hollow cinder block is far more brittle. The common telephone pole makes excellent cover from handgun and small caliber rifle rounds, but a 7.62 can chew through a telephone pole quickly. A fire hydrant is excellent cover, but it offers so very little of it that few people can make use of its solid construction. We could go on and debate the various objects that are present wherever you live. However, it is wise for you to take time to understand what is and what is not cover. By merely taking some of the more common objects and shooting them with ammunition and weapon styles that are common to your area, or those common to where you live and work, you can answer this for yourself. If you are a diplomat or military attaché working in a land where the AK-47 is a common cartridge, it would be wise to know what will and will not stop it, which are very few things short of actual armor plating. DO NOT underestimate the value of concealment, since few things are true cover and cover depends on what is being shot at you. Many instructors downplay concealment and how it can work to your advantage. Remember it is more difficult to shoot someone you cannot see. Think about the last time you went to the range and tried to hit a target in total darkness. And that was a target standing still! Try shooting at something that is moving and you have no idea exactly where it is and you will find what a challenge this can be. Understand concealment and use it to your advantage, as anything solid can be concealment.

Several years ago I talked to an undercover narcotics officer who told me of a situation in which he was in an adjoining motel room when a deal went bad. He determined later that the Confidential Informant he was using for the buy had turned him in to the dealer who panicked and started shooting through the wall. I have to commend this officer for being very "switched on." When he noticed the rounds were coming through the wall at the other end of the room and started tracking in his direction, he moved toward the gunfire. He felt that it was unlikely the suspect would fire back again at that end of the room where he started, so it was a safer place to be! He took a low position and moved to where the rounds had already come through the wall. He then quickly moved up on top of a table that actually put him in the location where the first rounds came through the wall. It was a calculated risk, but he figured it was all he had. While I know this is an extreme example, it is an excellent example of using concealment to your advantage. By keeping a cool head and understanding the concept of concealment, this officer was able to be an active participant in his own rescue.

Shooting around cover should be done as far back from the cover as practical. It should never be done any closer than arm's length. By doing so, this gives the shooter an enhanced field of vision, permits the use of an upright or kneeling shooting position and keeps the gun from being exposed beyond the cover. Keep the gun back from the edge so anyone on the opposing side cannot snatch it from your grasp. Also, keep in mind the "bouncing bullet" phenomenon. Bullets fired at a 45° angle or less, that impact a hard object will *not* deflect at the same angle. They will follow the plain of the hard object anywhere from a few inches to a foot-plus. For example, if hiding behind an automobile's engine block with the head sticking up above the car's hood, it is possible that a round that strikes the hood forward of the shooter could hit as the bullet follows the plain of the hood—be forewarned!

Since getting to cover or concealment has been established as important, it makes sense that moving while engaged in a gunfight is also important. To believe that everything will be a "High Noon" type situation where you can square off with your opponent in the street and expect them to engage in "fair gunplay" is not reality. Your opponent is going to do everything they can to beat you. When the fight begins, it is a good idea to not be where you were when your opponent first saw you. Thus, moving while shooting or moving to a better position to shoot is a good thing to know. Moving and shooting does take a certain degree of coordination. You should attempt to do it in a fashion that is the same, or as similar as possible, to your normal movements.

Figure 57

When moving laterally, do not try to side step more than a few strides. To move sideways quickly, turn to the side and walk normally. If the gun will be held to the support side, a two-hand position can be used. When moving with the gun on the gun side, shoot one-handed with the elbow rotated downward.

Proper tactics will require you to move laterally, forward and to the rear depending on the circumstances at hand. While shooting on the move in many firearms training courses translates to moving straight toward a target, this is not the norm in most armed confrontations. Shooting while going toward the target is normally the province of the tactical entry or SWAT team. This technique is used by tactical teams to run predetermined "routes" through a structure to get to a suspect or hostage taker. It is also standard in linear environments such as airplanes and buses. The technique is goal-oriented and in street level confrontations, shooting while moving toward your opponent is normally done to seek a position of advantage or greater cover as it *takes you closer to your opponent!* Otherwise, it is a good idea to try and disengage from the person who is trying to deliver bullets into your chest cavity. This normally means aggressive movement to the side or rear.

Lateral movements of just a step or two are an excellent way to remove oneself from incoming fire. As a matter of fact, it is a good idea to install a lateral step any time the weapon is drawn from the holster. Gunfights normally start when two people see one another and have reason to draw weapons. Your adversary will "key" on you and your location and direct hostilities in your direction. If you are suddenly not there, you have gotten inside their action/reaction loop and now they must react to the action that you have taken, which they did not anticipate....it may be all that is needed to turn the tide in your favor. Many people make the mistake of taking too wide a side step, trying to cover more distance than necessary. This large sidestep results in lowering the center of gravity too far for the shooter to draw their weapon and efficiently get an accurate shot as it takes them off balance. Not only is the large sidestep inefficient, it is also unnecessary to remove oneself from incoming fire. A sidestep of only 3 to 4 feet is more than enough to remove oneself from the path of a bullet that is no more than a ½" wide. In the interest of efficiency, two short lateral steps, quick shuffle steps really, are better than trying to take one large side step. If a large distance needs to be covered, the shooter would be wise to actually turn their body in the direction they are trying to go and walk straight ahead, keeping the weapon pointed in the direction of the threat. If the threat is to the strong side, the shooter will use one hand, utilizing a one hand shooting technique. If the threat is to the support side, hold the gun in a two hand grip stabilizing it for accurate fire. Both the side step and the side/forward shooting platform should be practiced on a regular basis.

What is most likely to happen during a gunfight is you will want to disengage from a suspect who is shooting at you. This will require a rearward movement while keeping your eyes on your opponent. Shooting while moving to the rear can be done with a great deal of accuracy, but like all things, it must be practiced. The shooting schools that I have attended all teach shooting while retreating, utilizing a rearward step where the toes come down first, roll back to the heel and then the next step is taken. I disagree with this technique, as I don't feel it will work as it is in direct contradiction to how the human body operates. Humans are designed to walk forward with their heel, ball and then toe coming in contact with the ground and the center of gravity works in this way. The problem with trying to walk in reverse is that the center of gravity will eventually overcome the feet and the body will fall back. Shooting on the move, going both forward and rearward, requires the knees to be bent to act as a shock absorber. If you try to walk upright in a normal stride, there is too much bounce to stabilize the handgun properly and get any type of accurate fire. Due to this requirement, when walking backward, the hips will be lower and will actually proceed the shoulders, chest and head region to the rear. While this technique works great on a nice flat range when no stress is evident, in a life threatening event, the body is going to move faster regardless of desire. Try this for yourself; go to a flat surface like a sidewalk, driveway or an open room in your house, and try to walk toes, ball, heel backward while sinking at the knees to add a shock absorbing effect to your outstretched arms. Pick up speed and you will quickly see that your hips will override your feet and you will fall backward. Add to this phenomenon uneven terrain, potholes, or objects lying to the rear of your feet that you cannot see and it's easy to see that trying to walk backward is filled with peril. And in a gunfight, the worst place to end up is laying on your back with your lower body and genital area exposed to incoming fire.

It's critical to stay upright in a confrontation and trying to walk backward is not going to work. It is best to try to keep your feet in contact with the ground when travelling backward. This will keep your center of gravity from overriding your feet, causing a fall. It will also give you warning to uneven terrain or objects in your way that are not in your field of vision. Two techniques that I have found to work well are what I call "step and drag" and "the shuffle step." When using the step and drag, the rear foot will step out as far as possible and will drag the forward foot while it stays in contact with the ground. With practice, this technique can be done quickly and will actually take the form similar to a shuffle step. Because of the shuffling action, the hips will never override the feet causing the shooter to fall. The draw back to this is that the upper body moves up and down in a piston-like action effecting accuracy. John Benner, Director and Chief Instructor of the Tactical Defense Institute in Ohio teaches the shuffle step technique in which the foot slides back staying in contact with the ground. The next foot slides back in a similar motion, so the feet do not cross one another, with one foot staying in contact with the ground at all times. John reports that he has had great success teaching this technique and has reports of it actually being used in the street effectively. Whichever technique is utilized is up to you, but I would strongly caution against using a technique that does not keep at least one foot in contact with the ground at all times. Additionally, when moving to the rear or laterally, it is a wise idea to never cross one foot over another as you will increase the risk of falling.

While these two techniques will help keep you from falling when trying to move backwards, understand that they are *not* limitless. If you try to move to the rear fast more than 20-25 feet, without looking, you will eventually fall. If lengthy rearward movement is needed to stay alive, you would be best served to move as the body was designed. Turn the feet and legs to move forward and rotate the upper torso to shoot to the rear with one hand. It won't be as accurate, but you will move faster. The question will be—which is more important?!

Now that I have explained how to shoot while moving in various directions, what about firing a few rounds at your opponent and just running to cover? While some may be a bit concerned about this, what is more important, shooting accurately or evacuating a hostile area? I realize there may be times that keeping an opponent at bay while quickly evacuating may be needed...that is why I discuss the above techniques. But how likely is this as compared to shooting AND THEN moving rapidly to the rear? To me, not getting shot is preferable to shooting a tight group. Turning and running away... after firing a few rounds...may just be the way to survive a sudden attack. Something to think about...

When shooting on the move in a forward direction, normal footwork should be used as it is always a good idea to do whatever is normal. Have you ever purchased a hot beverage and filled the cup right to the brim? In an effort not to spill the drink on your hands and floor, you bent you knees, flexed your hips and walked heel, ball, toe in order to stabilize the cup. When doing so, you have just performed the physiological action needed to shoot on the move going forward. You will find you cannot only move very quickly but with a great deal of stability. Remember, shooting on the move should be undertaken for a reason, normally to avoid incoming fire or gain a position of advantage...as with shooting while disengaging, moving is more important than shooting accurately. It is also wise to remember than when you move toward your opponent, you present a BIGGER TARGET! The technique should be used to keep your opponent engaged and to keep them from shooting back at you. But again, do not forsake rapid movement in the interest of trying to place a tight group on the target.

When both speed and accuracy are needed, consider shooting *then* moving. What I am talking about is rapid movement in any direction with a pause to fire a few accurate shots before resuming movement. You will be pleasantly surprised how fast and accurate this technique will allow you to be.

Similar in importance to shooting and moving is pivots and turns. Pivots and turns may sound like the same thing, but they are not quite. A turn is merely turning from one side to another, like walking down the street and somebody yells out your name, "hey, Joe" and you turn and you look at them. A pivot is a movement where you have to turn all the way around like someone is behind you, and now you have to pivot your body all the way around to see who it is. There is nothing magical about pivots and turns. Some may want to make them sound mystical, but when you are pivoting or turning into a threat, you are going to do nothing more than what you normally do. If something catches your eye, such as a movement or a sound, the normal thing to do is turn your head in that direction and look at it. That's fine, once you have looked, it's likely you're going to turn your body toward it which is a good thing. If you are walking down the street and someone yells at you from the right you will normally plant your right foot and turn on it. If it's from the left side the same thing will occur, you will plant the left foot and you will turn on that foot. Turning is releasing the pressure on whatever foot is going to leave the ground and shifting it to the foot that you are turning on and then squaring off with whatever it is your looking at. It's that simple. The necessary sequence of events is to look where you are going, turn your body in that direction and then draw the gun as you would for a normal stationary draw. Again, it is not magic, but it is one of those situations where, if you don't practice it, it will become complicated when you need it.

A pivot will require you to turn all the way around. Again, there is nothing magical here, you are going to do the same thing you did when you turned to the side, except you are going to turn your head as far around as you can and look. Then you are going to pivot on whichever foot you choose swinging the other foot around and moving into a stationary position. Once you are facing the threat, draw your handgun and drive it to the target as you would as if you had been originally facing it.

Use of cover, shooting on the move and pivots and turns all blend well into what we call room clearing or building search. What the tactically-oriented call "close quarter battle" or CQB, a military term for room to room fighting. Search techniques are normally the combination of using the handgun while moving and seeking cover and concealment along the way. As a general rule, searching a building by yourself is a HUGE mistake! There is no way you can keep track of your 360-degree environment at the same time you are trying to seek out a hostile adversary. Think about your own home and all of the places that someone can hide from you while your attention is diverted in another direction... and your home is the one location that you likely know best! Compound the problem by searching a location that is not familiar to you and you will see what a nightmare a building search can be. In reality, building searches should never be undertaken with less than two people, one to cover the front and one to cover the back, however, three and four man search teams are even better.

In the event of a home invasion, it is best to have a room designated as a safe room. This will normally be the master bedroom since the majority of home invasions (meaning the occupants are home) occur during hours of sleep. The safe room should have a solid core door with a deadbolt having at least a one-inch throw. There should be a cellular phone since telephones that require land lines can easily be disabled. A flashlight with at least 60 lumens of white light is a must. If leaving the safe room is unlikely, using a shotgun or carbine as the safe room weapon is a thought. The safe room should be decorated in such a manner that objects can be moved to utilize them as cover. Many people have the idea they can put a mattress up and use it for cover, however, the normal mattress and box spring are hollow objects and are very poor bullet stoppers. By having your bedroom furniture arranged in such a way that you can move it in line with the bed and take a position of cover behind both, a level of reasonable cover can be obtained in the event a breach of the room is attempted. If this happens, announce very loudly that you are in the room, that you are armed, and if someone enters the room that you will shoot! Call 911 and keep the line open as you do this.

If the suspects continue to force their way in, once they are in the room, it is reasonable to believe they pose a threat of serious physical harm since they did not heed your warning. At that moment, violence of action and a large volume of firepower will end the assault. However, many readers are parents, and since children do not sleep in the same room as their parents, it is very likely, no, it is essential, that when the home is penetrated parents will leave the master bedroom and work their way to the children. In the past, my wife would be left behind with her own firearm and a telephone to call 911. At that time, I would leave the master bedroom and work my way to the children's room clearing each as I go. I have selected a handgun for this mission because of the layout of my house. It offers a number of very hard corners and close quarter environments. If I had more room to maneuver, I would use a shotgun or carbine because of their greater power.

The type of weapon you select to clear rooms is going to be dependent on the environment in which you live. In my particular case, my bedroom is located down a hall that is very narrow and does not offer a lot of options as far as using a long gun. My best option, when clearing this hallway, is going to be using a handgun in a close retention position. From here I will try to take each corner using a method that is called "quartering" or "slicing the pie." When using this method you will be moving around each corner with your central focus being on the edge of the corner and what is beyond. Use as much set back distance as possible, much as we discussed when shooting around cover. Once that area is clear, additional lateral movement will be added slowly keeping the corner between you and

Figure 58
When "slicing the pie" or "quartering,"the shooter steps sideways in small increments, taking the time to see what is beyond their gun. The secret is to never move out farther than you can clear.

the potential threat. From above, this movement will look like a slice of pie, with the focal point being the point of the pie slice and the angle in which you are moving being the wide rounded crust area.

When slicing the pie or quartering a corner, it is a good idea to add to your skills what is called a "drop out" or "lunge" technique as well as a "roll out" or "lean" technique. The drop out requires you to plant your feet firmly in a solid stance, with the shooting side foot forward, and lunge (much like a fencer's lunge) your upper torso forward clearing the edge while pointing the gun in the direction of the threat. By doing this, you actually add to the reach of your quartering technique while keeping most of your upper body concealed from view. Once your lunge clears that particular area then you can let your feet follow and again continue working your way around your slice of the pie. Developed by John Benner of TDI, the drop out has proven to be very effective. The "roll out" or "lean" keeps the feet in a more conventional shooting position, but uses an outward lean of the upper torso to clear the edge. The lean is accomplished by keeping the upper body straight, but taking the outer knee towards the inner knee. This leans the upper body to the threat area. As Crucible founder Kelly McCann states, "your muzzle leads to danger" meaning you keep the muzzle of your gun pointed in the direction in which you most expect the threat. But at the same time, while you let your muzzle lead to danger, be cognizant of your 360-degree environment including up and down if your environment is such—maybe a high ceiling or walking on a cat-walk.

Figure 59
The drop out or lunge technique is used when a potential threat is detected. By placing the shooting side foot forward and lunging forward, the plain of cover is broken and the threat engaged from behind cover or concealment.

Figure 60
The roll out or lean technique can be used like the drop out but the foot placement is more conventional. To break the plain of cover, the rear knee bends toward the forward knee, leaning the body outward to engage the threat. Both the lunge and lean allow the shooter to return to cover quickly with little movement.

Once a corner is secured, then move, using the appropriate shooting on the move technique. Single corners offer the easiest challenge, however, when coming into a hallway that goes in both directions (a "T" intersection), a greater challenge is offered as you will have to actually clear two corners before you can venture into this open area. This is a situation in which multiple searchers would be worth their weight in gold. But, if you are alone, it is still possible to check the corner in both directions with a certain degree of "tactical safety." I'm not going to say it is going to be safe, because it is not. There will be a certain amount of risk no matter how you search or how many people are searching with you. When checking a two direction corner, you must slice the first corner as far as you can without exposing your back toward the open area. You will then drop back and check the other angle as far as permitted without exposing your back. Seeing as far as you can in both directions, you must then commit yourself to stepping out and checking the rest of it. It's a good idea at this point to do the unexpected. One suggestion would be to go low into a squatting position, moving out low since your adversary is likely to expect you at a higher level. By going low and moving out into the hallway you may give yourself that extra fraction of the second to check both directions and then get inside your opponent's action/response loop and shoot first, if appropriate.

Again, I cannot emphasize enough there is no way to search a building alone with any degree of safety. There are just too many hard corners, tough angles and entry and exit points and we don't have eyes in the front, back and sides of our heads. Even if we did, we wouldn't be able to turn our gun in every needed direction to engage all potential threats. There is just not enough time or space in this book to deal with every possible contingency. It is going to be up to your tactics, level of awareness and hopefully your superior level of skill and having a combative mind that helps you know which skill to pull out of your skill set(s) to best meet the need. Don't hurry, take your time and work the corners as best you can. Yes, I realize in a situation like this, where you are trying to get to your children's bedroom, there will be a sense of urgency. But let's be realistic, going fast and getting yourself hurt or killed means that you will never reach them, versus reaching them a little bit late. It's a tough call when trying to help loved ones. I have no definitive answers for you other than to just do the best you can.

Another common problem, when searching buildings, is clearing stairways. For many years it has been thought that when clearing stairways going from top to bottom was the best way. But over the last 30 years of law enforcement and spending more than my share of time in stairways, I have to disagree. When going down a stairway, your eyes and your weapon are on the opposite end of your body from what goes down the steps first. Your feet, your shins and your knees will be seen by any potential opponent long before you can bend over enough to engage them in combat, unless you are Gumby with a gun! Let's face it, no matter how young and flexible we are, it is difficult to get our gun and eye down to the same area as our feet. Very few people can bend over well and walk down a set of steps at the same time. It will require an almost pretzel-like flexibility. Going down steps will require going prone at the top of the stairwell before moving down. If possible, work your way around the steps trying to see as much as possible. If the steps are closed off due to walls or other construction, you will just do the best you can before proceeding. Going up the steps is really no different from clearing any typical hallway. The gun will lead you to danger, it will be at eye level and the only difference is that you will be going up the steps. This is easier done than many people realize by merely taking one step at a time with the same foot. Keep in mind you're not going to have the luxury of looking down at your feet, like many do when climbing steps. You're going to have to do the steps by feel. So it is a good idea to pick one of your two feet, depending on which side your going up the steps and which hand your gun is in, and take that step one at a time. Make sure that you raise your foot high enough to bring it down onto the step. Don't try to take it up high enough to slide it into place, pick it up, bring it down and when your foot contacts the step, use that inertia to push yourself upward and bring your next foot onto that same step working your way up. Stay to one side of the staircase or the other, but don't drag your back against the wall. This is sound practice in any kind of stairwell or hallway negotiation. Don't make noise by dragging your body against the wall as all that does is give away your location. By going up the steps, the only problem we really have is what is at the top. Once you get to the top, it is likely that you are going to have two hard corners, one in each direction since most steps empty into some type of common area or hallway. Once there, it will be no different from clearing any other dual hard corner. You will have to pie in one direction as far as you can and then flip around and pie in the other direction. Then make your move by trying to cover as much of that 360-degree environment as possible. Be fast, be aggressive, be ready and willing and it is very possible that if you move with enough speed you will get inside your opponent's action/response loop to utilize his startle response to your advantage.

Another tactical necessity is being able to shoot in alternate positions. It would be wonderful if we could always stand up with our feet planted firmly on the ground, but as we have already established in another chapter, it is quite possible that you may end up on the ground. Being able to shoot in alternate uncomfortable positions is sound training. Trying to figure out a new technique in the middle of a gunfight makes for a poor learning experience. It is wise to take the opportunity to experience these situations in the training environment, so you are less likely to succumb to panic. The first level of leaving your feet is a kneeling position. When doing so, do it quickly, by going to the knee that is on your shooting hand side. By going down on this knee, you maintain a level of balance that is quite similar to a normal shooting stance. Going behind low cover, such as the hood of the car or a low brick wall, would be a perfect example of having to go into a kneeling position. Since it is unlikely you will be wearing knee pads, kneel to where your foot was located as this might give you some advance warning to debris on the ground that might injure your knee. When going from standing to kneeling, use the foot to scrape away anything under the foot to help prep the ground for your knee. From an upright kneeling position to go lower all you need to do is rest your hip back on the foot on which you are kneeling. This pulls your support knee up into a high position in which you can take your support arm and rest it on this knee. Make sure that you do not put the ball of your elbow on the ball of your knee but slide the lower part of your upper arm down onto the knee. You may now return fire in a position that looks quite similar to the standard Weaver or Bent Arm Position. This braced kneeling position allows for a well-supported shot that can be used for distances longer than normal handgun engagements.

The prone position is probably the least advantageous position to be in. Lying on your stomach or back is the farthest thing possible from standing upright on your feet, severely limiting mobility. At the same time, going prone may be the only option you have to gain some degree of cover. I've had several stories related to me about military personnel in Central and South America who were walking across streets in crowded urban areas when gunfire erupted. In several of these cases these military officers were able to go prone in concrete gutters affording some degree of cover they would not have had standing up in the open. To go prone, the first thing you need to do is kneel. Many shooting schools instruct their students to immediately drop to both knees to get into the prone position. This works very well if you happen to have kneepads on, however, if you don't and you are older and less flexible, you may injure yourself at a bad time. My recommendation is to go down on one knee as previously explained, then lift up your support side foot, bringing it back while going down on your support side hand. Once your support hand has made contact with the ground, draw your pistol and drive it to the target in front of you.

Do not lay flat in a position where you are going to have to crane your head, neck and arch your back in order to see what is going on. Roll over onto your side bringing the top side knee out to stabilize your torso. You may then be able to rest your head on your shooting arm and line up your sights for a long shot. Known as the "roll over prone" position, it is possible to get reasonably flat in this position and remain stable. Try to maintain a position that will allow you to push yourself up into a kneeling position and then quickly into a standing position to gain mobility. A position similar to the roll over prone would be the roll over side position. A situation might arise where you have low, narrow cover that requires you to lie on your side and tuck your knees up in front of your chest. When doing so, place your arms in between your two knees, so the vice like pressing of the knees against your arms will stabilize your pistol allowing accurate fire from a very low, compact position. If this does not work, lay flat on your side and shoot one handed with your arm resting on the side of your leg. The disadvantage of this sideways position is it is the most difficult position to get up from. It will require you to spread your body to get upright and then get mobile. This will take several seconds and put you at a disadvantage while doing it. But it does offer a very compact position, very low to the ground, that is very stable to return fire. Going to the ground in any format whether it is kneeling, prone, or sideways, puts you at a serious disadvantage in regard to mobility. But again there may be those unique situations where it is your only option to protect your life.

The last thing we are going to discuss in this chapter is emergency handgun operation. More specifically – one hand reloads and manipulation. Before progressing, you should notice that I have not addressed what is known as off-hand or weak-hand shooting. The reason for this is, I have found with my own students, if you make a big deal about changing hands it tends to freak them out. The better way to deal with support or off-hand shooting is to merely mirror what you do with your primary hand. Remember NLP? If it is possible to model another person, it is possible for the off side of the body to model the primary side of your body. In essence, do the same thing with the support side that you do with the primary side. Yes, it feels different but feeling different is not the same thing as being different. Whatever you do with your strong hand, you should merely do with your weak hand. Practice it as such and don't make a big deal out of it. Work with your strong hand and FEEL what you do with your strong hand, how everything comes together, what your grip configuration is, your stance, your arm position and when it comes time to do that with your off hand then merely change the pistol to the other hand. Visualize your support side doing the same thing you have done with your primary side. Use a mirror to look at how you shoot primary and then off-side. Do this dry, of course. There is really nothing to it. You can figure this stuff out on your own. You don't have to make a big deal out of this. It's merely mirroring one side of your body from another. The muscular system on both sides of your body is the same, it just feels different.

The reason for off-hand shooting is because there could be times when your primary hand is injured and this will negate you from being able to use two hands to perform necessary functions such as clearing malfunctions, reloading, etc. When using the off-hand alone, it is no different from previously discussed. Lock the gun out in front of you, rotate the elbow down to six o'clock, locking the wrist, pointing the thumb toward the target and pressing the trigger straight to the rear. Reloading or clearing a malfunction can become interesting when using one hand. Clearing a malfunction, except the dreaded double-feed, is no different than with two hands. You are going to tap, rack and go back to the target. To tap the magazine well, tap it against a hard bony part of your body, say the side of your hip area around the waist to make sure the magazine is seated. Turn the gun's muzzle away from you and engage the rear sight on your belt, holster or any sharp edge, pushing forward to work the slide. There are many people who express a certain amount of concern about doing this with the popular Novak low-mount rear sight. Sure, the design of the Novak sight does make this more difficult to do if you try to push the gun straight down to cycle the slide. However, it can be done by hooking the rear Novak sight and bringing the muzzle out away from you further, so that you can engage that slope area. Then, instead of shoving the gun down, shove the gun out away from you and you will be surprised at how well that slide can be worked. Novak now offers a sight with a notch on top just for this purpose.

If the gun locks open, that tells you you're out of ammunition. I like to show two different ways of one hand reloading because you never know what situation or type of cover you will have. If you are going to reload while standing, you must first dump the magazine using whatever hand is available; whether it is your thumb or trigger finger, get the magazine out of the gun. Then turn the gun muzzle away from you, oriented so the magazine well is pointing up and lock it between your knees. Remove the spare magazine from the pouch and insert it in the gun. Then using either the slide stop, or engaging the rear sight on some sharp object and work the slide. Take the gun back to the target and get back in the fight.

Let's say you are behind low cover and you can't stand up without taking a round. It's a good idea to have a contingency reload. Turn the muzzle away from your body and lock the gun in behind your bent knee. Remove the spare magazine and insert it into the bottom of the grip, working the slide on some sharp object or using the slide stop lever and then back to the fight.

Have you ever tried to draw your pistol from your holster using your support side hand? This has happened in the street, so it is a good idea to know what works for you and your chosen equipment prior to the need to do it for real. Should you reach around the front or back? This depend on your girth and flexibility. Are you working in uniform and wear a triple retention holster? Can you manipulate the holster's safety devices with the off-hand? Certainly something to consider. This kind of stuff is not magic. It just requires some thought. You want to work this stuff out and plan your techniques on your own at the range under no stress. Again, trying to figure out a tactical option when the bullets are flying over your head will tend to affect the efficiency of your thought process.

Chapter Seventeen

DEALING WITH MULTIPLE THREATS

"40% of the time there will be more than one suspect"
Dave Grossi, Calibre Press Seminar

Statistics have shown that 40 to 45% of the time you will likely be attacked by multiple adversaries. I would not be a bit surprised if it was even higher. Criminals tend to draw courage from one another and do things a lone person will not do. So it only makes sense that they are more likely to attack another person when they have someone with them. Also by having someone with them, they have ready backup in the event they select a victim who is a little more "willing" than expected. Engaging multiple threats is something that you certainly need to prepare for.

Unlike the drills taught at many shooting schools, real multiple threats will not be standing side by side like pins in a bowling alley. Predators will split up and position themselves at varied distances. Techniques to shoot at multiple targets come down to two schools of thought. There is the Turret method, which has the shooter assume the chosen shooting stance and then turn the upper body as one unit, similar to a tank turret. The other is to shift your head and eyes and let your hands and gun move to what they are looking at. I have found that I have better luck moving my eyes and letting my hands follow them. Also, I find that letting my eyes lead my hands is more realistic to what really happens during any search situation. The head and eyes look for danger and the hands and gun follow. In real life, very seldom do they move as one unit like the Turret method. However, some people have difficulty doing this, so whichever technique you select really doesn't concern me. Try them both, find the one that works best for your eye-hand coordination and use it but remember, *you must find your attacker before you can counter-attack*...this is not a pistol competition in which you KNOW where the target will be. How well will you see your opponent as you turret, looking over your gun? There is nothing magical about this, just do what works best for you...but think hard about it, based on reality.

You also need to give consideration to effective scanning techniques. A lot of instructors will tell you that wherever your eyes look, the gun should be "looking"(i.e., muzzle direction) too. That sounds like a great idea in theory, but let's say that you're walking through a warehouse or down the hallway of a hotel and your head is moving back and forth quickly in multiple directions. This is not unusual when a potential threat is perceived and you want to cover as much territory as possible. Because there are so many things to check out and engage with your eyes, do you really want to be whipping the gun around, up and down, in and out? Do you want your gun potentially blocking your field of view? Probably not. Depending on the environment you may want to hold your gun in front of you, such as a third eye or low ready position and shift your head around as you go. It really depends on the number and complexity of the areas you have to see and cover. I really have no problems with this either way, but it is something to consider ahead of time.

Figure 61
By using three-dimensional targets, like these, available from Law Enforcement Targets, realistic multiple target scenarios can be trained using live fire.

Another subject that is discussed quite frequently is how many rounds should be shot at each target? This will depend on several things. Will one shot do it? Do you want to put two shots in each one of them? I can't say, that is going to depend on the situation at hand. What I will tell you is that nothing is absolute. You are going to have to deal with the threats as they show themselves. It is a common practice in many training programs to engage multiple targets based on weapon threat level. Which one has a gun? Which one has a knife? Another may have a club and you have to shoot the one that you feel is the most threatening. I'm not sure this isn't an exercise in futility. To me, the one that is closest to you is going to be the biggest threat. It's true that one suspect may be at 20 feet with a shotgun, but the other suspect may be at three feet with a knife. You tell me...which one is the biggest threat? The guy that is within arm's length that is going to cut you with a knife or the guy that is 20 feet away that is going to shoot you with a gun?

Figure 62

Avoiding altercations involving multiple adversaries is the best course of action. But once a situation presents itself, the only way to prevail will be quick and aggressive action. Here, the author strikes the closest adversary while using him as cover from the target on the left. He simultaneously shoots the antagonist on the right and then moves to shoot the remaining attacker. This is a nightmare scenario, but it is representative of what needs to be done.

Maybe the best alternative is to move so one suspect is in front of the other and deal with both, using one for cover. Don't worry about the number of rounds, shoot as needed. Regardless, the one thing you are going to want to do is engage and move away.

This being said, I also realize that not all hazardous situations can be avoided. Avoidance and evasion will not always be an option, but when countering is required we should do so to our advantage. One of these advantages should be a superior combative mindset. We should have the will and the skill to prevail in any confrontation. The will comes from mental attitude and the skill and confidence developed from quality training. Yes, superior training should be the other advantage.

If faced with multiple opponents and a withdrawal is not feasible, the first thing that should be sought is cover. Cover will give you the time and opportunity to launch a counter attack.

If nothing else...move! Don't just stand still and wait to be shot. Moving targets are harder to hit and it is likely your opponent has less training (if any!) in engaging moving targets. Don't just stand there and try to shoot it out. The problem here is many firearms training programs have advocated this very approach for a long time. Think about the last time you dealt with multiple targets on the range. It is probable you stood stationary, facing two or three targets and on a signal you drew your gun and shot each one of them twice. If it was a "real test of skill," you may have performed a reload or had to shoot the target with the most dangerous weapon first.

If shooting it out appears to be the only option, it's time to call upon a superior combative spirit and take the fight to them. Again, it is unlikely that the multiple attackers will be standing abreast. It is more likely that they will be standing apart in a staggered configuration. Use their position against them by moving aggressively in such a way they get into each other's line of fire. Not only are you doing the unexpected, creating lag time on their part, you are also giving yourself partial cover that you did not have before.

Once you have moved, shoot the suspect who is closest to you. He is the greatest threat regardless of the weapon in his or her possession. Hopefully this movement will allow you to move to a position of greater cover, or even better yet, out of the kill zone altogether, but nothing is assured.

While you may not have a choice on which way you move, try to do so in a way that will allow you to shoot in the direction of your support side. It is much easier to move your shooting hand toward your support side than it is to move it out and away from your shooting side. Practice both ways, but shooting to the "inside" is obviously easier. If you have access to a range that has a multiple direction shooting capability, use you imagination and set up a few likely scenarios and shoot and move through them. They don't have to be complex, as a matter of fact, they will likely be more realistic if they are not. I like the classic El Presidente' drill as it requires the shooter to perform a number of fundamental techniques at one time...not because it is a realistic multiple target engagement drill.

This short chapter is by no means the definitive answer on engaging multiple hostiles, but hopefully it is food for thought on how to prepare for such a probable situation. Train yourself to do something other than standing flat footed and shooting it out. Do something, move, seek cover, get the suspects in each other's way... do the unconventional! But fight back.

Chapter Eighteen

NIGHT WORK

"Damn I hate this, it's so damn dark down here.
A guy could get shot!"
Sgt. Bill Dillon to the Author
during a basement search for narcotics suspects.

hile numbers vary from year to year, FBI statistics show the majority of violent crimes (including armed confrontations involving police) occur in reduced-light environments. This is probably no different for the citizenry at large.

It should come as no surprise that the criminal predator likes to operate under the cover of darkness. Logically, criminals who are hard to see are harder to detect and apprehend. The human eye does not work efficiently in the reduced light environment. Conversely, this does not mean that the eyes are helpless in low light, but they do need some help.

When was the last time you had the 20 to 40 minutes necessary to allow your eyes to adjust to dim light before taking action? Have you ever had someone turn on the lights or shine a flashlight in your eyes once you had achieved "night vision?" Being so blinded would be very hazardous in an armed confrontation. Consider how consistent the light will be when you are out in reduced light. Seldom do we function in a consistently dark environment. As a matter of fact, it is likely that the light will fluctuate, meaning your eyes will never fully adjust to a single light or dark situation. Think about the last time you were walking down the street at night. There was probably a street light that illuminated part of the area, while at the same time there were pockets of darkness behind a bush, around a corner or just beyond the reach of the street light's beam.

While it's quite possible to see someone standing at the end of an alley, is it possible to see well enough to see what's in his hands? Shadows most certainly interfere with perception. What about back lighting? Isn't this also an inconsistent light situation? Imagine walking up to a front door on a dark night. As you near the door, it suddenly opens and a dark figure steps into the light pouring from the open door. You flinch at the sudden bright light and try to see what the dark shadow holds in its hand. Is it a TV remote control or a handgun?

Police officers and citizens alike are likely to encounter a poorly lit environment anytime and that includes daytime. Some examples would be deserted buildings without electricity, basements, closets, garages, or almost any place where sunlight can't penetrate. The street-smart thing to do is to cast light on a dimly lit situation. A good flashlight will most certainly do the trick. In some cases, a dedicated light system mounted on the weapon would be even better. Though a weapon-mounted light should be thought of as a supplement, not a replacement, for a hand held light. Fortunately, the current generation of "fighting lights" is better than ever before. In the past, a flashlight that produced enough light to be of any use was the size of a baseball bat. Today, lights are available that literally "outshine" the lights of just a few years ago, and they are no larger than the palm of your hand.

Think about what you are trying to accomplish with a tactical light. It is likely that you are trying to "shed light" on a dimly lit area that holds a potential threat. This area needs to be flooded with light so all threat locations can be seen with the naked eye. Most experts agree that 50 lumens is the minimum amount of light needed to accomplish this. If the threat area is so large that it will likely dwarf your 50-lumen light's output, it may be best not to illuminate the area and to withdraw until enough light is available.

Another necessary feature on a tactical flashlight is a momentary on/off switch. While a locking on/off switch can also be useful, it should be separate from the momentary switch. There are times when quick bursts of light will be needed. Having a switch that will lock on or off at the wrong time can be an invitation to disaster.

Additional worthwhile features include lightweight durable construction, non-glare color, pre-focused beam with no "dead spots" and a long battery life.

Tactical flashlight techni ques should not only address how to hold the light, but also when and how to deploy it. All too often, flashlight techniques deal with how to use the light in

Figure 63
The light mounted gun is the best way to engage hostile threats in a reduced light environment.

concert with the firearm and nothing more. While such techniques are certainly important, there is more that needs to be understood. A flashlight should be used to search, navigate and identify/locate threats and engage those threats in an inconsistent light environment. I like to emphasize the words "search and navigate" as it's far more likely that this is what you will do with a flashlight versus engaging hostile individuals with your firearm. As you practice your tactical flashlight techniques with the handgun, don't forget that there will be many times that you will use the flashlight without a handgun. The old FBI technique of holding the flashlight out away from your body is still a relevant technique to be used when a general search is being undertaken, and the weapon is not employed. Some instructors now call this technique "deceptive light." When would you use this technique? Imagine you are a patrol officer working the graveyard shift "shaking doors" at a local shopping complex. No trouble is expected, so the gun remains in the holster. However your job is to seek out trouble, so you are ever-vigilant. When turning a corner or looking through a window, hold the light away from you in case it draws fire. Additionally, as with all flashlight techniques, have the light on only when you really need to see something. Don't use it as a "crutch" against the dark. Using it as such will do nothing but "telegraph" your location.

It is a good idea, especially in hostile environments, to use the flashlight only long enough to see what you need to see and no more. Should your light draw fire, you want to be standing in a different location. If you use the light to locate a suspect, they have in turn located you! This is another reason to use a light with as many lumens as possible. If you locate a suspect in the dark, use the light to temporarily blind them by shining it in their eyes. This will increase their response time and give you more time to overcome them. This being said,

Figure 64
The Harries technique is the most battle proven of all flashlight techniques. It uses isometric tension to hold the back of the shooting hand against the back of the hand holding the flashlight.

lets talk about something that is missing in many of the Reduced Light training programs...when in a dark environment, how about *turning on the lights*, if possible. While many programs want students to "embrace the dark", it has been my experience that I function better in the light. Over the last thirty years, whenever I could, I turned on the lights because I could see better. Its not that I have anything against the "Demon of Darkness" techniques that are all the rage these days, its just that turning on the lights works so well and I don't have to worry about tripping over something or slipping on something while I do some "high speed-low drag" flash and move tactic. I can function like I would if it were day light. I have also found that criminals will try and seek the darkness if they are already in it. On one occasion, my SWAT Team was able to move a suspect into the room we wanted by turning on lights and allowing a suspect to flee the light. I know it was not very "tacti-cool", but it worked very well. While you will not always have control of the light, I prefer to leave darkness to vampires and work in a lighted environment, if at all possible.

Any defensive handgun-training program should include combative flashlight techniques so if they are needed, the shooter is prepared. Its also wise to consider any flashlight shooting technique to be a one hand shooting technique as the two hands *will* come apart when the gun is fired. The 1979 Federal Court decision POPOW v. MARGATE specifically calls for firearms training in a reduced-light environment. Many techniques have been developed over the years regarding the use of the flashlight in conjunction with a handgun. The following are those I feel are of the most benefit. Try each in turn and find one or two that work well. Use the technique consistently and master it. Trying to master them all will only cause confusion during a high-stress event, creating a delayed response.

The Harries Technique – Mike Harries, a former police officer, developed this technique for those who shoot with a bent support arm or Weaver stance. It works well with lights that have either an end-cap or side push-button on/off switch. The Harries uses the isometric tension of the two hands pressed back to back against one another. This keeps the light in line with the muzzle of the gun, supporting it for more accurate fire. The bent support elbow should be kept down below the pistol to add tension to the rear of the hands, which will give added support. Make sure that the flashlight always passes under the gun when assuming this position, so that the gun's muzzle is never pointed at the support hand.

The Chapman Technique – This technique was developed by Ray Chapman, retired law enforcement officer and former World I.P.S.C. Champion. This technique will work with either a bent or a straight support arm, making it a very popular flashlight shooting technique. It can be used with either a top or side activation button. The flashlight is held in a conventional manner with the thumb on the activation button and the index finger wrapped around the body of the light. The three remaining fingers are used to cup the shooting hand, creating a two-handed firing grip.

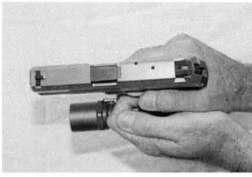

Figure 65
The Rogers technique requires the use of the Sure Fire combat flashlight. The light is held between the trigger and middle fingers of the support hand, which in turn pulls the flashlight back into the thumb of the shooting hand.

The Rogers Technique – Former FBI Agent Bill Rogers developed this technique for use with flashlights that have a rear activation button. Rogers first used the original Laser Products 6P light. Bill placed a rubber grommet around the body of the light and used the index and middle fingers of his support hand to press back on the grommet, in turn pressing the activation button against the large muscle under the thumb. The fingertips were free to grasp the shooting hand, while the light stayed in line with the gun's muzzle. The Rogers Technique has proven to be so successful that Surefire developed the 6Z Combat Light around it. The Rogers Technique, in conjunction with the 6Z light, is demonstrated at most major shooting schools. I personally like the Rogers Technique and have begun to use it. Like the Chapman Technique, the Rogers can be used with either bent or straight arm shooting technique.

The USMC Technique – While not an official technique taught by the U.S. Marine Corps, this technique was passed on to Smith & Wesson Academy Director Bert DuVernay who in turn passed it on

Figure 66
A modification of the Roger's technique
uses the thumb and trigger finger to push
the flashlight back into the shooting hand.

to me. In this position, the flash-light is again held in a traditional fashion, with the thumb on a side mounted activation button. The lip of the flashlight lens is then pressed into the fingertips of the shooting hand, locking it in place. This lock keeps the flashlight beam in line with the muzzle of the gun. By pushing forward on the flashlight, recoil control is also enhanced because the fingertips are locked onto the flashlight.

The Neck or Shoulder Mount Technique- The flashlight is held back by the neck or on the shoulder of the support side. This is a position that is commonly seen used by police officers who are on a traffic stop. When in this position, the light can easily be kept in alignment with the head and eyes, turning when they do. The gun is fired with one hand with the rear mounted light helping to illuminate the sights on the gun. I have become very fond of this technique and found it to work over a wide range of situations.

Regardless of which technique you select, it must be practiced before proficiency can be achieved. Don't fire a few rounds and expect to have a technique down pat. Additionally, practice getting into the flashlight position, especially from the holster. On the range, students tend to assume their flashlight shooting grip before live-fire practice and this is OK if your gun and light are always out and ready to fire. What about those times when the gun is in the holster? Aren't holster skills more often practiced in normal light? Disregarding holster skills, how likely is it that you will always have your gun next to your flashlight? Even when the gun is out of the holster? I have seen more than a few police officers check the outside of a building after an "alarm drop" with their flashlight, while their gun was down at their side. Though not tactically correct, that's what happens in real life. It makes sense to practice making the transition to the flashlight shooting position as well as shooting from it. And finally, let me ask you this, do we always want to point our gun at everything we point our flashlight at? If the answer is "no," then it's essential to practice getting into your chosen flashlight shooting technique before you shoot.

Should a weapon need to be deployed in a low-light scenario, then having the light mounted on the gun is the way to go. While this is not realistic for a daily carry gun, it is possible for a tactical response weapon—any gun that will be used only for a specific purpose. Actually, a dedicated light mount is probably a good idea on any long gun, since a rifle or shotgun will not go into a holster or be carried concealed. A light mount on a long gun is nothing more than another worthwhile accessory, like a good set of sights, optics or a quality sling.

When mounting a light to any handgun or long gun, be careful to avoid hanging wires or any other unnecessary appendage. Such wires will only snag and rip loose at the most awkward moments, rendering your light useless and announcing your arrival. Keep your light tight to the gun and easy to operate.

When using a light-mounted weapon, you must not only keep track of your muzzle but your light's beam trajectory as well.

Don't lean out from cover to take a shot and not allow your light to do its job. Light being reflected back into your eyes off the wall you are trying to shoot around could destroy your night vision!

Light-mounted handguns and long guns offer the following benefits:

- Light availability whenever your weapon is in your hand.
- Light availability without sacrificing shooting skill.
- On/Off capability without changing your firing grip.
- Capability to blind a suspect, denying him vision of yourself, your weapon, your movement. This could cause the suspect to surrender and resolve the situation.

Using a white light should also be given some thought and practiced. It is impossible to deal with every needed low light technique in just a few pages. Entire books have been written on this subject alone and I would suggest you read them. That said, here are a few principles of night work:

- Lights work both ways. If you light up an area, your light will not only affect your night vision, it will tell your opponent where you are.

■ If you use the light – move! Don't be where you were when
   the light was on. Also make sure you turn the light off *before*
   you move.

■ Use the light in short "blips" and then only to see what you
   need to see. Resist using the light like a night watchman.

Chapter Nineteen

AUTOMOBILES AND YOU:
HOW TO DEAL WITH THREATS WHEN IN YOUR VEHICLE

*"It's really simple, if you're threatened in your car forget your gun.
Step on the gas and drive over the S.O.B.!"*

Ed Lovette

More time is spent in automobiles than any other location with the exception of work and home. The automobile is used for transportation, regardless of the distance traveled. There could even be an argument made for the automobile being partly to blame for the low level of physical fitness that we as a society currently endure. The automobile can take us to pleasurable locations and it can take us into hostile environments. Unfortunately it can take us into hostile environments without being aware of it. All it takes is the wrong turn off the highway and suddenly we can be in a "no-man's land" that we didn't even know existed.

Unfortunately our driving skills are not what they should be. This is not because of lack of practice, because we practice all the time. It is due to an almost overabundant amount of time behind the wheel. We get complacent and lazy, our skills begin to evaporate due to the amount of time that we spend behind the wheel. Additionally, because we are so used to being in our car, we consider it our personal space and our level of awareness drops to a minimum. Being locked inside a car does not offer the same level of safety as does our home, but we tend to think of it as such. All that separates us from the outside world is some window glass and a bit of sheet metal. The one thing the car has to its advantage is that it is mobile. However, if we are not aware of what is going on around us, that level of mobility means nothing because if we are attacked, and don't see it coming, it is going to be too late to respond. The first warning that you may have is the window next to you shattering and a pair of arms reaching in to grab you or something inside your car.

This is a book about handgun combatives, but we cannot ignore the automobile as an environmental factor. The reality is we are in our cars a lot and we are in our cars when we are armed. But don't allow the handgun to give you a false sense of security. If you can see an attack coming, the best thing to do is to drive away from it. Countering is the last option as it is in any confrontation. This means an advanced level of awareness, not being trapped at traffic lights, always pulling up only far enough to allow a get away. It means, in urban environments, not trapping ourselves in a middle lane but using one of the side lanes where we can drive off, whether up over the curb and across the sidewalk or into the other lane of traffic.

Figure 67
Whenever removing yourself from a vehicle in a combat environment, make sure your foot holds the door open so that it doesn't close on your leg as you exit the vehicle.

In short, giving you an avenue of escape may be everything. And if the only avenue of escape is through your attackers, then so be it. Think about the vehicle versus the handgun. It offers a must larger target surface, it is much more accurate to guide to the target, and it offers a whole lot more foot pounds of energy than any handgun projectile. If at all possible, drive away–if not, use the car as a weapon and handle the situation.

While driving away is the best option, it is not always possible. A situation may develop where the car is disabled and now you must revert to the firearm. Unless you are in an armored vehicle, which is possible in some foreign lands, it's probably going to be wise to get away from the car. Vehicles, with the exception of the engine block, drive train, and tires offer very little cover to small arms projectiles and almost no cover to rifle cartridges like the 7.62x39 AK round. So your first priority is going to be removing yourself from the car, which is the immediate target. Getting out of the car and drawing a handgun while seated can be a very complicated task. If you're wearing your gun on your strong side in a belt holster, think about all the things that are going on in that one location. These days most vehicles have bucket seats with a console in the middle. There is a seatbelt and buckle joining together right there where your gun is located. Additionally, you probably have some type of garment covering the gun. And there is very little room to maneuver your upper body to clear the weapon because you have a steering wheel in front of your chest, a very "busy" location that requires some thought, visualization and practice prior to encountering a threat.

The first thing that needs to go is the seatbelt. I feel it is best to reach across your body using your support hand to release the seatbelt. As I say this, I am making the assumption that you are seated in the driver's seat and that you are right handed, which covers 80% of the world's population. If you are left handed, then it would still be your support hand releasing the seatbelt but you would not be reaching across your body. Using your support hand to release the seatbelt in one fluid motion, clear it away from your body and don't get tangled up in the seatbelt trying to exit the vehicle. Once the seatbelt is removed, use the support hand to then open the door. A word of caution, be prepared to use your left foot to trap the door open. If not, the spring tension of the door hinge will bring the door back violently. If it is an armored vehicle, there may be enough power to break your leg as it returns. As you push the car door open, use your left foot against the door trapping it. Then remove yourself from the vehicle in a low crouch position...as low as you can get!

There is very little cover in the passenger compartment of the vehicle but it does offer concealment. Try to keep yourself as low as possible and out of your attacker's view. Once your feet are firmly planted on the ground, this is the time to draw your weapon. Get back at least an arm's length from the car with your muzzle leading to danger, i.e., your muzzle coming up over the top at the same time. Try to determine where your threat is before you come up to shoot, as shooting into the unknown is both dangerous and foolhardy. There is no easy answer to this. Once you've left the vehicle, you may see better cover than what is offered by your car. You may opt to move quickly to that cover and then reassess your situation. I have no solid answers for this, as each situation will determine what is necessary.

Unless fire is coming from the direction of the engine block, it is a good idea to get yourself away from the open car door. Don't get trapped in the "v" of the door and body. When removing yourself from the car, you may have to use your shooting on the move skills to cover your withdrawal. If having to exit from the passenger side, the same process will be followed with the exception you will probably have to use your shooting hand (if you are right handed) to open the door. Getting the car door open and leaving the vehicle will be the same.

If the threat is coming from your side, you will have to exit the vehicle on the opposite side, which will require you to go across the seat and exit. This won't be fancy, it won't be pretty, but it can save your life. The first thing to do is to get down and out of view. Remember the door will not be good cover, but it will be concealment and it may be just enough to delay your opponent and give you a fraction of a second to get out and into a more secure position.

Once everyone has exited the car, you can then cover each other as you get away from the car. The person behind the engine block can cover first (best cover), allowing the person to the rear of the vehicle, the one with lesser amount of cover, to move to a position of greater cover. Once that person is in position, they can then cover the person behind the engine block while they leave the now disabled vehicle. This leap frog movement will help keep your attackers at bay.

Whenever returning fire from a vehicle, make sure that your muzzle is clear so that rounds do not skip off anything in front of you. It is not uncommon when shooting over and around barricades to see a clear sight but the short distance between the front sight and the muzzle hasn't cleared. When the gun is fired, the bullets will go into the cover instead of toward the attackers.

Practice vehicle operations at the range before they are needed. Visualize a response and practice so that it will be immediate. It is a good idea to use your own vehicle or the vehicle that you drive regularly. You don't have to do these drills fast, you can do them slow and careful so that you don't damage your vehicle during practice. Another good idea is to seek out some sort of defensive driving training. Knowing how to use your vehicle as a weapon can be quite advantageous in the event your vehicle comes under attack. This style of driving is far more advanced than what was learned in high school driver training. It is one of those things you may never need but when and if you do, it will be invaluable.

My friend and co-author of DEFENSIVE LIVING, Ed Lovette is a retired CIA operations officer and a former Captain in the U.S. Army Special Forces. He worked at the CIA's basic training school teaching evasive driving techniques and counter-surveillance. He was also Operations Manager at the Gryphon Group counter-terrorist driving school and a ten-year law enforcement veteran in which capacity he served as a patrol officer, a sheriff's deputy and a senior firearms/tactics instructor at the New Mexico Law Enforcement Academy.

D: Ed, thanks for taking the time to be here today and answering some questions. First of all, without a doubt the Gryphon Group driving course is one of the best, if not the best, known driving school in the world. What type of clients did you have at the school when you were there?

E: Dave, we had clients from a number of disciplines. Obviously we have police, we have military, particularly from the special operation community going to all the places that you see in the headlines these days. We also did a lot of training for the corporate market as well. And we had some programs that we just started when I was there, like the Carjack Counter Measures that is for the concerned private citizen.

D: Okay, that's a good place to go from here because this book is primarily intended for personal defense. I know you are really big on awareness. I have heard your lecture on the subject. But, beyond awareness, what type of skills do you think the individual should have when they are behind the wheel?

E: Well, obviously they need to have the standard driving skills, which we find lacking in a lot of people. This is something that we address early on in our course, give each student a sort of basic skills test. Find out how they handle the car, brake the car, all of that sort of stuff. And then the second level is evasive skills, which are actually quite basic. If they have just the concept, they don't need anything real fancy, but just to see it coming and what do I do when it does. Generally what they do is step on the gas. If we can get them to accept that, we're doing good. One of the things we find generally is, people only feel that they are armed and able to take care of themselves if they have a handgun and it's only because they don't know what they can actually do with a car.

D: Now, you see a lot of these fancy maneuvers in the movies. Is that the reality or not?

E: Nope, nope, you run into the same thing all the time, it's interesting that people don't seem to make this connection, but for all the same reasons that you can't make the fancy karate moves in a real fight. Most of us are not able to do this sort of thing unless we train extensively and frequently. And most of us, even people that do this for a living, are simply unable to do that, so, the simple stuff is best and we have at least a twenty year track record to show that the simple stuff works.

D: You also have an extensive personal background, so I know you have seen a lot of this kind of stuff in the field. When you're talking about simple maneuvers versus the complicated things, what are you talking about?

E: Okay, the simplest one, of course, is you see the threat, assuming the road ahead of you is not blocked. Then you just step on the gas and drive away. A lot of times we get reports that say that the individual was blocked. What we find is that a car stopped in front of them, but they had plenty of room to go around them and didn't. So the second part of the course is simply to go around it. The third part, which we teach in some of the classes, generally for the military and police is to go through, which takes care of ramming. The fourth piece of this is to go backward. Just put the car in reverse and back up until you think you're okay and then turn around and leave. And then the one that sort of fits in the middle of all this is just do a big U-turn. We did not teach this for years and people did it anyway, if they see a problem, they don't feel they can go backward, they don't feel they can go around, they just do a U-turn. Use the whole road, whatever they needed, end up going in the other direction in the other lane. It's really that simple.

D: We talked one time about the J turn. Apparently you guys have disregarded that now and have gone to something called a Y turn?

E: Well, we constantly look at everything that we do. We need to be able to document it, just like any other sort of training. We teach techniques that are relevant and valid. This started when I was with the government and had access to a lot of incident reporting and especially for those people trained in J turns and we're still waiting to see one. Quite frankly, I haven't seen one yet. Not to say it hasn't happened. Just after looking at lots and lots of these we haven't seen it. It has to do with how people react in stress, brake conditions, traffic, etc. What we teach is obviously step on the gas and go forward is part A and part B is if you have to back up, you back the car up until you feel that your off the "X" or out of the kill zone. Then you just do a very simple turn around like you do every day of your life when you back out of your driveway. It's really that simple.

D: Okay the book is about the use of handguns in personal defense. I was fortunate to see the actual program that Gryphon Group and the SIG-Arms Academy attempted to put together, but could not really get off the ground...too bad as it was an excellent concept. This in mind, what brief suggestions can you give to people if the car is disabled and they can't use it?

E: Okay, good point. We put so much emphasis on the car and, of course, either you can't get it started, it's totally blocked in, etc. The short answer is that you have to get away from the car. Of course, there are all sorts of tactics and techniques for that. The main thing is the car is the target, that's where the rounds are going, get away from it. You have to get out as best you can. One of the things you need to do, depending on where you are is see if you can get to parked vehicles, for example, you've got cars parallel parked along the side of the road, you can get behind those and you can move from car to car with cover. You can do the same thing in a big parking lot. You have Wal-Mart, K-Mart, etc., the main thing is to get away from the car and get under cover. Shoot when you have to. The biggest thing is not to stand and fight. Biggest thing is to disappear.

D: Okay. You made the comment to me that one of the best things that I could do is just never get so close to the vehicle in front of me so that I couldn't see the rear tires, so I could always have an option out. Any other simple suggestions like that you could share?

E: There are a couple things. One is like your talking about, we like to, when you pull up behind a car, if possible, be able to see the rear tires actually on the pavement. That way we know that we have plenty of maneuvering room if we have to get away. The other thing, it's really being alert. You really need to practice that. But one of the things that I have found that is very helpful, is that there are dead spots in your side mirrors. I like to use the "fish eye" mirrors. Those little round mirrors that are about two bucks apiece in a Wal-Mart. Stick those on there and that opens up those dead spots and you can truly, with two outside mirrors and the rearview mirror, watch 360 and that's really the only other suggestion.

D: Where exactly on the side view mirrors should you put these contact mirrors. Inside? Lower corner?

E: Yeah, lower outside corner on the mirrors. What that does is reveals the dead spots to the rear of the vehicle. When I see the whole thing in that little mirror, I know it's too close.

D: You have made me believe that vehicle skills are probably as important, if not more important, than shooting skills. You are in the car a whole lot more than running around with a gun in your hand. Ed, listen, I really want to thank you for taking some time here today. I really appreciate it.

Chapter Twenty

COMBATIVE CLOSE QUARTER SHOOTING:
ESSENTIAL SKILLS

55% of officers killed in the line of duty are shot at distances under ten feet.
— FBI Officer Killed Statistics

I have heard it said that "liars figure and figures lie," but I don't think you can ignore statistics collected over the last several decades that state the majority of law enforcement shootings occur at extremely close distances. Such statistics are not kept on legally armed citizens involved in gunfights, but I think they too follow this trend. What distances are we talking about? From the statistics compiled over the last 30 years as many as 80 to 85% depending on the year occur within 20 feet. Of that 80% 55% occur within 6 feet, almost arm's length. It doesn't take a great deal of skill to shoot someone who is a double arm's length away, all you have to do is be first on the trigger. Another reason why awareness, or seeing the threat coming, can be the difference between life and death. The interesting thing about this is that we have known it for long time. But firearms instruction still takes place at 7, 10 and 15 yards. Why is that? Well, quite frankly, tradition and it's easy to do.

When training at longer distances we can get into our preferred stance, use our perfect grip and we can draw and fire with less pressure. However, when we are very close to the target everything changes and we can't use the stance, grip and other techniques that we have worked so hard to perfect. The fact is, training people at close quarters is difficult as well as dangerous. Much of firearms training is undertaken in static line environments. Training people to side step and shooting guns next to their chest can become problematic for the person standing next to them. What it requires is beyond the comfort zone of many. The gun cannot be held straight out at arms length, we cannot find the perfect sight picture, or put our feet in a traditional position. We have to hold the gun back against our pectoral, we may have to lean back, forward, or side step. We're going to do a lot of the things that are not part of the static line drills we are used to. At the same time, we may not be using a gun, we may be fighting hand to hand and that's not firearm training. The

193

fact is, people like to look good and this is difficult when fighting hand to hand.

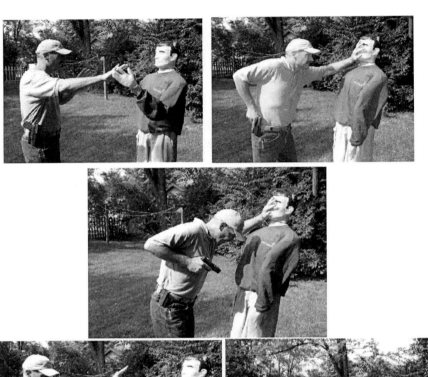

Figure 68
Where the head goes, the body will follow. When shooting at extreme close distances, the time and opportunity must be created and a strike, smash or rake to the face will do just that. It does not require a lot of skill and works on most everyone as the ability to see and/or breathe is needed to fight. It requires aggression and a fast draw to a close retention position. Multiple shots are delivered to the torso with a sudden disengagement followed by shots to the head.

Let's consider for a moment how the law enforcement officer operates, since this is where the quoted statistics come from. They are constantly in close contact with just about everyone. They ask for driver's licences, issue tickets and summons, talk with citizens, handcuff those arrested and so on. Close contact is a police reality. Can you imagine the public outcry if officers stood back 20 or 30 feet and shouted at citizens to throw their I.D. to them so the officer could maintain a "reactionary gap." I think that I can safety state that the chief or sheriff's phone lines would be busy. The legally armed citizen may say that "I NEVER let anyone get that close to me!" Really!? You never ride escalators, shake hands, share an elevator or taxi, go to a movie, wait in line at a bank, etc., etc., etc. EVERYONE makes close contact with other people, so is it really a surprise that shootings are also up close and personal affairs?

Close confrontation is a reality, so knowing hand-to-hand tactics are to your advantage. When you are engaged at distances of double arms' length, it's not a gun problem. *Even if deadly force is justified, when fighting inside "the hole" (double arms length) you run the risk of giving your gun to your opponent! Also realize that you cannot out draw a pointed firearm without some type of diversion. Action will always be faster than reaction. It is wise to realize that at extreme close distances, it will be the weapon and not the person you will need to attack. It needs to be handled in this order:*

1. Control the weapon (gun, knife, club, etc.)
2. Aggressive Counter-Attack
3. Break contact, gain distance and employ firearm

Think about how fast you can draw your gun from concealment. Can you draw in 1.5 seconds and get on target? That is terrific, but you should remember that the average person can travel 7 yards in 1.5 seconds and that's not incredibly fast. It breaks down to 13 seconds for a 100-yard dash, a time that would not make the high school track team. Think about the people who have greater reflexes and are even faster than average. 1.5 seconds may not be fast enough. The answer may be hand-to-hand techniques, body movement, fighting and gouging until you can create enough distance to bring your gun into action. Hand to hand techniques are not the subject of this book. But I would strongly encourage anyone interested in personal defense to learn some type of hand-to-hand combat. Instead of going from shooting school to shooting school, vary your training. Take handgun training, take some driver's training, some knife training, some hand-to-hand training. This type of training will be what is necessary to make yourself well rounded in personal defense.

In the last few years, well-known instructor and researcher Ralph Mroz has conducted research into close shooting techniques. Over several years he took a critical look at exactly what we're doing in firearms training for CQ situations. This research resulted in a videotape that is available from Paladin Press called "*Extreme Close Quarter Shooting: A critical examination of close in shooting techniques.*" While you may not agree with everything Ralph discusses, his videotape should not be ignored. Ralph does a good job of showing that many things we consider doctrine and do not question, may not be as good as originally thought. Another good resource is Kelly McCann's "*Combative Pistol,*" also from Paladin Press.

The most common close quarter technique and the one I was taught over 30 years ago is the "speed rock." The speed rock requires the shooter to arch their back, drawing their pistol and trying to fire into their opponent's midsection as they are being attacked. The gun is fired as soon as it clears the holster and the wrist indexes against the shooter's torso. Proponents of this technique have rightfully pointed out that it is used for special situations only, such as when you have been backed up against something, like the hood of a car or the vanity in the bathroom. In such a situation, you are trapped and can't move any further back, so the speed rock may have certain applications. However, it is not the only technique. The problem with the speed rock is there is little clearance from the holster so you could easily shoot yourself. Additionally, rounds generally tend to hit low in the abdomen, which are not stopping shots with a handgun. When using the speed rock , it is almost as easy for your opponent to take your gun away from you as it is to draw, provided your opponent sees it coming.

Another technique, known as the "shove and shoot" is quite common and I admit it is one that I use. When using this technique, you try to create distance by either striking your opponent in the chest, shoving him back, while at the same time you step back clearing distance for you to draw your weapon. The technique is somewhat instinctive in that if someone violates your personal space, it is normal to step back out of their path and also try to limit any forward movement. One area of concern is it requires the user to step back into the unknown. We discussed this briefly when talking about shooting on the move and trying to walk backward. Again, I would suggest a shuffle step be used so that falling will not be the end result. Massad Ayoob has pointed out that striking someone in the chest or face oftentimes has no effect. He asked the questions, "Have you ever struck someone with all your might and it had no effect?" "Have you ever taken a solid blow yourself and not been affected?" So, can we rely on a blow to stun an attacker who is charging us at full speed?

Although Ralph and Mas make some good points about the shove and shoot technique, I still feel it has merit based on my own experience. The technique's success is totally dependant on where and how you strike. In reality, it should not be called the "shove and shoot" it should be called the "strike and shoot" or "smash and shoot" with the strike being to the face or neck. The fact is, I have shoved my hand into the face of three people over the thirty years I was in law enforcement and it worked each time. On all three occasions, the offenders were going for my gun and a straight arm to the face was done without thought. On one occasion, the suspect was quite a bit bigger than I and I caught his nose between my middle and ring fingers, using it to push him over on his back. Based on my experience, I am skeptical when someone tells me that such a technique will not work. Hmmm...

The face and neck are vital and largely unprotected areas of the body. It is impossible to fight if you cannot see and/or breath...body functions that are affected by strikes to the face and neck. I once had a lengthy conversation with a WWI veteran who had fought in the extreme close combat of trench warfare. He sat with a drink in his hand, that was shaking as he spoke and with a tear running down his cheek, he gave me a piece of advice that I will never forget. "Those German were a fierce bunch as they came over the edge of the trench. Their eyes were a' blaze and they were screaming...I was scared out of my mind. But you can't let that control you. You have to get around their bayonet and attack their ability to see or breathe. If you can stop one or the other, you will win the fight." This is from the mouth or someone who has been there, done it under the most extreme of circumstances and WON!

A hard strike to the shoulder can actually turn an opponent changing their attack path. Visualize the human body with a post extending up from the ground between the legs to the neck with the head sitting on the top. When the body is pushed on either side, it will rotate around the post while if the head is struck, it will push the post back. If you try to push the post in the middle, it will not move because it is solid. This is the problem with the shove and shoot to the chest. Trying to shove the largest body mass with a single arm, especially if this mass is moving forward, will meet with failure regardless of how strong the arm is. Picture a person moving at you as you strike, claw or poke them in the face...better yet, you get your hand under their chin...and you lock the arm. Where the head goes, the body will follow. If the fingers enter the eyes, better yet! Smash the nose or impact the throat? Sorry to hear about their luck! Such an action will need to apply aggressive forward motion, but keep it simple and easy to do.

In the past, I have been a advocate of trying to side step an aggressive forward attack but I have come to realize that this precisely timed movement is not the panacea that many state or believe. If you move laterally too soon, your opponent will re-direct their attack. A lateral step is not so large that an attacker cannot adjust accordingly. If you move too late, well...the problem here is fairly obvious, you would probably have more success just going low and letting them trip over you than trying to "play Matador." However, this being said...MOVE...standing still is always wrong.

Another technique that has been proven effective is called the "spearing elbow." This involves dropping your center of gravity, taking a small step either forward or backward and stabbing your non-shooting elbow sharply into the attacker's chest area while covering your head with your hand and forearm. At the same time you draw your handgun bringing it up close to your chest and shoot your attacker in the torso or the pelvic area. This technique has shown to be very easy to accomplish due to startle response that everyone will experience to some degree. Crouching and covering the head is something that is done naturally whenever an individual is startled. One downside of the technique is having your elbow and your forearm up over your head restricts vision to a degree. However, fights are fluid situations in which movement is constant. How much your vision is restricted will be dependant on the situation at hand.

The "drop to the ground" technique is what it sounds like, when you are attacked, you drop down to the ground on your back, using your feet and legs to push your attacker back away from you. Without a doubt this would catch your attacker by surprise as it is one of the last things he would expect. The downside is being on the ground certainly restricts your mobility. Additionally if multiple suspects are involved, you are now on the ground in a situation where you can't pivot or move very well and you may now have to engage multiple suspects. On seconds thought, DON'T DROP TO

THE GROUND...you will just get the shit kicked out of you...I don't care which "expert" advocates it!

Whichever technique you use is up to you based on your operational parameters, your environment and your skill level. But do not disregard close contact shooting techniques, as they are more likely to be used than other techniques commonly taught. Ralph Mroz offers several principles that address the CQS problem and I think they are worth repeating here:

1. At less than 7 feet, speed wins, not skill.
2. Attitude, smoothness and control will probably determine who wins the encounter.
3. People will naturally want to move their gun toward the threat, so any technique requiring shooting from a close body position must incorporate locking the gun arm to the body.
4. When designing close shooting techniques, assume a 5' tall, 100 lb. defender against a very strong opponent.
5. Make sure your technique will work in a crowded cramped area. Anything will work on nice, flat open controlled range space.
6. You always want to move off the center line of the attack. As a matter of fact, moving is always good!
7. Assume multiple adversaries, incorporate multiple targets and multiple lines of fire into your training exercises.
8. Use dummy guns to train on uneven terrain.
9. Incorporate continual verbalization into your training.

Extreme close quarter shooting is down, dirty, ugly, bloody, muddy fighting. Don't lose track of what combatives are, whether they're handgun, open hand, or knife, it's fighting. The implement you use doesn't make a difference. Again, if the confrontation is so close that you can't bring your gun up to eye level...then maybe it's not a "gun" fight. Training for CQS situations requires you to shoot your chosen handgun close to YOUR body and at target. I like to use three dimensional targets like the TAC-MAN or full size mannequin targets available from Law Enforcement Targets. These targets allow the shooter to strike and shoot while adding a more human like feel to the exercise. LE Targets also offers a manually pulled cart for their mannequin that allows the shooter to incorporate movement to the CQS drill. Of course, Airsoft and Simunitions equipped firearms offer the most realistic method for engaging in mock close quarter shooting situations.

What drills should you use to train for close contact shooting? Think about the type of close contact you have on a daily basis and recreate them with a close attack. Do you work across a public service counter? Make traffic stops? Clean office buildings? Your normal world is a good place to start. The first thing you need to establish is a close retention shooting position. It needs to be obtained from the holster and it must be back far enough that it is protected from a grab as much as possible. It should be tight against the pectoral muscle and ***obtained by feel so that it can be recreated on demand without looking at the gun!*** Make sure the gun is clear of any fabric or tissue, but do not lay it sideways as it could become unstable and jam during rapid fire. Work from concealment if this is your real world!

Start slow to find your version of the close retention position. Hold the gun up next to your chest and look at it. Make sure that it will fire and that nothing that you do not want to shoot gets shot. Then work on drawing from the holster to this position and firing a double tap. Again, go slow and build into speed. CQS skills are an essential part of Handgun Combatives. Don't ignore them because they are not fun to do.

Chapter Twenty-One

KEEPING SHARP

"Perfect practice makes perfect"
John Shaw, Founder of the
Mid-South Institute for Self-Defense Shooting

Reading this book is only a beginning. You need to seek out hands on training in handgun combat. Seek as much training as possible, don't follow one individual trainer or school and go through all of their courses. I suggest that you seek the knowledge of numerous trainers as not everyone has the perfect plan or the best idea. A combination of ideas may be the exact ticket to combative success.

Practicing your combative skills is essential. Get to the range and fire live rounds as often as possible. However, I realize that many of us do not have the time or the money to go to the range as much as we would like. Ammunition is expensive, even when you reload. And how many of us have the time to get to the range, let alone the time to reload ammunition. In the hectic lifestyle of the new millennium, time is at a premium and is almost as valuable as money.

The best training might be dry fire training. Unloaded weapon training in the privacy of your bedroom or garage, performing drills and developing the skills that you will need to win an armed confrontation. It's amazing how good you can get with a handgun and never actually fire a shot. The only downside to dry firing is that you really get no feedback about accuracy. You can get very good at holster skills, speed loading and other skills, but you have no feedback as to where the gun is pointing and whether or not what you are doing will actually increase on-target accuracy. Getting such feedback will only make you a better shooter.

No doubt the person that can draw fast, reload, clear malfunctions and other necessary skills will have more time to place the shot. By practicing handling drills dry, you will have more time at the range to actually launch bullets at a target, working on trigger press and recoil control. However, what if there was a device available that would allow you to get this accuracy feedback in a dry drill environment? You certainly could not work on recoil control because live rounds fired in your bedroom will irritate your spouse and your neighbors. But if you knew that your shots were accurate, that your trigger press was true, that your presentation to the target was correct, would it not help you develop motor skill, so when you did go out and fire rounds recoil control would be your primary concern? It would certainly increase your skill, cut down on your ammo budget and make you better prepared.

For the cost of another handgun, such a device does exist. It is called "Beamhit™." The first time I saw a Beamhit™ unit was at the Ohio Peace Officer Training Academy in London, Ohio. I was attending a defensive tactics instructor update when lead instructor Sam Faulkner called me into his office. Sam told me he wanted to show me the neatest firearm training aid that he had ever seen. He pulled out a box with a black plastic case that had a small bulls-eye target in the center. Next to it was a Smith & Wesson 5906 with an attachment on the muzzle. Sam explained that the Beamhit™ unit allowed more realistic dry fire training due to the laser unit attached to the barrel. I looked at the unit and gun and thought—"video game"! Nothing could have been further from the truth. Since that time I have learned Beamhit™ has been adopted as a training solution by the U.S. Military, State Police Training Academies, Foreign Governments and major Law Enforcement Agencies worldwide. It is also being used by many citizen shooters for both competition and firearm skills practice. I was a little skeptical, but interested enough to call Beamhit® to discuss my concerns about the unit. I was told that the Beamhit™ 110 portable unit was ideal for defensive handgun dry fire training, as that was its original mission. The Beamhit™ Laser Trainer was developed for a foreign government Special Defense Forces who had been tasked with protecting their prime minister and staff when traveling overseas. While these agents couldn't train where they stayed, it was at these locations where they were most vulnerable to attacks. "The officers were in places where such scenarios could happen, but they couldn't prepare for it." I was told. Thus, this government search for means to train with their 9mm service pistols, no matter where in the world they were located was initiated. The Beamhit™ 110 is a battery powered 4-inch target that receives a laser beam transmitted from a mandrel inserted into the barrel of the firearm. In previous models the mandrel or laser transmitter was a large contraption on the muzzle of the training weapon. This made the gun muzzle heavy and holstering impossible. This is no longer the case. The current Beamhit™ unit uses a bore sleeve, which is caliber specific, and a laser module or mandrel that fits inside the sleeve, a battery and a muzzle end cap. All this fits into the gun's barrel with the bright orange end cap protruding from the muzzle about a ½ inch. This makes it easy to verify that the gun's muzzle is plugged and is a safe dry fire practice weapon. The laser module is activated by dry firing the training weapon. The vibration travels down the barrel from the falling hammer activating the laser beam. With the proper caliber sleeve firmly seated the unit is aligned within ¼ inch at 50 yards. An adjustment screw is fitted in the rear of each unit to insure a tight fit.

A number of years ago, I attended a defensive handgun course at the Thunder Ranch Training Facility in Mountain Home, Texas. After a variety of challenging exercises and drills, I shot more than 1,000 rounds and returned to Ohio and put myself through several skills tests to determine exactly where I stood in regard to my skills.

With a PACT Club Timer II against 8 inch plates at 7 yards, I performed a number of drills, as follows:

> 1 round   ready position
> 1 round   holster
> 1 round   concealed holster
> 1 round   speed load   1 round

These are your typical dry fire drills. I returned to Ohio to incredibly bad weather. I found that for the next several months I could not fire real ammunition due to lack of a range. After several months of using the Beamhit™ as my principal training tool, I returned to the range and fired the same drills and discovered that I had actually improved in the areas that I mentioned. This experience encouraged me so much that I continue to use the Beamhit™ as my principle dry fire training tool to this day.

Since that time I have created a number of various training scenarios and target systems around the Beamhit™ unit. I mounted a humanoid photographic target on a wood frame and mounted the Beamhit™ unit high in the chest cavity with a four-inch circle representing the heart. Using this threat, I have been able to do vehicle drills, seated shooting drills, holster drills, reload drills and even vehicle debus drills inside the comfort of my own garage. I have even been able to make the target move by purchasing a nylon chord and two pulleys from a hardware store. The pulleys were attached at opposite ends of the garage and the nylon chords fed through them. Remove the cardboard backer and target and attach it to the chord. I then had my son move the target back and forth and both at and away from me inside the garage area allowing me to actually engage a moving target.

This Beamhit™ unit has been a great success and I would strongly urge anyone who is interested in developing their skills to purchase such a unit for their own use.

Dry fire practice, without a doubt, enhances skills. Accuracy feedback in these dry fire skills can actually improve your live fire practice. Is there any downside to the Beamhit™ System? Sure. First, there is no recoil impulse, so rapid shooting recoil control can't be simulated. Second, with many pistols, like the Glocks and the Heckler and Koch LEM pistols, only one shot can be fired before the gun must be reset by cycling the slide. However, I have come to realize that for the amount of skill development I get from the Beamhit™, this is a small price to pay.

No, the Beamhit™ is not a replacement for live fire shooting, but it's here to stay and it's certainly a worthwhile supplement. Just five or ten minutes working on a specific thing, whether it be magazine exchanges, malfunction drills, holster skills or weapon presentation, can greatly enhance your ability to defend your own life. I think you would agree after working with the Beamhit™ unit that not only is it worth its money, but if you're attacked, it's worth its weight in gold.

Since I wrote the last edition of HANDGUN COMBATIVES I have continued to train with the Beamhit™ unit with great success. I continue to be a big proponent of laser-based dry-fire training due to the feedback it offers. The one down side of this tool is that it only offers one "round" of training, i.e., the slide must be cycled in order to reset the trigger. Over the years I could not help but think how much better the dry-fire experience could be if I could work the reset of the trigger to simulate multiple shots. As it turns out, just such a tool has been recently introduced and I have been doing some serious real world dry-fire training since I have received it.

The Ready Shot takes the laser technology found in the Beamhit and has added the ability to work the trigger multiple times. Currently available for the Glock, Springfield XD and Smith & Wesson M & P, the Ready Shot gives instant feedback via a barrel mounted laser that interacts with a square target that can be set up most anywhere. For those who do not have one of the listed guns, the Ready Shot unit will work with your laser unit, though you won't have the multiple shot capability. I'm not totally sure how the technology works, but the Ready Shot comes with a replacement magazine that has a wire that fits on to the trigger draw bar of the Glock. In addition, a magnet is fitted to the rear of the trigger and the combination of the two allows the gun to be used dry while offering multiple shot capability. No, the trigger action is not exactly like it will feel when you shoot the gun live, so you won't be able to work on your sub .20 second splits for IPSC, but you will offer greater reality to your dry fire simulation.

The Ready Shot is not inexpensive, but is a worthwhile addition to your training tool kit. If you check the internet, you will find a number of dry fire training aids that will help you prepare for armed conflict. If you don't have the money for such devices don't worry, just do the "old-fashioned" version of dry fire and "shoot" at a spot on the wall. It doesn't matter but in the end, dry fire...it's worth the time and effort regardless of what any "expert" says.

Chapter Twenty-Two

PUTTING IT ALL TOGETHER

"Aim at nothing and you will probably hit it!"
"Luke" 14 Intelligence Company,
British Army in Northern Ireland

I admit that I am not a big fan of training standards. I believe in practicing to be correct. What I mean by standards is a certain amount of accuracy in a certain amount of time doing a particular drill. What I am most interested in for my students and me, is being able to accomplish a particular skill as fast as humanly possible with as much accuracy as can be obtained. To me, accuracy is everything while speed is secondary. If you continue to practice and work on accuracy while at the same time work to eliminate unnecessary motion from your shooting, speed will come on its own.

I can remember when I worked day after day trying to develop a 1.5 second draw from the holster. I was able to get the 1.5 seconds but not with the degree of accuracy that I wanted each and every time. My version of combat accuracy is being able to hit an 8-inch circle at 20 feet/7 yards. As time went by and I began to understand the dynamics of the draw (keeping the elbows straight to the rear and bringing your hand to the gun instead of trying to seek it out) I realized that with repetitive practice, eliminating excessive movement and performing the technique half-speed, that when I did try to add speed, I was actually faster than if I try to beat the clock in a spastic manner. The same is evident when presenting the gun to the target trying to get a fast and accurate shot. I found that when coming from the ready position and delivering the gun to the target by following my thumbs, I could get accurate shots without even looking at the sights because I had developed a familiar task transfer. Once the motor skill was developed and I eliminated all excessive movement, I realized that I would be fast without trying. The problem with standards is the student goes so fast to better the standard, that he/she never develops the motor memory and skill to do it without conscious thought, which is the key to fighting in the street. Thus, I have tried not to make standards "all important." I am concerned with developing the skill properly than trying to be fast.

At the same time, I realize that students seem to like standards. They want to measure themselves against the clock the same way athletes want to know how far they can jump or throw. Students want something to measure their skills against, so I have developed some drills that I use to stay sharp. I have found that my students enjoy them as well. They are based on skills I feel may happen in the real world, but at the same time can be done anywhere. I have put them in a chart at the end of the chapter, so if the reader likes these drills, they can cut them from the page, laminate them and keep them with them at all times. Since the first edition, I have modified the times based on student feedback while keeping them both relevant and realistic.

A word of caution, don't be too overly concerned with meeting the time. Emphasize accuracy. These drills are intended to be done at 20 feet on an 8- inch target. If you get to the point where the speed is not a problem, don't try to speed up, use a smaller target. Go to a 6-inch plate and continue to work on accuracy and economy of motion.

Figure 69
The author uses simple training props to keep his skills honed. All is available from Law Enforcement Targets including the dueling tree, PNZ steel plate, TAC-Man 3D target and the full-size mannequin on a wheeled cart that can be moved in any direction.

Practice time is important for me. I admit that I do not get as much as I would like, so I try not to waste any. I am not a grand master like Rob Leatham or Todd Jarrett and I never will be and neither will most of you reading this book. What we do have in common is wanting to shoot well enough to save our own lives. I feel that I have obtained this level of skill. A practice session for me will involve 200 to 250 rounds over a several hour period. I will start my session by visualizing what I am working on, whether it be trigger control, follow through, holster skills or weapon presentation.

I have developed a visual image of what I want myself to look like based on several of my past instructors. I have videos of many of the well known instructors and I have watched them over and over. I have noted their movements and have placed in my mind's eye how I want to model their actions. I have taken videos of my performance and have tried to incorporate their movements into my motion. I have been able to "feel" what I want to accomplish by combining all of these representations. It sounds weird, I know, but it does work.

I then start out slowly and take the time to give my body a felt representation of what I am doing. All of us have been able to "feel" when a shot is off. I try to stay really in touch with the kinetic aspects of shooting. I will look and feel the proper grip, when it shifts during a volley of fire I will know it. I will go slowly through my draw taking the time to feel what it feels like when I do it right. I will speed up keeping this proper feel intact. If I lose the feel, I will slow down. If it feels "herky-jerky," it is not correct. John Shaw says that "smooth is fast" and while I can appreciate what he is trying to say, I think it is better said that "lack of unnecessary movement is fast." It's probably just semantics, but I like to be as verbally/visually descriptive as possible.

Don't fall into the trap of thinking you had a good practice session just because you hit the target on a particular day. You may have just been lucky and shot well in spite of your lack of sound fundamentals. You are having a good practice session when you continue to shoot well when you shoot without having to concentrate on it. You have begun to "shoot by feel." Get a visual image of what you want to do and then feel yourself do what is in your mind. If you like what you have read in this book, use the pictures to lock a visual image in your mind and then let your body do what the mind thinks about. This same process can be used during both live fire and dry-fire training. Again, I know it sounds weird, "new age" and all that. But it does work ...give it a try!

Discussing this subject, I can't help but remember a quote from many years ago. Famed Border Patrol officer and gunfighter Bill Jordan said it in his book *NO SECOND PLACE WINNER* and I will never forget it. "Speed is fine, but accuracy is final." The history of gun fighting, going all the way back to the days of the wild west has shown that the person that gets the first solid hit on their adversary is usually the winner of the gun battle. Hitting what you're shooting at is everything.

I have covered a lot of ground in just a few short pages and I realize that I have not covered every possible situation. No book or training program ever will. Please realize that all training is artificial to some degree and it is up to each and every one of us to learn as many skills as possible and store them away in our personal defensive "skill set." When a situation develops, the person who will win is the one who can pull the needed skill from the set with the least amount of lag time and bring it into play. Practice is the key to eliminating the need to "orient" to the situation. Practice is also part of developing a combative mind.

This book is about violence. Let me be the first to tell you that violence is never the answer. Unfortunately, all too often, it is the only solution. Thanks for reading. I hope you enjoyed it and most important, got something out of it. I care about you and I want you to PREVAIL!

Please stay safe and "Check 360 often!"

Close Quarter/Covert Pistol Skill Drills		
Drill #1	From ready, one shot on one target:	1.0
Drill #2	On Target, two shots on one target:	1.0
Drill #3	On Target, one shot on two targets:	1.3
Drill #4	From ready, fire/reload/fire on one target:	3.0
Drill #5	Draw from concealment, one shot on one target:	2.0
Drill #6	Draw from concealment/one shot on three targets:	2.8
Drill #7	Draw from concealment/side step/two rounds on one target:	2.3
Drill #8	Draw from concealment/kneel/ two rounds on one target:	2.3

Note: Each drill is fired twice and the average time recorded. As times are achieved use smaller target. Start with an 8" target at 20 feet.

A Closing Word
by Captain Mike Boyle, Retired
New Jersey Fish and Game, Bureau of Law Enforcement
Contributing Editor,
GUNS AND WEAPONS FOR LAW ENFORCEMENT
Board member, the International Association for Law
Enforcement Firearms Instructors

I t has been said that a little information can be dangerous. This is especially true of combative skills. A well intentioned individual may dabble in the traditional martial arts or attend a shooting school and come away with the notion that he is invincible. Reality has a nasty way of kicking us in the teeth and the unprepared or under prepared person will usually find himself on the short end of the stick.

Incomplete information often rears its ugly head in the training world as well. Although things have changed for the better in those institutions that train law enforcement officers, I still encounter "we've always done it that way' attitudes. Tradition is no guarantee that the right information is coming across. Fortunately, there is a great deal more continuity in public sector training these days and today's police recruit is far better prepared to function in a violent world.

The private sector remains a mixed bag. There are of course highly capable individuals and organizations that offer cutting edge training. On the other hand, there are those unscrupulous individuals attempting to pass themselves off as something they never were.

Considering that this information may literally be a matter of life or death, always ask yourself, what qualifies this person to deliver the message? Although being a real world practitioner of the craft helps, having the ability to effectively convey information is just as important.

Naturally, real world experience helps but that too has its limits. Sometime ago, I was observing a group of firearms instructors work out in a class taught by a world class instructor. One of the participants was clearly having a problem executing some relatively simple techniques which quickly caught the eye of the instructor. When he attempted to correct this individual, his sage advice fell on deaf ears. "I survived a deadly encounter," the errant shooter announced. I can only surmise by dumb luck. Considering this individual's lack of commitment in attempting to improve himself, I don't suppose he has much to offer his own students.

When teaching handgun fighting skills, information must come from a credible source and be believable. I know of no better person to deliver this message than Dave Spaulding.

I first met Dave many years ago while attending the annual conference of the American Society of Law Enforcement Trainers. We were both on the agenda to give a presentation and by chance crossed paths in the exhibit hall. Although we engaged in casual conversation, it's safe to say we were pretty wary of one another. Long careers in law enforcement make one suspicious of the motives of others, especially writers.

In time, those walls came down and we became friends. I've been out to Dave's turf to teach classes and he has been to mine to do the same. On other occasions, we've found ourselves teaching together on the road for someone else. What I have come to find out is that Dave Spaulding is the real deal.

Dave is recently retired from his police job where he served a long career and excelled in a number of diverse assignments including patrol, training, and as a supervisor. Toward the tail end of his career, he quarterbacked an interagency narcotics interdiction team. While most of us who have been at the game for some time find ourselves in some cushy air conditioned backwater, Dave was kicking in doors. The techniques and tactics he used to keep himself and his teammates safe can be used to your advantage as well.

Best of all, Dave breaks it all down and has it make sense. I have not known him to blindly accept what has come before as the gospel truth, but to dissect and analyze and try to make something better.

Over the years, there have only been a few definitive texts on fighting with a handgun. Handgun Combatives is one of them. The information contained herein is simple, makes sense, and is street-proven. I hope you drank from the well of tactical knowledge.

APPENDIX

T he following list is not all-inclusive. It is a list of manufacturers and trainers that I have personal experience with and that I highly recommend. It does not mean that there are no other excellent establishments or companies, it's just that I have not personally dealt with them.

Training Schools:

Thunder Ranch
www.thunderranchinc.com

Smith & Wesson Academy
www.smithwesson.com

Gunsite Academy
www.gunsite.com

SIG Arms Academy
www.sigsaveracademy.com

Tactical Defense Institute
www.tdiohio.com

A.P.P.L.E. P.I.T.T.
Police Training Institute
www.racstraining.com

Mid-South Institute for Self Defense
Shooting
www.weaponstraining.com

DTI (John Farnum)
www.defense-training.com

U.S. Training Centers
www.ustraining.com

Crucible
www.cruciblesecurity.com

Manufacturers:

I will not list the major firearms manufacturers as I think they are all good. It can be argued that one brand is better than another, but they are not. It is all up to the individual to select the gun that best meets their needs. If you have a Glock, Beretta, S & W, H & K, Ruger, Colt, Kimber, Springfield Armory, SIG-Sauer, Browning, Kahr, FN or other well-made firearm, just treat it well. It will do the same for you!

Comp-Tac Holsters
866-441-9157
www.comp-tac.com

The Wilderness
800-775-5650
www.thewilderness.com

Chestnut Mountain Sports
802-438-5732
www.chestnutmountainsports.com

Alessi Holsters
716-691-5615
www.alessiholsters.com

XS Sight Systems
800-734-7939
www.xssights.com

Hoffner's Holsters
877-463-3637
www.huffners.com

FIST, Inc.
800-443-fist
www.fist-inc.com

Beamhit/MPRI
800-232-6448
www.beamhit.com

Law Enforcement Targets
888-489-7830
www.letargets.com

Blade Tech
253-655-8059
www.blade-tech.com

Mitch Rosen
Gun Leather
603-647-2971
www.mitchrosen.com

Bowie Tactical Concepts
937-544-4606
www.bowietacticalconcepts.com

Milt Sparks Holsters
208-377-5577
www.miltsparks.com

Robar Companies
623-581-2648
www.robarguns.com

Ameriglo
770-390-0554
www.ameriglo.com

Advanced Design
and Engineering
530-913-2565
www.speedsights.com

Ready Shot
877-973-2399
www.readyshot.com

INDEX

OTHER TITLES OF INTEREST
FROM LOOSELEAF LAW PUBLICATIONS, INC.

Defensive Living
by Dave Spaulding

Crucial Elements of Police Firearms Training
by Brian R. Johnson

Essential Guide to Handguns
Firearm Instruction for Personal Defense & Protection
by Stephen R. Rementer and Bruce N. Eimer, Ph.D.

Instinct Combat Shooting 3rd Edition
Defensive Handgunning for Police
by Chuck Klein

Armed Response
A Comprehensive Guide to Using Firearms for Self-Defense
by David Kenik

Deadly Force
Constitutional Standards, Federal Guidelines and Officer Survival
by John Michael Callahan, Jr.

Developing the Survival Attitude
by Phil L. Duran

Tactical Attitude
Learn from Powerful Real-Life Experiences
by Phil L. Duran and Dennis Nasci

Use of Force
Expert Guidance for Decisive Force Response
by Brian A. Kinnaird

Processing Under *Pressure*
Stress, Memory and Decision-Making in Law Enforcement
by Matthew J. Sharps